MORAL LESSONS FROM GANDHI'S AUTOBIOGRAPHY AND OTHER ESSAYS

Gandhian Studies for Peace and Research Series

1. Gandhian Model of Development and World Peace - *R.P. Misra*
2. Conflict Resolution Through Non-violence : Role of the Univ. Vol. 1 : Science and Ethics - *K.D. Gangrade* and *R.P. Misra*
3. Conflict Resolution Through Non-violence : Role of the Univ. Vol. 2 : Development without Destruction - *K.D. Gangrade* and *R.P. Misra*
4. The Social Philosophy of Mahatma Gandhi - *K.S. Bharathi*
5. Gandhian Humanism - *Mohit Chakraborty*
6. Gandhian Holestic Economics - *Shashi Prabha Sharma*
7. Gandhian Spiritualism : A Quest for the Essence of Excellence - *Mohit Chakraborty*
8. Gandhian Perspective on Population and Development - *A.K. Sharma*
9. Thoughts of Gandhi and Vinoba : A Comparative Study - *K.S. Bharathi*
10. Economic Philosophy of Mahatma Gandhi - *Shanti Swarup Gupta*
11. The Political Thoughts of Mahatma Gandhi - *K.S. Bharathi*
12. Gandhi and 21st Century - *Janardan Pandy*
13. Gandhian Philosophy of the Spinning Wheel - *Mohit Chakraborty*
14. Gandhian Satyagraha : An Analytical and Critical Approach - *Ajay Shanker Rai*
15. Gandhi and His Religion - *P.A. Raju*
16. Mahatma Gandhi : Vichar Vithika (Hindi) - *S.P. Agarwal*
17. Poverty of Gandhian Philosophy - *Himansu Roy*
18. Right to Equality in the Indian Constitution - *S.N. Saraswati*
19. Meditations of Gandhi : A Ravindra Varma Festschrift - *M.P. Mathai, M.S. John* and *Siby K. Joseph*
20. Politico-Economic Ideas of Mahatma Gandhi - *Sukhendu Mazumdar*

About the Author

Prof. K.D. Gangrade (*b*. 1926), Vice-Chairman of Gandhi Smriti and Darshan Samiti, New Delhi, has been a former Pro-Vice-Chancellor, Dean, Faculty of Social Sciences, and Head, Department of Social Work, University of Delhi. He has also taught at the University of Manchester, U.K. and Tata Institute of Social Sciences, Mumbai. He has served the United Nations as well in various capacities. Prof. Gangrade has 12 books to his credit. He is recipient of Samaj Gaurav (1988) from the Bhartiya Sangthan, Rashtra Ratna (1998) from Viswa Jagriti Mission, and Radha Raman Award (2000) for outstanding contribution to education.

MORAL LESSONS FROM GANDHI'S AUTOBIOGRAPHY AND OTHER ESSAYS

K.D. GANGRADE
Gandhi Smriti and Darshan Samiti
Gandhi Darshan, Rajghat, New Delhi

Published for
GANDHI SMRITI AND DARSHAN SAMITI, NEW DELHI
By
CONCEPT PUBLISHING COMPANY, NEW DELHI-110059

ISBN 81-8069-084-9

First Published 2004

Published and Printed by
Ashok Kumar Mittal
Concept Publishing Company
A/15-16, Commercial Block, Mohan Garden
NEW DELHI-110059 (India)

Phones: 25351460, 25351794
Fax: 091-11-25357103
Email: publishing@conceptpub.com

FOREWORD

Mahatma Gandhi's autobiography, *My Experiments with Truth*, has attracted worldwide attention as a classic of modern times for the remarkable insights it offers into the progression of human soul in its resolute march to relate itself to the ever-changing ethos in the course of life's journey. Over the years, this record of Gandhi's perception of a part of his own life has become a masterpiece winning universal acclaim for the honesty with which the author interprets his life upto the first quarter of this century. Surprisingly, Gandhi did not conceive it to be an elaborate treatise. He described it as "My Experiments with Truth".

The big question is: Do the experiments conducted by Gandhi hold out any message or lesson to the present generation or to the generations to come? Were they not personal, about himself?, critics might ask. Is Gandhi, who tried to look at men and matters from an ethical, moral and spiritual angle, relevant in an age conditioned to a large extent by materialistic and consumeristic considerations and by a generation who is nurtured in the invincibility of the power of money? The contemporary decay of vital human institutions such as religions and the callous indifference with which morality and ethics are viewed by the protagonists of unlimited growth are taking humanity to a cliff of what promise and consequence, nobody knows. The computer boys are promising humanity such wonders that would set even the most balanced brain on fire. In this jungle of madness and frenzied rush, which in a different way reminds us of the initial stages of colonialism, what is the relevance of Jesus, the Buddha, Prophet Mohammad or for that matter any of the teachers of humanity? We measure all of them on the basis of our own needs, which are now by and large material and physical. Ethics, morality and spirituality all seem to have become things of the past. Still we gloat over such endearing concepts such as 'global human family', 'global village', 'warless world' and a 'world without boundaries'. Yes, physical boundaries we have been able to dismantle, but what about the mental and psychic boundaries which still prevent the rich nations from sharing their excess wealth with the less privileged humanity? It is estimated that with the diversion of one-third of what the rich nations spend on armaments, malnutrition could be wiped out in several Afro-Asian countries and safe drinking water could be provided. But who listens?

Gandhi never took refuge in any scriptures or shastras blindly and those who approach him with closed minds would see only their own visages and would miss the essential Gandhi who was an uncompromising experimenter. To experiment requires great courage, conviction and clear perception and a readiness to court inconvenience or even failure. The arm-chair critic does not have or require any of these attributes. Gandhi described himself to be lost in the ivory-tower of contemplation. Like an inspired experimenter he tested his ideas in the laboratory of his own life in order to gain insights and knowledge by living it and not repeating what others said or copying from others. The freshness of his ideas inspired millions and even those who came to scoff at him became lifelong associates and admirers.

He called his autobiography "The Story of My Experiments with Truth". This reveals his readiness to subject his own life as the testing ground and his approach is that of a scientist who will neither compromise truth nor forsake his efforts to arrive at the truth he is searching for, whatever be the other temptations. He looked at the vast vicissitude of philosophy not from the conventional angles of contemplation but on the hard realities and challenges of everyday life, with man at the centre and man as the prime concern. Philosophy for him, as in the Indian tradition, is not a set of formulations, it is transformation of the spirit, soul and the whole life-style which will elevate humankind in order to live happily and shed rays and lights of happiness around. It surely does not mean anything to those who want to flourish in human misery and to whom individual contribution to better human life does not mean anything.

"What I want to achieve—and what I have been striving and pinning to achieve these thirty years—is self-realization, to see God face to face, to attain *Moksha.* I live and move and have my being in pursuit of this goal. All that I do by way of speaking and writing, and all my ventures in the political field, are directed to this same end. But as I have all along believed that what is possible for one is possible for all, my experiments have not been conducted in the closet, but in the open; and I do not think that this fact detracts from their spiritual value. There are some things which are known only to oneself and one's Maker. These are clearly incommunicable. The experiments I am about to relate are not such. But they are spiritual, or rather moral; for the essence of religion is morality." Gandhi stated in his autobiography. While there is some substance in the argument that one has to be a Gandhi to understand Gandhi, it is an over-simplification and an effort to miss the obvious.

No major concept or practices of Gandhi could be understood fully unless they are internalised in the crucible of human life. For instance, the concept of 'Swaraj' as used by Gandhi has many layers of meaning. Political independence could be described to be what it is only at a very superficial level. It means mastery over oneself, one's thought and action. There cannot be any type of freedom so long as a person or a society is unable to get rid of fear. The 'inner voice' about which Gandhi often talked about and which many of even his closest friends and disciples could not comprehend has to be the sole guide and consultant in the progression of both mind and soul. Besides mustering sufficient courage to stand up and fight for what the inner voice dictates as Gandhi demonstrated with convincing success one has to be ready to 'walk alone'. This will not be possible if our approach is through our conditioned minds. Would it be possible for us to uncondition our minds and try to look at the achievements of leaders like Gandhi dispassionately? Just as the attempts to look at Gandhi infallible and god-like is reprehensible, the attempt to describe him in the fashionable parlance 'an enigma', just because some people are not able to comprehend the full import of what he symbolised or what he achieved is beyond their understanding, betrays a type of intellectual hypocrisy or a laboured effort to eminence by dissecting the life of popular icons.

Gandhi wrote, "I simply want to tell the story of my numerous experiments with truth, and as my life consists of nothing but those experiments, it is true that the story will take the shape of an autobiography. But I shall not mind, if every page of it speaks only of my experiments. I believe, or at any rate flatter myself with the belief, that a connected account of all these experiments will not be without benefits to the readers. My experiments in the political field are now known, not only to India, but to a certain extent to the 'civilised' world. For me, they have not much value; and the title of 'Mahatma' that they have won for me has, therefore, even less. Often the title has deeply pained me; and there is not a moment I can recall when it may be said to have tickled me. But I should certainly like to narrate my experiments in the spiritual field which are known only to myself, and from which I have derived such power as I possess for working in the political field. If the experiments are really spiritual, then there can be no room for self-praise. They can only add to my humility. The more I reflect and look back on the past, the more vividly do I feel my limitations." Many detractors of Gandhi did not find anything unusual or great in the work. Such iconoclastic efforts did not prevent the Autobiography from becoming one of the most sought after books which is still being read with interest in almost all continents.

A comforting thought that would come to anyone in this connection is the simple truth that many of the reformers of humanity from Aristotle to Martin Luther King, Jr. who were either ridiculed, scoffed at, crucified, burned or stoned to death or assassinated, exiled or excommunicated for the 'sins' of speaking out truth, did not live and die in vain. These 'rebels' as they were called are the torch-bearers of human civilisation and no amount of intolerance, jealousy, ignorance and arrogance could efface their importance in any manner. These men and women dared the powers that be to raise human life to lofty levels and helped others who did not allow themselves to be blinded by the idiosyncrasies of their times. These great souls, by whatever name you may call them, fearlessly held aloft the lamps of reason and never allowed to blind their reason and it was for this definance they had to pay dearly. And Gandhi was no exception to this. His martyrdom at the hands of a fanatic further illustrates this running steak of lunacy which surfaces periodically and unabated.

Gandhi loved life and looked at life as something precious. His life offers valuable lessons to each one of us who desperately looks for suitable anchors in our bid to survive in the mad rush for wealth and power which alone appear to be the guiding principles of contemporary society. It is here the significance of what Gandhi narrates assumes importance. It has been pointed out that each line in the Autobiography is a gem of infinite wisdom. The personal experiences of Gandhi ceases to be his own travails and one could see that most of the incidents narrated in the book have universal application and undoubtedly it emerges as the undiluted and honest record of one of the most sensitive humanists who in turn becomes the Universal Man, notwithstanding the other titles such as Mahatma, Saint, Martyr for Peace, and so on.

Professor K.D. Gangrade, one of India's widely acclaimed professional social work educator and sociologist, and scholar of considerable repute, looks at the autobiography of Gandhi from a refreshingly new angle to identify the lessons Gandhi's experiments offer to each individual in the moral reconstruction of our society along Gandhian lines. If Gandhi looked at his own life like a scientist, Professor Gangrade analyses the autobiography here from an angle of an inspired social scientist who is very much aware of the fact that at no stage all the teachings of any of the great men and women of any age would have perennial value. Yet the core of their teachings constitute the fulcrum around which human life revolves.

Professor Gangrade does not look at the autobiography as a sacred text. His approach is essentially that of a social scientist. He finds the autobiography as an ocean of infinite importance in shaping one's life. Never before has any scholar or admirer of Gandhi looked at the autobiography from this refreshingly original angle and it is hoped that this work of Professor Gangrade would encourage readers, particularly the young, to look at the achievements of Gandhi beyond the stereotyped image of the Father of the Nation and the champion of nonviolence and a few other concepts and practices associated with Gandhi. The present work stands out in many respects as a significant contribution to Gandhian and is a reliable handbook and a textbook to rediscover Gandhi through his autobiography.

The Gandhi Smriti and Darshan Samiti has great pleasure in presenting this work of immense significance as a tribute during the Fiftieth Anniversary of Gandhi's martyrdom and it is hoped that this will help the young readers to discover the Revolutionary Gandhi who offered a healthy alternative vision of life and a creative blue-print for the emergence of a new social order. We thank Professor Gangrade for undertaking this work on our behalf.

Dr. B.N. Pande, Vice-Chairman of Gandhi Smriti and Darshan Samiti, encouraged us at every stage of this work and we thank him for his guidance. Sri N. Vasudevan, Director of the Gandhi Media Centre, offered valuable help in making this book available in the present format

Gandhi Smriti and Darshan Samiti
New Delhi

N. RADHAKRISHNAN
Director

PREFACE

My book *Gandhi's Autobiography: Moral Lessons* in English, was published by Gandhi Smriti and Darshan Samiti, Rajghat, New Delhi, in 1998. I am extremely happy that it was very well received by the people in general and youth in particular. All copies were exhausted by the end of 2001. Its Hindi and Mongolian (by Mr. G.T. Tegshbureu) edition is also available.

I was not able to bring out immediately the second edition of the book as I was preoccupied with other assignments.

The title of the second edition of the book is *Moral Lessons from Gandhi's Autobiography*. I have also given references under each lesson to serve as a guide to researchers and others who are interested to know their derivatives and source. I have also included some essays on pertinent questions and issues often raised by people.

I am specially thankful to my colleague Mrs. Gita Shukla who prepared references for each lesson. Dr. Sita Ojha deserves to be given special thanks for her help in editing and finalizing the essays. Mr. Ramesh has helped in comparing the material from the main text. Thanks are also due to Mr. Rizwan, Mrs. Samiksha and Mrs. Seema Sharma who prepared the draft and final manuscript of the volume. My special thanks are also due to Dr. Savita Singh, Director, GSDS for providing a very congenial environment to accomplish this task.

I trust this new edition will be found useful by all those who are interested in finding Gandhian ways to deal with societal problems.

Gandhi Smriti and Darshan Samiti
Gandhi Darshan, Rajghat
New Delhi

K.D. GANGRADE

CONTENTS

1

INTRODUCTION

We generally believe that it is beyond us to practice Gandhian values and principles in our thoughts, speeches and deeds in the contemporary world in general and India in particular. Gandhi in his *Autobiography* or *The Story of My Experiments with Truth* writes:

> "I have all along believed that what is possible for one is possible for all, my experiments have not been conducted in the closet, but in the open; and I do not think that this fact detracts from their spiritual value.
>
> . . . The experiments I am about to relate [in the *Autobiography*] are . . . spiritual, or rather moral. . . . I claim for them nothing more than does a scientist who, though he conducts his experiments with the utmost accuracy, forethought and minuteness, never claims any finality about his conclusions, but keeps an open mind regarding them. . . . One claim I do indeed make as it is this. For me they appear to be absolutely correct, and seem for the time being final. . . . So long as my acts satisfy my reason and my heart, I must firmly adhere to my original conclusions."

The story includes experiments with nonviolence, celibacy and other principles of conduct believed to be distinct from Truth. But for Gandhi Truth is the sovereign principle, which includes other principles. This Truth is not only truthfulness in word, but truthfulness in thought also, and not only the relative Truth of our conception but the absolute Truth, the eternal principle, that is God. ". . . I worship God as Truth only. I have not yet found Him, but I am seeking after him, I am prepared to sacrifice the things dearest to me in pursuit of this quest. Even if the sacrifice demanded be my life, I hope I may be prepared to give it. I have faint glimpses of the absolute Truth, God and the daily conviction is growing upon me [Gandhi] that he alone is real and all else is unreal. The farther conviction growing."

Gandhi also said: ". . . whatever is possible for me is possible even for a child, and I have a sound reason for saying so. . . . They may appear impossible to an arrogant person. . . . The seeker after truth should be humble than the dust. The world crushes the dust under its feet, but the seeker after truth should be so humble himself that even the dust could crush him. . . ."

Thus it has been made abundantly clear by Gandhi that we must give up our ego to achieve ultimate Truth. That is to see God face to face in the service of people. Are our present-day leaders ready to sacrifice and shed their narrow self-interest and loyalties for the good of larger goal of development and building of the nation to wipe out tears from every eye of poor and down-trodden people?

The assessment of fifty years of our Independence reveal that the fruits of political independence have not reached all the huts of people in India specially those living in urban slums and rural hutments. The rise and fall of the country essentially depends on the calibre of leaders who are trustworthy in all respects and honoured by almost all the citizens of the nation. The leaders must cultivate and imbibe the values and principles pronounced by Gandhi in his autobiography.

In the present book these values and principles have been distinctly and clearly distilled for ready reference for everybody who is in search of Trutn. The lessons deduced from each Chapter from the experiments of Gandhi if adopted and followed will provide a clean administration; create a social order in which everybody gets social justice; prevent exploitation of poor and weak by the dominant and powerful; and stop corruption and scams in high, middle and low places.

In India of today there is nexus and collusion for corruption and exploitation of people between bureaucrats-businessmen-politicians to an unimaginable degree. India finds a place in the top most ten corrupt countries in the world. People have lost faith and confidence in their political leaders in whose hands their destiny lie. The question therefore arises—and has to be answered—as to what kind of values the present generation will focus on and transmit to the future generation. The coming generation do not find any model either in their parents or teachers or leaders to follow and emulate.

In the words of Gandhi, "role models should be pure as a crystal, meek as a lamb, brave as a lion and chivalrous to a fault."

There is a growing intolerance at all levels—in the family, society and country. Families are breaking up and its effect would be felt by the future generations, who will not pardon us.

I hope and trust the fragrance of the lessons drawn and deduced from Gandhi's autobiography will spread far and wide and will bring solidarity, tranquillity and lasting peace in the world as we march towards the twenty-first century.

Objective and Purpose of Gandhi's Autobiography

The objective of writing this Autobiography in the words of Gandhi is:

> "I am not writing the autobiography to please critics. Writing it is itself one of the experiments with Truth. One of its objects is certainly to provide some comfort and food for reflection for my co-workers."
>
> ". . . It is not my purpose to attempt a real autobiography. I simply want to tell the story of my numerous experiments with truth, and as my life consists of nothing but those experiments, it is true that the story will take the shape of an autobiography. But I shall not mind, if every page of it speaks only of my experiments. I believe, or at any rate flatter myself with the belief that a connected account of all these experiments will not be without benefit to the reader. My experiments in the political field are now known, not only to India, but to a certain extent to the 'civilized' world. But I should certainly like to narrate my experiments in the spiritual

field which are known only to myself, and from whom I have derived such power as I possess for working in the political field. If the experiments are really spiritual, then there can be no room for self-praise. The more I reflect and look back on the past the more vividly do I feel my limitations.

My uniform experience has convinced me that there is no other God than Truth. And if every page of these chapters does not proclaim to the reader that the only sources for realization of Truth is Ahimsa, I shall deem all my labour in writing these chapters to have been in vain. And, even though my efforts in this behalf may prove fruitless, let the readers know that the vehicle, not the great principle is at fault. After all, however, sincere my striving after Ahimsa may have been, they have still been imperfect and inadequate. The little fleeting glimpses, therefore, that I have been able to have of Truth can broadly convey—are idea as illustrations of the indescribable lustre of Truth, a million times more intense than that of the sun we daily see with our eyes. In fact what I have caught is only the faintest glimmer of that mighty effulgence. But this much I can say with assurance, as a result of all my experiments, that a perfect vision of Truth can only follow a complete realization of Ahimsa."

Emphasis on Fundamental Duties

We are currently observing the fifty-second *Puniya tithi*—Martyrdom Day—of Mahatma Gandhi. He was shot dead on 30th January, 1948 while on his way to his daily communion with the Creator. Godse shot Gandhi dead, the godly or so he thought. But he could only liquidate the messiah's mortal coils—'worn-out/garments'—*jeernani vasami*, in the language of the Gita. He is Mahatma, whose thoughts, words and deeds are in perfect harmony with each other.

According to Gandhi, instead only talking of fundamental rights, we should lay stress on fundamental duties and obligations. The true source of right is duty. If we discharge our duties, rights will not be far to seek. What we can do and what we must do is to imbibe the spirit of Gandhi's view of life. The Gandhian spark should glow in every Indian soul. The Gandhian ideals should be lived up to by each one of us in our individual family and institutional life, irrespective of what others do or fail to do. This will usher in transparency, purity and probity in public life, which are the basic ingredients of clean, efficient and democratic governance. [S. Ramakrishnan, "Attend to Fundamental Duties and Obligations," *The Hindustan Times*, 25 January, 1998, New Delhi, p. 13.]

It is only when the paramount duties are performed that the individual and society can exist and flourish. Duties and the performance of duties create the conditions in which rights can be exercised. Rights also imply an external authority or power that assures them. In the absence of such a power that assures or ensures, rights will remain notional and aspirational. So the assuring power and its viability have to be first created or sustained and that can be done only by the performance of the paramount duties. In this sense, therefore, rights flow from the performance of duties. It is the performance of duties that creates the pool and the power on which rights depend. Moreover, for the performance of one's duties one is not dependent on others. For the assurance of one's rights, one is dependent. Gandhi, therefore, believed that the performance of one's duty in conformity with the Higher Law is one of the basics on which society depends. No society can survive or ascend to higher levels of achievements if self-indulgence becomes its motto. (Ravindra Varma, "Gandhian Perception of the Ethical Foundation of Society," *Gandhi Marg*, October-December 1997, pp. 285-86.)

National Flag and Truth

Indian tricolour is symbolic of the three universal concepts of *Satyam* (Truth), *Sivam* (Goodness), *Sundaram* (Beauty). The motto of free India is *Satyameva Jayate* (Truth Alone Triumphs). Thus the ideal of India and Indian society is Truth and Righteousness.

The National Flag has three colours—scarlet, white and green. With *Dharma Chakra* inscribed in the middle is in blue colour. The flag represents the idealism of the country.

The French conjured up the ideals of Equality, Fraternity and Liberty with their tricolour banner.

In India and perhaps everywhere else in the world, the white colour is associated with purity, knowledge and light. The green connotes prosperity and plenty. The red signifies smartness and sacrifice and brotherhood. The wheel denotes the concept of Time-Destiny-Existence. The wheel also signifies comprehensive movement and progress, spiritual as well as secular. Thus, the *Dharma Chakra* is the symbolic epitome of Indian aspirations and ideals.

The significance of the Flag lies in giving Truth central place in the total and holistic approach to reach the cherished goal of *Sarvodaya* (development and welfare of all).

2

LESSONS FROM GANDHI'S AUTOBIOGRAPHY

I have drawn some lessons from the *Autobiography* of Mahatma Gandhi. I feel these lessons are highly relevant and universal and worth following as we enter the twenty-first century.

Introduction

1. What is possible for one is possible for all.
[Introduction, pg. *x*, para 1, line 6]
2. Truth is the Sovereign Principle.
[Introduction, pg. *xi*, para I, line 7-8]
3. The seeker after truth should be humbler than the dust. The world crushes the dust under its feet, but the seeker after truth should be so simple that even the dust could crush him.
[Introduction, pg. *xii*, lines 1-4]

PART I

Chapter I: Birth and Parentage

1. Gandhi's father was incorruptible and impartial in family as well as outside matters. [pg. 3, para 4, lines 4-6]
2. Mother was deeply religious and of saintly qualities. She would take the hardest vows and keep them unflinchingly.
[pg. 4, para 3, lines 2, 6]
3. Gandhi had model parents. He had imbibed good qualities from them. [pg. 45, para 1, line 1]

Chapter II: Childhood

1. Teacher prompted young Mohan to copy correct spelling of 'Kettle' from his neighbour's slate. But he would not be prompted. He thought the teacher was there to supervise against copying. He could not learn the art of copying. Elders' wrong advice need not be followed. However, this did not in the least diminish his respect for the teacher. He was by nature blind to the fault of elders. [pg. 5-6, para 3]
2. The book 'Shravana Pitrubhakti Natak' (a play about Shravana's devotion to his parents) made an indelible impression on his mind. That is, to respect and serve parents. One has to sacrifice all happiness and pleasure to serve parents. [pg. 6, para 2]
3. Similarly, another play—Harish Chandra—had inspired him to go through the ordeal, as Harish Chandra did, for upholding the ideal of Truth. One must be ready to face difficulties to follow the path of Truth. [pg. 6, para 3]

Chapter III: Child Marriage

1. Marriage among Hindus is no simple matter. It brings parents of both the parties almost to the verge of ruin. [pg. 7, para 4]
2. Child marriage for child does not mean anything more than the prospect of good clothes, rich dinners and a strange girl or boy to play with. [pg. 8, para 2]
3. But boys in general immediately assumes authority over the wives as husbands. This shows male's superiority over female. [pg. 9, para 1, last line]

Chapter IV: Playing the Husband

1. Nothing is impossible for pure love.[pg. 11, para 3, last line]
2. Jealousy does not wait for reasons. [pg. 10, para 10, line7]

Chapter V: At the High School

1. Early marriage generally results in wasting a year in education (Gandhi and his immediate elder broker wasted a year. His brother gave up studies altogether. One does not know how

many youth are in the same plight as he.) Child marriage must be avoided at all cost. [pg. 12, para 2]

2. Physical and mental training should have equal importance in the curriculum. [pg. 13, para 1, last line]
3. A man of Truth must also be a man of care. [Gandhi's desire to dislike gymnastics was because of his keen desire to serve as nurse to his ailing father. As soon as the school closed, he would rush home and begin serving/ministering him. Compulsory exercise came directly in the way of this service. Now it happened that one day (Saturday), when school was held in the morning, he had to go from home to the school for gymnastics at four O'clock in the afternoon. He had no watch and the clouds deceived him. Before he reached the school the boys (students) had all left. The next day Mr. Gimi—the gymnastics teacher—examined the roll, found him marked absent. On being asked the reason for absence, he (Gandhi) told him what had happened. He (Gimi) refused to believe him and ordered Gandhi to pay fine. He was convicted foı lying. That pained him deeply. How was he to prove hi: innocence. There was no way. He cried in deep anguish. H‹ saw that a man of Truth must also be a man of care. This wa: the first and last instance of his carelessness in school.] [pg. 14, line 1]
4. Good handwriting is a necessary part of education. Ba‹ handwriting should be regarded as a sign of an imperfec education. [pg. 14, para 1, lines 8-9]
5. Children should first be taught the art of drawing befor‹ learning how to write. [pg. 14, para 1, lines 13-14]
6. Every Hindu boy and girl should possess sound knowledge o Sanskrit language. [pg. 15, para 2, last line]
7. In all-India curricula of higher education there should be place for Hindi, Sanskrit, Persian, Arabic and English, besides of courses, the vernacular. [pg. 15, para 3, lines 1-3]

Chapter VI: A Tragedy

1. A reformer cannot, afford to have close intimacy with him whom he seeks to reform. [pg. 16, para 4, lines 1-3]

2. True friendship is an identity of souls rarely to be found in the world. [pg. 16, para 4, lines 4-5]
3. In friendship there is very little scope for reform. [pg. 16, para 4, line 6]
4. Man takes to vice far more readily than virtue. [pg. 16, para 4, line 8]

Chapter VII: A Tragedy Continued

1. Women is an incarnation of tolerance. [pg. 21, para 2, line 9]
2. Man, as soon as he gets his consciousness of right should be thankful to the Divine mercy for the escape. [pg. 20-21, para 4, last line]

   [A friend once took Gandhi to a brothel. He sent him in with the necessary instructions. Gandhi went into the jaws of sin, but God in his infinite mercy protected him against himself. Gandhi was almost struck blind and dumb in this den of vice. He sat near the woman on her bed, but he was tongue-tied. She naturally lost patience with him and showed him the door, with abuse and insults. He could recall four similar incidents in his life, and in most of them his good fortune, rather than any effort on his part, saved him. From a strict ethical point of view, all these occasions must be regarded as moral lapses, for the carnal desire was there, and it was as good as the act. But from an ordinary point of view, a man who is saved from physically committing sin is regarded as saved.]

Chapter VIII: Stealing and Atonement

1. A clean confession, combined with a promise never to commit the sin again, when offered before one who has the right to receive it, is the purest type of repentance. [pg. 24, para 2, lines 4-7]
2. Don't allow lust to overpower you. [pg. 26, para 3]

Chapter IX: My Father's Death and My Double Shame

1. When death is imminent, who can think of the right remedy? The inevitable has to be accepted. [pg. 25, para 1, lines 13-14]

[Every night his hands were busy nursing his father's legs, but his mind was hovering about the bedroom and that too at a time when religion, medical science and conscience alike forbade sexual intercourse with a pregnant woman. He was always glad to be relieved from his duty, and went straight to the bedroom. [pg. 25, lines 3-5]

The dreadful night came. But Gandhi was with his wife. The servant knocked the door. "Get up", he said, "Father is very ill." Gandhi guessed what 'very ill' meant at that moment. He sprang out of bed. "What is the matter? Do tell me!" "Father is not more!" [pg. 26, para 3]

The grip of lust did not allow Gandhi at the critical hour to be with his father so that his father could have died in his arms. This was a blot he had never been able to efface or forget.]

Chapter X: Glimpses of Religion

1. Impressions formed at childhood strike roots deep down into one's nature. [pg. 28, para 1, lines 9-11]
2. Morality is the basis of things and that Truth is the substance of all morality. [pg. 29, para 4, lines 1-3]
3. Return good for evil. [pg. 30, para 1, line 2]

Chapter XI: Preparation for England

1. Blessings of mothers and elders are really matters for Godspeed. [pg. 32, para 3, last 2 lines]

Chapter XII: Outcasts

1. Solemn promises made to mother to abstain from wine, women and meat will keep one safe from various temptations and lust. [pg. 33]

[A general meeting of the caste was called and Gandhi was summoned to appear before it. He was told "In the opinion of the caste, your proposal to go to England is not proper. Our religion forbids voyage abroad. We have also heard that one is obliged to eat and drink with Europeans!" To which Gandhi replied: "I do not think it is at all against our religion to go to England. I intend going there for further studies. And I have solemnly promised my mother to abstain from three things you fear most (wine, women and meat), I am sure the vow will keep me safe! I cannot alter my resolve to go to England."] [pg. 34, para 3]

Chapter XIII: In London at Last

1. Lawyers should have a long tongue. [pg. 36, para 2]
2. If the word of lawyer is not to be trusted, where is the use of possessing a certificate in the matter. [pg. 37, para 4, lines 7-8]
3. Don't touch other people's things. [pg. 38, line 7]
4. Don't ask questions in first acquaintance. [pg. 38, lines 7-8]
5. Don't talk loudly. [pg. 38, line 9]

Chapter XIV: My Choice

1. A vow is a vow. It cannot be broken. [pg. 40, para 3, last line]

Chapter XV: Playing the English Gentleman

1. A student ought to go on with studies. Character makes a gentleman and not dress. [pg. 44, para 2]

Chapter XVI: Changes

1. Make it a point and habit to account for every pie and for everything that comes into and goes out of your pocket. [pg. 45, lines 10-11]
2. Long walks may practically free oneself from illness and give a fairly strong body. [pg. 45, para 2, last line]
3. Latin is very useful to lawyers. [pg. 45, lines 17-18]
4. Knowing and understanding Latin means greater command over the English language. [pg. 46, lines 20-21]
5. Plain living will save plenty of time. [pg. 47, lines 20, 21]
6. Change should harmonize inward and outward life. [pg. 47, para 2, lines 6-10]

Chapter XVII: Experiments in Dietetics

1. Ethically man's supremacy over the lower animals meant not that the former should prey upon the latter, but that the higher

should protect the lower, and there should be mutual aid between the two as between man and man.

[pg. 47, para 2, lines 6-10]

2. Man should eat not for enjoyment but to live. [pg. 48, line 1]
3. A vegetarian diet is the least expensive. [pg. 48, line 10]
4. The real seat of taste is not the tongue but the mind. [pg. 48, last line]
5. Nobody can dare do harm a person whom God protects. [pg. 49, para 2, last line]
6. Despite pledge may be very explicit, people will turn and twist the text to suit their own purposes. This should not be done and people must adhere to the pledge taken by them. [pg. 49, last para]
7. Selfishness burns people who take pledge blindly, and by a use of ambiguous interpretation; they deceive themselves and seek to deceive the world and God. One golden rule is to accept the interpretation honestly put on the pledge by the party administering it. [pg. 50, lines 1-4]
8. A convert's enthusiasm for his new religion is greater than that of a person born in it. [pg. 50, para 2, lines 1-2]

Chapter XVIII: Shyness My Shield

1. One should not be drone. The bees are very busy, the drone is a thorough idler. [pg. 50, last para, last line]
2. Silence is part of the spiritual discipline of a votary of Truth. [pg. 53, para 1, lines 11-12]

Chapter XIX: The Canker of Untruth

1. It is never too late to mend. [pg. 56, para 1, line 3]

Chapter XX: Acquaintance with Religions

1. Renunciation is the greatest religion. [pg. 58, para 2, last line]
2. *Sermon on the mount:* The verses say that ye resist not evil: but whosoever shall smite thee on the right cheek, turn to him the other also. And if any man take away thy coat let him have thy cloak too. [pg. 58, para 2, lines 4-6]

3. For a bowl of water, give goodly meal.
[pg. 58, para 2, lines 7-8]

Chapter XXI: Nirbal Ke Bala Rama

1. Prayer is an unfailing means of cleansing the heart of passions. Prayer needs no speech. It is in itself independent of any serious effort. [pg. 61, para 2]
2. Supplication, worship, prayer are no superstition; they are acts more real than the acts of eating, drinking, sitting or walking. It is exaggeration to say that they alone are real, all else is unreal. [pg. 61, para 1]
[In England even in respectable households in play of rubber bridge every player indulged in innocent jokes with the landlady as a matter of course, but Gandhi's companion and their hostess began to make indecent ones as well. Gandhi did not know that his friend was an adept in the art. It captured Gandhi and he also joined in. Just when Gandhi was about to go beyond the limit, leaving the cards and the game to themselves, God through the good companion uttered the blessed warning: "Whence this devil is in you, my boy! Be offquick!" Gandhi was ashamed. He took the warning, and expressed within himself gratefulness to his friend. Remembering the vow he had taken before his mother, he fled the scene.]

Chapter XXII: Narayan Hemchandra

1. Civilized fellows are generally cowards. Great men never look at a person's exterior. They think of his heart.
[pg. 64, para 2]

Chapter XXIII: The Great Exhibition

1. The Eiffel Tower (Paris) was a monument of man's folly, not of his wisdom. [pg. 66, para 1, lines 4-5]
2. Tobacco is the worst of all intoxications inasmuch as a man addicted to it is tempted to crime which a drunkard never dared to do. Liquor made a man mad but tobacco clouded his intellect and made him build castles in the air.
[pg. 66, para 4, lines 1-3]

Chapter XXIV: "Called"—But Then?

1. The curriculum of study to the bar is easy, barrister being humorously known as 'dinner barristers'! Everyone knew that examination has no value. [pg. 67, para 4, lines 1-3]
   [There are two conditions which had to be fulfilled before a student was formally called to the bar: 'Keeping terms'; twelve terms equivalent to about three years and passing examinations. 'Keeping terms' means eating one's terms, *i.e.*, attending at least six out of about twenty-four dinners in a term. Eating did not mean actually partaking of the dinner, it meant reporting oneself at the fixed hour and remaining present throughout the dinner.] [pg. 66, para 3, lines 1-7]

Chapter XXV: My Helplessness

1. It is easy to be called to the bar but it is difficult to practise. Legal maxims, "use your property in such a way as not to damage that of others", is one of them, but Gandhi was at a loss to know how one could employ this maxim for the benefit of one's client. [pg. 68, para 6, lines 1-7]
2. A Vakil should know human nature. He should be able to read a man's character from his face. And every Indian ought to know Indian history. This has no connection with the practice of law, but you ought to have that knowledge. [pg. 7, lines 5-9]
3. Honesty and industry are enough to become a successful lawyer. [pg. 69, para 2, last three lines]

PART II

Chapter I: Raychandbhai

1. The outer storm must be considered as a symbol of the inner. [pg. 73, para 2, line 1]
2. There is a great deal of Truth in the doctrine that true knowledge is impossible without a Guru. (An imperfect teacher may be tolerable in mundane matters, but not in spiritual matters.) [pg. 75, para 2, lines 2-3]

3. Only a perfect Gnani (a knowing one, a seer) deserves to be enthroned as a Guru. There must be ceaseless striving after perfection. For one gets the Guru that one deserves. Infinite striving after perfection is one's right. It is its own reward. The rest is in the hands of God. [pg. 75, para 2, lines 5-9]

Chapter II: How I Began Life

1. The barrister's profession is a bad job—much show and little knowledge. [pg. 78, para 4, lines 1-2]

Chapter III: The First Case

1. For a barrister to vegetate for five to seven years is not unusual. [pg. 78, para 8, lines 1-2]
2. Make a virtue of necessity. [pg. 78, para 7, lines 5-6]

Chapter IV: The First Shock

1. Don't compromise principle by any means. [pg. 8, para 2]
2. Selfishness is blind. [pg. 82, para 1, line 15]

Chapter V: Preparing for South Africa

1. Power intoxicates to an inordinate extent. [pg. 83, last para, line 6]
2. Petty intrigues between states and intrigues of officers for power were and are the order of the day. [pg. 84, para 2, lines 3-4]

Chapter VI: Arrival in Natal

1. Chess is a game in which there is plenty of scope for the exercise of one's intelligence. [pg. 86, last para, lines 6-7]
2. Many a youth, must have fallen into sin by a false sense of shame. This must be avoided. [pg. 88, last para, lines 1-3]

Chapter VII: Some Experiences

1. Man may be practically unlettered, but he may have rich fund of experiences. He has to be respected and one must learn from his vast experiences. [pg. 89, para 1, lines 1-2]

Chapter VIII: On the Way to Pretoria

1. It is cowardice to run away without fulfilling obligation and resolving problem. [pg. 94, para 1, lines 3-4]
2. Root out the disease and suffer hardship in the process. [pg. 94, para 1, line 7]
3. Redress for wrongs should only be to the extent that would be necessary for the removal of the prejudice. [pg. 94, para 1, line 8]

Chapter IX: More Hardships

1. Don't pocket insults for making money. [pg. 97, para 2, lines 2-3]

Chapter X: First day in Pretoria

1. Some people believe:
   (*a*) It is impossible to find eternal peace, unless one accepts Jesus as the only Son of God and Saviour of mankind. [pg. 100, para 3, lines 6-8]
   (*b*) The book of books is the Holy Bible. [pg. 101, line 1]
2. One should learn to respect all religions. [pg. 100, para 4, last line]
3. One should not embrace another religion unless one understands his own. [pg. 101, para 8, lines 3-6]

Chapter XI: Christian Contacts

1. The prayers are supplications to God for various things, according to each person's desire. The prayer for God are to open the doors of heart. [pg. 101, last para]

Chapter XII: Seeking Touch with Indians

1. Truth is inconsistent with business. Business is a very practical affair, and Truth is a matter of religion. [pg. 105, para 2, lines 11-15]

   [The merchants or businessmen must be awakened from this fallacy. Their responsibility to be truthful is all the greater in a foreign land because the conduct of a few Indians is the

measure of that of millions of their fellow countrymen.]
[pg. 105, para 2, lines 11-15]

2. Don't lose patience with pupils. [pg. 106, para 1, line 9]

Chapter XIII: What It Is To Be A 'Coolie'

1. Don't go to Court in respect of any personal grievance.
[pg. 109, line 1]

Chapter XIV: Preparation for the Case

1. Facts are three-fourths of the law. [pg. 110, para 4, line 1-2]
2. If we take care of the facts of a case the law will take care of itself. [pg. 110, para 4, lines 8-9]
3. Facts mean Truth, and once we adhere to Truth, the law comes to our aid naturally. [pg. 111, para 2, lines 15-16]
4. True functioning of a lawyer is to unite parties.
[pg. 111, para 2, lines 15-16]

Chapter XV: Religious Ferment

1. God could not but listen to prayer fervently offered.
[pg. 112, para 3, lines 3-4]
[For example, George Muller of Bristol of England depended entirely on prayer even for his temporal needs.]
[pg. 113, line 1]
2. One must learn to follow the inner voice. [The Kingdom of God is within you.]
[book written by Tolstoy pg. 114, last para, line 9]

Chapter XVI: Man Proposes and God Disposes

1. There can be no fee for public work. [pg. 116, para 7, line 2]

Chapter XVII: Settled in Natal

1. One must not accept any salary for public work.
[pg. 116, para 7, line 2]

Chapter XVIII: Colour Bar

1. When at Rome do as Romans do. [pg. 123, para 2, line 5]
[Gandhi while practising in the court of Natal did not wear

the turban to obey the law of the country as it would have been ill becoming of him to disregard a custom of the court in the province of Natal.] [pg. 123, para 2]

2. The very insistence of Truth required that one must appreciate the beauty of truth. This is an essential part of Satyagraha. [pg. 123, para 3, lines 5-6]

Chapter XIX: Natal Indian Congress

1. Sustained agitation is essential for making an impression on the authority. [pg. 123, para 5, lines 4-5]
2. Not to carry public work with borrowed money. [pg. 124, last para, line 1]
3. One could rely in people's promises in most matters except in respect of money. [pg. 125, lines 1-2]
4. Carefully kept accounts are *sine qua non* for any organization. [pg. 126, para 2, lines 5-6]

Chapter XX: Balasundram

1. Indentured labour is generally considered the property of his master. [pg. 128, line 6]

Chapter XXI: The £ 3 Tax

1. The indentured labour could be tolerated as independent agriculturists, but their competition in trade could not be brooked. [pg. 130, para 1, lines 3-4]
2. Truth will ultimately triumph in the end. [pg. 131, para 3, line 1]

Chapter XXII: Comparative Study of Religions

1. God can be realized through service. [pg. 132, para 1, line 4]

Chapter XXIII: As a Householder

1. Howsoever one may want to repair, a rift is a rift. [pg. 137, line 4]

Chapter XXIV: Homeward

1. Religion and morality were/are synonymous. [pg. 136, para 1, line 2]

Chapter XXV: In India

1. The authors of Smriti's have laid the greatest emphasis on cleanliness both—inward and outward.
[pg. 142, para 3, lines 4-5]

Chapter XXVI: Two Passions

1. Service which is rendered without joy helps neither the worker nor the served. [pg. 145, para 3, lines 3-4]

Chapter XXVIII: The Bombay Meeting

1. A patriot cannot afford to ignore any branch of service to the motherland. [pg. 147, para 4, lines 5-6]

Chapter XXVIII: Poona and Bombay

1. Leaders should be like river Ganges. [pg. 148, para 2]
[Gandhi regarded Sir Pherozeshah Mehta like the Himalaya, the Lokmanya Tilak like the Ocean, and Gokhale as the Ganges. One could have a refreshing bath in the holy river. The Himalaya was unscaleable, and one could not easily launch forth on the sea, but the Ganges invited one to its bosom.] [pg. 148, para 2, lines 5-9]
2. There is no barrier that love cannot break.
[pg. 149, para 5, last line]

Chapter XXIX: 'Return Soon'

1. The aggrieved party imagines that the editor of a newspaper or a magazine is a power in the land. Only he knows that his powers can hardly travel beyond the threshold of his office.
[pg. 151, para 1, lines 4-6]
2. We win justice quickest by rendering justice to others.
[pg. 151, para 4]

PART III

Chapter I: Rumblings of the Storm

1. A Hindu wife regards implicit obedience to her husband as the highest religion. A Hindu husband regards himself as lord

and master of his wife, who must ever dance attendance upon him. This type of attitude must stop. The women must be given right place and status in the Hindu society.

[pg. 155, para 2]

2. All become one in face of the common danger. They forget their differences and begin to think of the one and only one God—Mussalmans, Hindus, Christians and all.

   [pg. 156, para 2, lines 9-11]

3. The name of God disappears from the lips of people with the disappearance of danger. [pg. 156, para 2, lines 24-25]

   [The momentary mood of earnest prayer gives place to *maya* as soon as fear of death disappears.]

Chapter II: The Storm

1. Western civilization, unlike the Eastern is predominantly based on force. [pg. 159, para 1, line 9-10]

   [I (Gandhi) said: "I hope God will give me the courage and the sense to forgive whites for their violent threats and acts and refrain from bringing them to law. I have no anger against them. I am only sorry for their ignorance and their narrowness. I know that they sincerely believe that what they are doing today is right and proper. I have, therefore, no reason to be angry with them. When truth becomes known they will be sorry for their conduct."] [pg. 159, para 2]

Chapter III: The Test

1. It is idle to adjudicate upon the right and wrong of incidents that have already happened. It is useful to understand them and, if possible, to learn a lesson from them for the future.

   [pg. 161, last para, lines 1-3]

Chapter IV: The Calm after the Storm

1. It is not good to run public institutions on permanent funds. A permanent fund carries in itself the seed of the moral fall of the institution. A public institution means an institution conducted with the approval, and from the funds of the public.

When such an institution ceases to have public support, it forfeits its right to exist. [pg. 165, para 2, line 6-11]

2. The ideal for public institutions is to live, like nature, from day to day. The institution that fails to win public support has no right to exist as such. [pg. 165, para 2, line 16-18]

Chapter V: Education of Children

1. The young children should not be separated from their parents. The education that children imbibe in a well ordered household is impossible to obtain in hostels. The children should not be deprived of the training that can be had from contact with the parents. [pg. 166-67, last para, lines 10-11]
2. A choice has to be made between liberty and learning, who will not say that former has to be preferred a thousand times to the latter. [pg. 168, para 2, last three lines]
   [The youth whom I (Gandhi) called out in 1920 from those citadels of slavery—their school and colleges—and whom I (Gandhi) advised that it was better to remain unlettered and break stones for the sake of liberty than to go for a literary education in the chains of slavery will probably be able now to trace my (Gandhi's) advice to its source.] [pg. 168, last para]

Chapter VI: Spirit of Service

1. A careful study of any subject is inestimable help. [pg. 170, parà 1, lines 5-6]
2. In order to the proper upbringing of children, the parents ought to have a general knowledge of the care and nursing of babies. [pg. 170, para 2, lines 1-3]
3. The education of the child begins with conception. The physical and mental states of the parents at the moment of conception are reproduced in the baby. Then during the period of pregnancy it continues to be affected by the mother's moods and temperament, as also by her way of life. After birth the child imitates the parents and for a considerable number of years entirely depends on them for its growth. [pg. 170, para 2, lines 9-16

4. We labour under a sort of superstition that the child has nothing to learn during the first five years of its life. On the contrary, the fact is that the child never learns in after-life what it does in its five years. [pg. 170, para 2, lines 6-9]
5. It is the height of ignorance to believe that the sexual act is an independent function like sleeping or eating. The world depends for its existence on the act of generation, and as the world is the playground of God, and a reflection of his glory, the act of generation should be controlled for the ordered growth of the world. He who realizes this controls his lust at any cost, equips himself with knowledge necessary for the physical, mental and spiritual well bring of his progeny and give the benefits of that knowledge to posterity.
[pg. 170-71, last para]

Chapter VII: Brahmacharya I

1. The devotion of a servant is a thousand times more praise-worthy than that of a wife to her husband.
[pg. 171, last two lines]
2. It should be important conviction with the public man that procreation and consequent care of children are inconsistent with public service. [pg. 172, last para, lines 9-10]
[In order to devote myself (Gandhi) to the service of community I decided to relinquish the desire for children and wealth and live the life of a *vanaprastha*—of one retired from household cares.]

Chapter VIII: Brahmacharya II

1. The vow is a sure shield against temptations.
[pg. 174, para 1, lines 6-7]
2. In *Brahmacharya* lies the protection of the body, the mind and the soul. [pg. 174, para 2, lines 5-6]
3. The *Brahmachari*'s food should be limited, simple, spiceless and if possible uncooked. His ideal food is fresh fruit and nuts. [pg. 175, para 1, last line; para 2, line 1]
4. The *Brahmachari* must control his mind as it (mind) is at the root of sexuality. *Brahmacharya* means control of the senses in thought, word and deed. [pg. 176, para 1, line 1]

Chapter IX: Simple Life

1. It is difficult to make friends and people to appreciate the beauty of self-help. [pg. 178, para 2, lines 1-2]

Chapter X: The Boer War

1. The average Englishman believed that the Indian was (and is) a coward, incapable of taking risks of working beyond his immediate self-interest. [pg. 179, para 4, lines 1-3]
   [This is evident from the current scams and scandals prevalent in the country. Corruption has become all pervasive. Indians must rise in the twenty-first century and prove to the world that nobody can match their honesty and integrity.]
   [Author's own comment]
2. Human nature shows itself at its best in moments of trial and crisis. [pg. 181, para 1, line 2]

Chapter XI: Sanitary Reform and Famine Relief

1. Indians are not good in keeping their houses and surroundings clean. Habit of cleanliness must be inculcated in people. [pg. 181, para 3, lines 8-9]
2. It is very difficult to help the community in getting to do its own duty as against claiming for its rights. [pg. 182, para 1, lines 2-3]
3. One has to have infinite patience to get the people to do any work. [pg. 182, para 1, lines 8-9]
4. It is the reformer who is anxious for the reform, and not society, from which he should expect nothing better than opposition, abhorrence and even moral persecution. [pg. 182, para 1, lines 9-11]
5. Truth is like a vast tree, which yields more and more fruit, the more you nurture it. The deeper the search in the mine of Truth, the richer the discovery of the gems buried there, in the shape of opening for an ever greater variety of service. [pg. 182, para 4, lines 2-6]

Chapter XII: Return to India

1. The voice of the people is the voice of God. Service has its own reward. [pg. 183, para 3, lines 2-3]

2. A public worker should not accept costly gifts. [pg. 185, last line]
3. For gifts a trust may be created in favour of the community. [pg. 185, para 6, lines 5-6]

Chapter XIII: In India Again

1. Service is no mushroom growth. It presupposes the will first and then experience. There is no lack of will on the part of good simple hearted young men, but they lack experience. [pg. 187, para 2, lines 4-7]
2. The National Congress before the entry of Gandhi would meet three days every year and then go to sleep. The organization should remain active rather than just have a conference or meeting for three days or so in a year. [pg. 187, para 2, lines 7-9]

Chapter XIV: Clerk and Bearer

1. Always respect elders. [pg. 189]
2. Work of an organization must be properly rationalized. [The Congress secretary in those days was so busy that he had no time even to button his shirt. There was little regard for economy of energy. More than one did the work of one, and many of an important thing was no one's business at all. The work of an organization must be properly rationalized and distributed amongst various functionaries.] [pg. 189]

Chapter XV: In the Congress

1. Resolution(s) moved by an important leader generally get unanimously passed without understanding or discussing them. [pg. 190-91]

Chapter XVI: Lord Curzon's Darbar

1. Heavy is the toll of sins and wrongs that wealth, power and prestige exact from man. [pg. 193, para 3]

Chapter XVII: A Month with Gokhale I

1. Some leaders' private relations and friendship are all for public good. [pg. 194, para 1, lines 2-3]

[Gokhale's private relations and friendship are all for public good. All his talks has reference only to the good of the country and are absolutely free from any trace of untruth or insincerity. India's poverty and subjection are matters of constant and intense concern for him. He is a person whose example needs to be emulated.] [pg. 194, para 1]

2. There are some leaders who will spend very little from the salary on themselves and spend the rest on public purposes. [pg. 194, para 6]

   [Prof. P.C. Ray (now Sir), who having a monthly salary of Rs. 800, keeps just Rs. 40 for himself and devotes the balance to public purposes. He is not, and does not want to get married.] [pg. 193, para 6]

3. Attend court in the interest of client(s).

   [There is an example of Mandlik. He once having missed the train, engaged a special train so as to be able to attend the court in the interest of his client.] [pg. 194, para 3]

4. There is no reason to suppose that everything what the leaders do is with a view to personal comfort.[pg. 195, para 1, line 7]

   [Gokhale used to have a horse-carriage in those days. Gandhi remonstrated him, "Can't you make use of the tram-car for going about from place to place? Is it derogatory to a leader's dignity?" Slightly pained he (Gokhale) said, "So you also have failed to understand me! I do not use my council amount for my personal comforts. I envy your liberty to go about in tram-car, but I am sorry I cannot do likewise. When you are the victim of as wide a publicity as I am, it will be difficult, if not impossible, for you to go about in tram-car.]

5. No matter, what amount of work one has, one should always find sometime for exercise, just as one does for one's meals. It does not take away from one's capacity for work, it adds to it. [pg. 195, para 5, lines 3-7]

Chapter XVIII: A Month with Gokhale II

1. One must oppose giving alms to sturdy beggars. [pg. 196, para 6, line 8]

2. All places are equally good for us. The people are like a flock of sheep, following where leaders lead them.
[pg. 196, last para]
3. The killing of animal(s) as a part of religious worship is very cruel. [pg. 197, para 2, lines 2-3]
4. The life of a lamb is no less precious than that of a human being. [pg. 197, para 4, lines 4-5]
5. The more helpless a creature, the more entitled it is to protection by man from the cruelty of man.
[pg. 197, para 4, line 4-5]

Chapter XIX: A Month with Gokhale III

1. There should be an intense desire to know life of people to understand and work with them. This is possible by living with them. [pg. 198, para 5]

Chapter XX: In Benaras

1. Third class passengers, in railways, are treated like sheep and their comforts are sheep's comforts.
[pg. 200, para 2, lines 6-7]
[We have abolished third class, but situation has not changed much.]
2. The indifference of the railway authorities to the comfort of the third class [now second class] passengers, combined with the dirty and inconsiderate habits of the passengers themselves make third class travelling a trial for a passenger of cleanly ways. [pg. 200, para 3, lines 1-4]
3. One remedy for awful state of things—that educated men should make it a point of travelling third class and reform the habits of the people, as also never letting the railway authorities rest in peace, sending in complaints wherever necessary, never resorting to bribes or unlawful means for obtaining their own comforts, and never putting up with infringement of rules on the part of anyone concerned. [pg. 200, last para]
4. The surroundings of Kashi Vishwanath Temple are full of the dirt and the noise. Gandhi went in search for God but failed to find Him. He was not in a particularly good mood. He had no

mind to give any *dakshina*. So he offered a pie. The *panda* incharge got angry and threw away the pie. "Go away," he replied. "I (*Maharaj*) don't care for your pie." And then followed a volley of abuse. "I (Gandhi) took the pie and went away my way, flattering myself that the Brahmin had lost a pie and I had saved one." But *Maharaj* was hardly the man to let the pie go. He called me back and said, "All right, leave the pie here. I would rather not be as you are. If I refuse your pie, it will be bad for you." I silently gave him the pie and, with a sigh, went away. If anyone doubts the infinite mercy of God, let him look at these sacred places. [pg. 202, para 2-5]

5. God (Sri Krishna) in Gita had proclaimed long ago: "Whatever a man sows, that shall he reap! The law of *Karma* is inexorable and impossible of evasion. [pg. 203, para 1]

Chapter XXI: Settled in Bombay

1. One should hate as poisonous the use of flattery for getting briefs. [pg. 203, para 5, last line]
2. As the elephant is powerless to think in terms of the ant, in spite of best intentions in the world, even so is the Englishman powerless to flunk in the terms of, or legislate for, the Indian. [pg. 205, line 4-7]

Chapter XXII: Faith on its Trial

1. It is only during events of crisis that a man's faith is truly tested. One must face the crisis boldly and adhere to one's faith. [pg. 206, para 2, lines 5-6]

   [Gandhi was advised by the doctor to give eggs and other non-vegetarian diet, to his ailing son to pick up his health. Gandhi was in a great dilemma because he could not ascertain his son's wish as he [son] was not grown up to decide for himself. Gandhi decided against the advice of the doctor. He felt that there should be a limit even to the means of keeping ourselves alive. Even for life itself we cannot to do certain things. Religion, as he understood did not permit him to use meat, eggs and the like.] [pg. 206, para 2]

2. The thread of life is in the hands of God. Why worry and let us entrust it to Him, and in His name go on with the treatment one has thought is as the right treatment.
[pg. 207, para 1, lines 5-7]

Chapter XXIII: To South Africa Again

1. Enterprising youth may emigrate to other countries if they could not find an opening in their own country.
[pg. 209, para 6]
2. It is wrong to expect certainties in this world, where all else but God, that Truth, is an uncertainty. The quest for Truth is the summum bonum of life. [pg. 209-10, last para]

PART IV

Chapter I: "Love's Labour Lost?"

1. The rule of might being right or the law of sword.
[pg. 213, para 4, lines 3-4]
2. But sword we had none.
3. We scarcely had the nerve and the muscle even to receive sword-cuts.

Chapter II: Autocrats from Asia

1. Public departments are maintained for the good of the people and should be responsive to public opinion.
[pg. 215, para 4, lines 6-7]

Chapter III: Pocketed the Insult

1. One may not look forward to any reward for one's labours, but one should be certain that a good action is bound to bear the fruit in the end.

Chapter IV: Quickened Spirit of Sacrifice

1. Some people go for life insurance due to fear of death and want of faith in God. [pg. 219, para 2, lines 2-3]
2. The spirit of sacrifice is tempered by the desire to lay by something for the future. [pg. 219, para 1, lines 1-3]

3. The chief thing about theosophy is to cultivate and promote the ideas of brotherhood. [pg. 220, para 2, lines 10-11]

Chapter V: Result of Introspection

1. The Gita can become an infallible guide of conduct and dictionary of daily reference. [pg. 221, para 1, lines 2-3]
   [Gandhi turned to this dictionary of conduct for a ready solution of all his troubles and trials. Words like *aparigraha* (non-possession) and *samabhava* (equability) gripped him.]
2. The Gita's teaching of non-possession to mean that those who desire salvation should act like Trustee, who though having control over great possession, regards not an iota of the possession as his.
   [pg. 221-22, para 1, last two lines and first two lines]

Chapter VI: A Sacrifice to Vegetarianism

1. One most important way of carrying out missionary work is by personal example and discussion with searchers for knowledge. [pg. 223, para 2, lines 4-6]
2. A man's reforming zeal ought not to make him exceed his limits. [pg. 224, para 4, lines 4-5]

Chapter VII: Experiments in Earth and Water Treatment

1. Fresh fruit and nuts are the natural diet of man.
   [pg. 225, para 3, lines 6-7]
2. A writer almost always presents one aspect of a case, whereas every case can be seen from no less than seven points of view, all of which are probably correct by them.
   [pg. 226, para 3, lines 4-6]

Chapter VIII: A Warning

1. In the legal profession, the Indian proverb says that as a man eats, so shall he become. [pg. 227, para 3, line 8]
2. For the seeker of truth who lives on fear of God and who will see him face to face, restraint in diet both as to quality and quantity is as essential as restraint in thought and speech.
   [pg. 228, para 3, lines 6-9]

Chapter IX: A Tussle with Power

1. In the legal profession, the very intellect sometimes becomes an abomination to one inasmuch as it could be prostituted for screening crime. [pg. 230, para 1, lines 2-4]
2. Hate the sin and not the sinner. [pg. 230, para 6, line 4]
3. It is quite proper to resist and attack a system and not its author. [pg. 230, last para]

Chapter X: A Sacred Recollection and Penanace

1. One should not make any distinction between relatives and strangers, countrymen, and foreigners, white and coloured, Hindu and Indians of other faiths, whether Mussalmans, Sikhs, Parsis, Christians, *Dalits* and Jews. [pg. 231, para 1, lines 4-7]
2. One should not use husband's authority to harass one's wife out of one's blind love for her. [pg. 231, last para, last three lines]
3. One should not use taunting language or words which may pierce wife's ears like an arrow. [pg. 232, para 2]
4. A woman having matchless powers of endurance will always be the victor. [pg. 232, para 4, last 2 lines]
5. One should think that the wife is a helpmate, a comrade and a partner in the husband's joys and sorrows. Giving her equal respect will make domestic life more and more graceful, sweet and happy. [pg. 232, para 6, lines 3-4]

Chapter XI: Intimate European Contacts

1. It is extremely difficult to describe and characterize one's belief in God. [pg. 233, para 3-4]
2. One should follow the sage maxim that nothing once begun should be abandoned unless it is proved to be morally wrong. [pg. 234, para 3, lines 4-5]

Chapter XII: European Contacts (*continued*)

1. A person's character should be as clear as crystal and courage that would shame a warrior. [pg. 237, para 2, lines 4-5]
2. One knows neither night nor day in toiling for a cause. [pg. 237, para 3, line 1]

Chapter XIII: Indian Opinion

1. The sole aim of journalism should be service. The newspaper press (media) is a great power, but just as an unchained torrent of water submerges whole countrysides and devastates crops, even so uncontrolled pen serves but to destroy. If the control is from without it proves more poisonous than want of control. It can be profitable only when exercising control from within. [pg. 239, para 2, lines 6-7]
2. Satyagraha would probably have been impossible without Indian Opinion [a journal]. [pg. 239, para 1, lines 16-17]
3. The aim of the editor has to be to establish intimate and clear bond between him and the readers.
   [pg. 239, para 1, lines 21-22]

Chapter XIV: Coolie Locations or Ghettoes

1. People usually migrate abroad in search of wealth and trade.
   [pg. 241, lines 6-7]
   [But the bulk of the Indians who went to South Africa were ignorant, pauper and agriculturists. The traders and educated Indians who followed them were very few.]
   [pg. 24, lines 7-11]

Chapter XV: The Black Plague I

1. If one's heart is pure, calamity brings in its train men and measures to fight it. [pg. 243, para 3, lines 1-2]
2. The indefatigable zeal and fearlessness with which youth work will rejoice everyone beyond measure.
   [pg. 244, para 1, lines 1-2]

Chapter XVI: The Black Plague II

1. Once awakened to a sense of their duty, the official(s) of any government or non-official body will not delay in taking prompt measure(s). [pg. 244, para 4, lines 5-7]

Chapter XVII: Location in Flames

1. When people are in a terrible fright, the leader's constant presence is a great consolation to them.
   [pg. 247, para 3, lines 1-2]

Chapter XVIII: The Magic Spell of a Book

1. Anything that appeals to intellect must be translated into practice. [pg. 248-49, last line and first line respectively]
2. A public worker should not make statements of which he has not made sure of their authenticity. [pg. 249, para 2, lines 1-2]
3. A book's influence can be so much upon the reader that it can change his life in accordance with the ideals contained in it. [pg. 249, para 5, last two lines]
4. The limited reading may help thoroughly to digest what one reads. [pg. 250, lines 2-3]
5. A poet is one who can call forth the good talent in the human breast. Poets don't influence all alike, for everyone is not evolved in an equal measure. The teachings of *Unto This Last* made Gandhi realize:
   (*a*) That the good of the individual is contained in the good of all.
   (*b*) That a lawyer's work has the same value as the barber's, inasmuch as all have the same right of earning their livelihood from their work.
   (*c*) That a life of labour, that is, the life of the tiller of the soil and craftsman, is the life worth living. [pg. 250, para 1-2]

Chapter XIX: Phoenix Settlement

1. Followers, co-workers follow the leader in his ethical experiments without much argument and discussion. [pg. 251-52]

Chapter XX: The First Night

1. No use of shedding tears if the things don't work the way we like. We should do whatever is humanly possible. [pg. 253, lines 1-2]
2. People cooperate and do respond in an emergency. [pg. 253, para 7]

Chapter XXI: Polak Takes the Plunge

1. It is found by experience that man makes his plans to be often

upset by God, but at the same time where the ultimate goal is the search of truth, no matter how a man's plans are frustrated, the issue is never injurious and often better than anticipated.
[pg. 254, para 2, lines 6 to 10]

2. There are some persons who are not conscious of their own capacities. They need be awakened to their capacities.
[pg. 255, First three lines]
3. There are some who by their sociability win the hearts of all and soon become the members of the family. They take to hard work like duck takes to water.
[pg. 255, para 3, lines 3-4]

Chapter XXII: Whom God Protects

1. Experience has shown that all experiments involve obvious risks. [pg. 257, first two lines]
2. He who will go in for novel experiments must begin with himself. This will lead to quicker discovery of 'truth' and God always protects the honest experimenter(s).
[pg. 257, para 1, lines 4-7]
3. Common religion is the religion of ethics.
[pg. 257, para 3, last line]
4. The distinction between heterogeneous and homogeneous is discovered to be merely imaginary. We are all one family.
[pg. 258, para 1, lines 10-12]
5. True beauty consists in purity of heart.
[pg. 258, para 2, lines 12-13]

Chapter XXIII: A Peep into the Household

1. Character building is the bounden duty of every parent.
[pg. 260, lines 28-29]
2. Children inherit the qualities of the parents no less than their physical features. Environment does play an important part, but the original capital on which a child starts in life is inherited from its ancestors. [pg. 260, para 1, lines 1-4]
3. The Indian parents who train children to think and talk in English from their infancy betray their children and their country. They deprive them of the spiritual and social heritage

of the nation and render them to that extent unfit for the service of the country. [pg. 261, lines 1-5]

Chapter XXIV: The Zulu Rebellion

1. British and some of their subjects believed that the British Empire existed for the welfare of the world. [The Zulu rebellion was against the new rule and the tax imposed on them.] [pg. 261, para 1, line 7]

Chapter XXV: Heart Searching

1. *Brahmacharya* is necessary for one who aspires to serve humanity with his whole soul. [pg. 264, para 2, lines 10-11]
2. Life without *Brahmacharaya* appears to be insipid and animal-like. The man, brute by nature, knows no self-restraint. Man is man because he is capable of, and only in so far as he exercises self-restraint *Brahmacharya*, which is so full of wonderful potency, is by no means an easy affair, and certainly not a mere matter of the body. It begins with bodily restraint, but does not end there. The perfection of it precludes even an impure thought. A true *Brahmachari* will not even dream of satisfying the fleshly appetite, and until he is in that condition, he has great deal of ground to cover. [pg. 265, para 1-2]
3. There is a key to lock out undesirable thoughts, but everyone has to find it out for himself. Saints and seers have left their experiences for us, but they have given us no infallible and universal prescription. [pg. 265, para 3, lines 6-9]

Chapter XXVI: The Birth of Satyagraha

1. *Satyagraha* (*sat:* truth, *agraha:* firmness) is a form of nonviolent struggle against exploitation, oppression, subjugation and repression. It is an ethical value. It is of moral pressure, where the volunteers or activists submit to discomfort, suffering, or punishment as an expression of their position and depth of their conviction.
   [Examples will include fasting, lying down in front of a bulldozer to halt or prevent an unwanted project, or blocking a street or engaging in other illegal activities likely to lead to

police action.] This approach emphasizes goodwill rather than hostility towards the opponents.

Chapter XXVII: More Experiments in Dietetics

1. Passion in man is generally coexistence with a hankering after the pleasures of the palate. One should eat not in order to please the palate, but just to keep the body going. When each organ of sense subserves the body and through the body and soul, its special relish disappears, and then alone does it begin to function in the way nature intended it to.
[pg. 267, para 2, lines 2-3]

Chapter XXVIII: Kasturba's Courage

1. Kasturba refused to take beef and tea despite the advice of the doctor. This shows women's determination. [She gave a resolute replay: "I will not take beef tea. It is a rare thing in this world to be born as a human being, and I would rather die in your (Gandhi) arms than pollute my body with such abominations."] [pg. 270, para 6]

Chapter XXIX: Domestic Satyagraha

1. Inhibition imposed from without rarely succeed, but when they are self-imposed, they have decidedly salutary effect.
[pg. 272, para 2, lines 3-4]
2. Salt is not a necessary diet for man, that on the contrary saltless diet is better for the health.[pg. 272, para 3, lines 4-5]
3. Self-denial is good for the soul. The diet of a man of self-restraint must be different from that of the man of pleasure, just as their ways of life must be different.
[pg. 274, lines 2-4]

Chapter XXX: Towards Self-restraint

1. Milk stimulates animal passion. [pg. 274, para 2, line 2]
2. There is an intimate connection between the mind and the body, and the carnal mind always lusts for delicacies and luxuries. [pg. 275, para 4, lines 7-9]

3. Those whose minds are working towards self-restraint, dietic restrictions and fasting are very helpful. In fact without their help concupiscence cannot be completely rooted out of the mind. [pg. 275, para 5, last four lines]

Chapter XXXI: Fasting

1. It is better to have always one's co-worker's cooperation in anything that appeals to one as being good. [pg. 277, para 3, lines 4-5]
2. Fasting and similar discipline is one of the means to the end of self-restraint, but it is not all, and if physical fasting is not accompanied by mental fasting, it is bound to end in hypocrisy and disaster. [pg. 278, para 1, lines 1-4]

Chapter XXXII: As School Teacher

1. Under ideal conditions, 'true education' can be imparted only by parents and that there should be the minimum of outside help. [pg. 278, para 3, lines 13-14]
   [The Tolstoy Farm in South Africa was a family, in which Gandhi occupied the place of father. He therefore assumed so far as possible the responsibility for the training of the young.] [pg. 278, para 3, lines 15-18]
2. Character building is the proper foundation for the education of children. If the foundation is firmly laid, the children could and would learn all other things themselves or with the assistance of friends. [pg. 279, para 1, lines 5-9]
3. Building body should not be underrated as such physical labour should become an integral part of education system. [pg. 279, para 2, lines 3-4]
4. Every youngster must learn at least some useful vocation. [pg. 279-80, last and first line respectively]
5. As a rule the youngsters should not be asked to do what the teachers did not do. [pg. 280, para 2, lines 1-2]

Chapter XXXIII: Literacy Training

1. As far as possible mornings should be devoted to physical work and domestic duties, so school hours must be kept after the mid-day meals. [pg. 280, para 5, lines 8-10]

2. One should never attempt to disguise one's ignorance from one's pupils. [pg. 281, para 3, lines 7-8]
3. It is not necessary to load the boys and girls with the quantities of books. [pg. 281, last para, lines 3-4]
4. The true text book for the pupil is his/her teacher. [pg. 281, last para, lines 4-5]
5. Children learn or take in much more without labour through their ears than through their eyes. Reading is a task for them, but listening is pleasure. [pg. 282, para 2, lines 9-10]

Chapter XXXIV: Training of the Spirit

1. All training without culture of the spirit is of no use and may be even harmful. [pg. 282, para 2, last two lines]
2. The training of the spirit is a thing by itself. [pg. 282, para 2, lines 9-10]
3. To develop the spirit is to build character and to enable one to work towards a knowledge of God and self-realization. [pg. 282, para 2, lines 10-11]
4. It is a matter of common knowledge that those who defer preparation for this invaluable experience until the last stage of life attain not self-realization but old-age amounting to a second and pitiable childhood/living as a burden on this earth.
5. It is not through books that one can impart training of the spirit. Just as physical training is to be done through physical exercise, the intellectual through intellectual exercise, even so the training of the spirit is possible only through the exercise of the spirit. And the exercise of the spirit entirely depends on the life and character of the teacher. It is possible for a teacher situated miles away to affect the spirit of the pupils by his way of living. A teacher has to be an eternal object-lesson to the boys and girls. [pg. 283, para 1, lines 4-11]

Chapter XXXV: Tares Among the Wheat

1. One should not make one's own children feel that they are superior to other boys and girls. To put that sense of superiority into their heads will be to lead them astray. The association

with other boys and girls will be a good discipline for them. They will, of their own accord, learn to discriminate between good and evil. [pg. 285, lines 3-7]

2. Children wrapped up in cotton wool are not always proof against all temptation or contamination. It is true, however, that, when boys and girls of all kinds of upbringing are kept and taught together, the parents and teachers are put to the severest test. They have constantly to be on the alert. [pg. 285, para 3]

Chapter XXXVI: Fasting as Penance

1. It is very difficult to bring up and educate boys and girls in the right way. If one wants to be their real teacher and guardian, one must touch their hearts. One must share their joys and sorrows, one must help them to solve their problems that faced them, and must take along the right channel the surging aspirations of their youth. [pg. 285, para 3]
2. The guardian or teacher is responsible, to some extent at least, for the lapse of his ward or pupil. Teacher may have to take to penance for the guilt of his boys and girls. [pg. 286, para 1, lines 2-3]
3. The guilty party or parties can be made to realize their sin by inflicting some penance on the teacher or the guardian. [pg. 286, para 3]

   [So I imposed on myself a fast of seven days and a vow to have only one meal a day for a period of four months and a half. I felt greatly relieved, for the decision meant a heavy load off my mind. The anger against the guilty parties subsided and gave place to the purest pity for them. My penance pained everybody, but it cleared the atmosphere. Everyone came to realize what a terrible thing it was to be sinful and the bond that bound me to the boys and girls became stronger and truer.]
4. Where there is no true love between the teacher and the pupils, where the pupils delinquency has not touched the very being of the teacher and where the pupils have to respect for the teacher, fasting is out of place and may even be harmful. [pg. 286, last para, lines 5-9]

Chapter XXXVII: To Meet Gokhale

1. In the march towards truth, anger, selfishness, hatred, etc., naturally give way, for otherwise, Truth would be impossible to attain. A man who is swayed by passion may have good enough intentions, may be truthful in word, but he will never find the Truth. A successful search for Truth means complete deliverance from the dual throng such as of love and hate, happiness and misery. [pg. 288, para 8, lines 2-7]
2. A man emerging from a long fast should not be in a hurry to regain lost strength, and should also put a curb on his appetite. More caution and perhaps more restraint are necessary in breaking a fast than in keeping it. [pg. 288-89, last para]

Chapter XXXVIII: My Part in the War

1. There is a world of difference between Indians and the English. We are slaves and they are masters. How could a slave cooperate with the master in the hour of the latter's need? However, England's need should not be turned into our opportunity. That is, one's misery should not become other's opportunity. [pg. 289-90, last para]

   [London in those days was a sight worth seeing. There was no panic, but all were busy keeping to the best of their ability. Able-bodied adults began training as combatants, but what were the old, the infirm and the women to do? There was enough work for them, if they wanted. So they employed themselves in cutting and making clothes and dressings for the wounded. One can draw a good lesson from the experiences of London people to face the situation boldly.]

   [pg. 291, para 4, last line]

Chapter XXXIX: A Spiritual Dilemma

1. A votary of Truth is often obliged to grope in dark. [pg. 291, para 4, last line]
2. *Ahimsa* is a comprehensive principle and the unity of all life. [pg. 291, para 4, last line; pg. 292, para 1, line 1]
3. When two nations are fighting, the duty of a votary of *Ahimsa*

is to stop the war. He who is not equal to that duty, he who has no power of resisting war, he who is not qualified to resist war, may take part in war, and yet wholeheartedly try to free himself, his nation and the world from war.

[pg. 292, para 1, line 5-9]

4. A votary of Truth may not do anything in defence to convention. He must always hold himself open to correction, and whenever he discovers himself to be wrong he must confess it at all costs and atone for it.

[pg. 293, para 1, lines 6-9]

Chapter XL: Miniature Satyagraha

1. A *Satyagrahi* is born to be deceived. But ultimately a deceiver only deceives himself. [pg. 294, para 1, lines 2-5]
2. One should not be surprised if one of these days one has to go to the gallows for the sake of truth.

[pg. 294, para 3, lines 3-5]

Chapter XLI: Gokhale's Charity

1. One should decide for oneself according to the dictates of one's inner voice. [pg. 297, para 3, last line]

Chapter XLII: Treatment of Pleurisy

1. The treatment of pleurisy (Gandhi suffered from this disease) and cure lay not in taking medicine internally but in dietetic changes assisted by external remedies.

[pg. 298, para 6, lines 2-3]

Chapter XLIII: Homeward

1. There is always a difference between the ruler and the subject or ruled. [pg. 301, para 2, last four lines]
2. It is a joy to get back to the homeland after an exile of long years. [pg. 301, para 5]

Chapter XLIV: Some Reminiscences of the Bar

1. It is generally believed that the lawyer's profession is a liar's profession. [pg. 302, para 4]

[This had no influence on Gandhi. He had no intention of earning either position or money by lying. He warned every client at the outset that he would not take up a false case or coach the witnesses. The result was that no false case used to come to him.] [pg. 302, para 4]

Chapter XLV: Sharp Practice

1. It is important to practice law without compromising truth. [pg. 305, para 2, last two lines]
2. Do not vitiate truthfulness. [pg. 304, para 3]

Chapter XLVI: Clients Turned Co-workers

1. One's devotion to truth enhances one's reputation among the members of the legal profession. [pg. 305-6, last para]
2. The object of all professions should be service to the community and not conspiracy against laity. For this purpose winning the confidence of the people is an indispensable condition. [pg. 306, para 2]

   [In South Africa hundreds of Gandhi's clients became his friends and real co-workers in public life.]

Chapter XLVII: How a Client was Saved

1. To save or not to save anybody from the wrong done by one can be saved by means of confession. [pg. 307, para 2]
2. The shame lies not so much in going to Jail as in committing the offence. [pg. 308, lines 3-4]

   [The deed of the shame has already been done. Imprisonment should be regarded as penance. The real penance lies in resolving never to do wrong or commit crime again.] [pg. 308, lines 4-7]

PART V

Chapter I: The First Experience

1. The reception given to strangers in foreign land by local people make them at home. [pg. 311, para 3, last three lines]
2. It is necessary to enter protest against established practices to make people conscious of their mistakes. [pg. 312, para 1]

Chapter II: With Gokhale in Poona

1. As a rule, as a *Satyagrahi*, onc must understand the viewpoint of the party he proposes to deal with.
[pg. 312, last two lines]
2. It is faith in people that sustains the *Satyagrahi*.
[pg. 313, para 3]
3. In order that workers concentrate on work they must be made free from financial responsibility. [pg. 313, para 8]
4. One may commence work from one's familiar place.
[pg. 313, para 7]

Chapter III: Was it a Treat?

1. There are some youths who do not think before speaking.
[pg. 315, para 2]
2. No reform is possible unless some of the educated and the rich voluntarily accept the status of the poor.
[pg. 316-17, last para]
3. A nation that wants to come into its own ought to know all the ways and means to freedom. Usually they include violence as the last remedy. *Satyagraha*, on the one hand, is an absolutely nonviolent weapon. It is the duty of the leader to explain to people its practice and its limitations. [pg. 316-17, last para]

Chapter IV: Shantiniketan

1. Self-help experiment contains the key to *Swaraj*.
[pg. 318, para 2, last line]
2. Before understanding and gaining experience, one must not express opinion on public questions.
[pg. 319, para 4, lines 3-4]

Chapter V: Woes of Third Class Passengers

1. The face of truth is hidden behind the golden veil of *maya*.
[pg. 321, para 1, last two lines]

Chapter VI: Wooing

1. Physical relationship divorced from spiritual is body without soul. [pg. 322, para 4, last line]

Chapter VII: Kumbha Mela

1. Life based on disciplinary resolutions will add a few years to life and will save one from many an illness.
   [pg. 325, last para]

Chapter VIII: Lakshman Jhula

1. Hinduism must purge itself of untouchability.
   [pg. 328, line 7]
2. So long as there are different religions, everyone of them may need some outward distinctive symbol. But when the symbol is made into a fetish and an instrument of proving the superiority of one's religion over others', it is fit only to be discarded. [pg. 328, para 1]
3. One will be charmed with the natural scenery about Rishikesh and the Lakshman Jhula, and one's head will bow in reverence to ancestors for their sense of the beautiful nature, and for their foresight in investing beautiful manifestations of nature with a religious significance. [pg. 328, para 3]

Chapter IX: Founding of the Ashram

1. Our creed is devotion to truth, and our business is the search for and insistence on truth. [pg. 330, para 4, lines 7-8]
2. Service without humility is selfishness and egotism.
   [pg. 330, para 5, last line]

Chapter X: On the Anvil

1. Do not return abuse with abuse. The man showering abuses will become ashamed and will cease to bother.
   [pg. 331, para 6, last two lines]
2. Trust in management and good work will bring money.
   [pg. 332]

Chapter XI: Abolition of Indentured Emigration

1. People tolerate the wrong system through sheer negligence. They must be awakened to agitate and fight the system.
   [pg. 334, para 1, lines 7-10]

2. Patience is rewarded. [pg. 336, para 3, line 10]
3. God does send help when needed. [pg. 336, para 3, last line]

Chapter XIII: The Stain of Indigo

1. Leader must take the rein in his own hands rather than expect guidance from elsewhere. [pg. 339, para 1, last two lines]

Chapter XIII: The Gentle Bihari

1. Where the ryots are so crushed and fear-stricken, law courts are useless. The real relief for them is to be free from fear. [pg. 341, para 2, line 3-5]

Chapter XIV: Face to Face with Ahimsa

1. People yield obedience to the power of love. [pg. 343, para 3, last three lines]
2. One should aim at work and not name, substance and not shadow. [pg. 344, para 1, lines 2-3]

Chapter XV: Case Withdrawn

1. The disinterested service of the people in any sphere ultimately helps the country politically. [This has been amply proved by the Champaran struggle.] [pg. 346, last para, last iine]

Chapter XVI: Methods of Work

1. Method of inquiring must be a bold experiment with Truth and *Ahimsa*. Each peasant (case) must be closely cross-examined, and whoever failed to satisfy the test may be rejected. [pg. 347, para 1, line 3-4]

Chapter XVII: Companions

1. One must have capacity—specially an outsider to merge oneself in the province (state) of his adoption. [pg. 349, para 3, lines 3-4]
2. Work of a permanent nature is impossible without proper village education. [pg. 350, para 1, lines 2-3]
3. In order to involve villagers and to get their active participation in education they (villagers) must provide teachers with board and lodging. [pg. 350, para 2, lines 3-4]

4. Don't entrust children to commonplace teachers. Their literacy qualifications is not so essential as their moral fibre.
[pg. 350, para 3, lines 3-6]
5. Teacher is expected to teach the children not grammar and the three Rs so much as cleanliness and good manners.
[pg. 350, para 5, lines 2-3]
6. Villagers must be made conscious and aware of cleanliness and sanitary work. [pg. 351, para 1]
7. One must penetrate in every department of villagers' lives.
[pg. 351, para 1, last two lines]

Chapter XVIII: Penetrating the Villages

1. Sanitation is a difficult affair. Even in the field labourers are not ready to do their own scavenging.
[pg. 352, para 2, lines 1-2]
2. Sanitation must be made integral part of all works in villages.
[pg. 352, para 2]

Chapter XIX: When a Governor is Good

1. The recommendations of the committee cannot be accepted and implemented without the cooperation and firmness of a person of the status of Governor. [pg. 354, para 4]

Chapter XX: In Touch with Labour

1. One must not dare to give advice on any issue or problem without proper inquiry on the spot.
[pg. 355, para 1, last two lines]
2. Conditions for a successful strikes are:
(a) Never to resort to violence. (b) Never to molest black legs. (c) Never to depend upon alms. (d) To remain firm, no matter how long the strike continues, and to earn bread during the strike period, by another honest labour. [pg. 357, line 4-5]
3. One must recognize the principle of arbitration in a dispute between two parties.

Chapter XXI: A Peep into the Ashram

1. Human language can imperfectly describe God's ways. They are indescribable and inscrutable.
[pg. 358, para 4, lines 10-11]

2. As a rule one should not kill snakes.

[pg. 358, para 3, lines 5-6]

Chapter XXII: The Fast

1. The fast can touch the hearts of people in authority. They may set about discovering some means to settle the strike.

[pg. 360, last para]

[The fast by Gandhi touched the hearts of mill owners. They set about discovering some means for a settlement to call off the strike.] [pg. 360, last para]

2. The grinding poverty and starvation with which our country is afflicted is such that it drives men and women every year into the ranks of the beggars, whose desperate struggle for bread renders them insensible, to all feelings of decency and self-respect. And our philanthropists, authorities, instead of providing work for them and insisting on their working for bread, give them alms.

Chapter XXII: The Kheda Satyagraha

1. One has to suspend or give up splendid and growing practice at the bar to join the struggle. (This was done by Sardar Vallabhbhai Patel to join the Kheda *Satyagraha.*)

[pg. 363, para 1, lines 4-5]

Chapter XXIV: The Onion Thief

1. The Gujaratis are deeply interested in the fight. They are ready to pour forth their riches for the success of the cause. It is not easy for them to see that *Satyagraha* cannot be conducted simply by means of money. Money is the thing that it least needs. The *Satyagrahi* has to learn the new lesson of simplicity.

[pg. 364, para 1]

2. The main thing is to rid the agriculturists of their fear by making them realize that the officials are not the masters but the servants of people, inasmuch as they receive their salaries from the tax payers. [pg. 364, para 4, lines 1-4]
3. The most difficult part in *Satyagraha* is to fully learn the lesson of civility. Civility does not mean the mere outward

gentleness of speech cultivated for the occasion, but born quietness and desire to do the opponent good.

[pg. 364, para 4, lines 1-4]

4. When the fear of jail disappears, repression puts heart into the people. [pg. 365, para 2, lines 3-4]

Chapter XXV: End of Kheda Satyagraha

1. It is the people's right to determine who is poor.

[pg. 366, para 1, line 6]

2. The end of a *Satyagraha* campaign can be described as worthy, only when, it leaves the *Satyagrahi* stronger and more spirited than he was in the beginning. [pg. 366, para 2]
3. The Kheda *Satyagraha* marks the beginning of an awakening among the peasants of Gujarat and the beginning of their true political education. [pg. 366, para 3, lines 3-6]
4. The successful completion of Kheda *Satyagraha* indelibly imprinted on the public mind that the salvation of the people depend upon themselves, upon their capacity for suffering and sacrifice. [pg. 367, lines 1-5]
5. The people have found *Satyagraha* the true and infallible method for redressal of their grievances.

[pg. 367, para 1, lines 4-5]

Chapter XXVI: Passion for Unity

1. One should not miss a single opportunity to remove obstacle in the Hindu-Muslim unity. [pg. 368, para 1, lines 3-5]
2. The young men and women have to be ready to become *fakirs* for the service of the motherland.

[pg. 368, para 2, last line]

3. In matters of religion beliefs differ, and each one's is supreme for himself. [pg. 368, para 4, lines 8-9]

[If all will have the same belief about all matters of religion, there will be only one religion in the world.]

[pg. 368, para 4, lines 10-12]

Chapter XXVII: Recruiting Campaign

1. There is no trust between the government and the people.

[pg. 371, para 1, lines 7-10]

2. There are times when optimism may receive rude shock. [pg. 371, para 2, lines 2-3]
3. Distress may disappear by rendering voluntary help to government in the hour of its trial. [pg. 372, para 2, lines 2-3]
4. No government can afford to disregard the leaders, who represent the large masses of the people. [pg. 372, para 4, liens 12-15]
5. Educated classes do influence the masses. [pg. 373, para 2, lines 89]
6. Disappointment of hope means disillusion. [pg. 374, lines 4-5]

Chapter XXVIII: Near Death's Door

1. To eat too much butter is to injure one's health. [pg. 374, para 3, lines 3-4]
2. One loses interest in living when one is in that helpless state, doing nothing, receiving the service of friends and co-workers and watching the body slowly wearing away. [pg. 377, para 1, lines 7-9]
3. One should not be hasty in arriving at certain conclusions. [pg. 377, last line]
4. Some people believe eggs are as harmless as milk. [pg. 377, last line]

Chapter XXIX: The Rowlatt Bills and My Dilemma

1. Some people are liked and admired for the instantaneous capacity to take decisions. [pg. 378, para 1, last line]
2. The ideal of truth requires that vows taken should be fulfilled in letter and spirit. [pg. 378, last para, last line]

Chapter XXX: That Wonderful Spectacle

1. One can wake a man if he is really asleep; no effort will produce any effect upon a man who is pretending to be asleep. [pg. 381, para 3, lines 1-3]
2. *Satyagraha* is a process of self-purification. [pg. 383, para 1, lines 2-3]

Chapter XXXI: That Memorable Week I

1. Civil disobedience can be offered in respect of such laws as easily lent themselves to being disobeyed by the masses. [pg. 384, para 3, lines 4-6]
2. All is not gold that glitters. [pg. 385, para 3, lines 3-4]
3. One should not worry much about paucity of attendance in meetings. [pg. 385, para 3, lines 9]

Chapter XXXII: That Memorable Week II

1. People by nature are peaceful and not violent. [pg. 389, para 1]
2. *Satyagraha* is essentially a weapon of truthful. A *Satyagrahi* is pledged to nonviolence and unless people observe it in thought, word and deed one cannot offer mass *Satyagraha*. [pg. 389, para 8, lines 6-8]
3. One must suspend *Satyagraha* so long as people have not learnt the lesson of peace. [pg. 390, para 5, lines 2-4]
4. Those leaders who want to lead the people to *Satyagraha* ought to be able to keep the people within thc limited nonviolence expected of them. [pg. 391, line 2-5]

Chapter XXXIII: A Himalayan Miscalculation

1. Ideally it is only when one sees one's mistakes with a convex lens and does just the reverse in the case of others, that one is able to arrive at a just relative estimate of the two. A scrupulous and conscientious observation of this rule is necessary for one who wants to be a *Satyagrahi*. [pg. 391, para 1, lines 13-18]
2. A *Satyagrahi* obeys the laws of society intelligently and of his own free will, because he considers it to be his sacred duty to do so. It is only when a person has thus obeyed the laws of the society scrupulously that he is in a position to judge as to which particular rules are good and just and which are unjust and iniquitous. Only then does the right accrue to him of the civil disobedience of certain laws in well defined circumstances. [pg. 392, lines 2-9]

Chapter XXXIV: '*Navajivan*' and '*Young India*'

1. The journals will help expound the inner meaning of Satyagraha to the reading public. [pg. 393]

Chapter XXXV: In the Punjab

1. One's self-confidence must be infectious. [pg. 396]
2. In enquiry reports there should not be a single conscious exaggeration in it anywhere, and every statement made in it must be substantiated by evidence. The aim of a report should be solely with a view to bringing out the truth and nothing but the truth. [pg. 398]

Chapter XXXVI: The Khilafat Against Cow Protection?

1. Non-cooperation or to withhold cooperation from government is inalienable right of the people. [pg. 402]

Chapter XXXVII: The Amritsar Congress

1. The reforms, though may be defective, may still be acceptable as a strategy. [pg. 403]
2. One will find it extremely difficult, out of respect, to differ from reasoned, well tried and universally revered leaders. In such case(s) one must hear the inner voice. [pg. 404]

Chapter XXXVIII: Congress Initiation

1. One's capacity as a draftsman and a faculty to condensed expression will be generally found useful in seminars and conferences for drafting resolutions and writing proceedings. [pg. 406]
2. One may have to be satisfied in the work of committees with the nominated members of the leaders for want of time at their disposal. [pg. 407]

Chapter XXXIX: The Birth of Khadi

1. The objective of Khadi set before all Indians is to be able to clothe ourselves entirely in cloth manufactured by our own hands. [pg. 408, para 1, lines 1-2]

[We should forthwith discard the use of mill woven cloth, and all the Indians should wear hand-woven cloth made from Indian yarn only.] [pg. 408, para 1, 2-5]

Chapter XL: Found at Last

1. One becomes so much self-possessed of the spinning wheel that one gets lost in it and it is difficult to distract one's attention, and even much more difficult to draw one's eyes from one's beloved *charkha* (spinning wheel). [pg. 412, line 4-6]

Chapter XLI: An Instructive Dialogue

1. The price of an article is governed by the demand for it. Who can check the law of demand and supply? [pg. 412, para 6, lines 3-5]
2. *Khadi* can provide work to semi-starved semi-employed women of India and to clothe the people of India with *Khadi* woven out of it.
3. One has to think very hard and ask a question as to whether the spinning wheel can weave its way in the age of power-driven machines.

Chapter XLII: Its Rising Tide

1. Once people are convinced and are able to overcome their scepticism they throw themselves heart and soul into the movement or any task. [pg. 416]
2. Death of an esteemed leader leaves a deep void as people are deprived of his counsel very much needed in that hour of crisis in the nation's history. [pg. 417]

Chapter XLIII: At Nagpur

1. We should not be obsessed with numbers. The participants in a conference should be manageable to get better output. [pg. 418]
2. The goal of the Congress was the attainment of Swaraj within the British Empire if possible and without it if necessary. [pg. 418]
3. The means for attainment have to be peaceful and legitimate.

Farewell

1. One must know and understand that there is no other God than Truth. The only means for realization of Truth is *Ahimsa*. [pg. 419, para 4, lines 1 to 4]
2. To see the universal and all pervading spirit of Truth face to face must be able to love the meanest of creatures as oneself. And a man who aspires after that cannot afford to keep out of any field of life. [pg. 420, para 1, lines 1-4]
3. People who say that religion has nothing to do with politics do not know what religion means. [pg. 420, para 1, lines 6-7]
4. Identification with everything that lives is impossible without self-purification; without self-purification the observance of the law of *Ahimsa* must remain an empty dream; God can never be realized by one who is not pure of heart. Self-purification, therefore, must mean purification in all the walks of life. And purification being highly infectious, purification of oneself necessarily leads to the purification of one's surroundings. [pg. 420, para 2]

   [The path of self-purification is hard and steep. To attain perfect purity one has to become absolutely passion-free in thought, speech and action; to rise above the opposing currents of love and hatred, attachment and repulsion. One must reduce oneself to zero. So long as a man does not of his free will put himself last among his fellow creatures, there is no salvation for him. *Ahimsa* is the farthest limit of humility.]

   [pg. 420, para 3]
5. One must pray to the God of Truth that He may grant us the boon of *Ahimsa* in mind, word and deed. [pg. 420]

3

GIST OF LESSONS

The lessons scattered in different Chapters have been brought together at one place as Gist of Lessons under the following four broad sections:

Section I : Workers and Public Service
Section II : Education
Section III : Legal Profession and Practice
Section IV : Parents

SECTION I

Workers and Public Service

1. Workers working with people have to be humbler than the dust. The world crushes the dust under its feet. But the worker has to be so simple that even the dust could crush him.
2. There can be no fee or charge for public work.
3. One must not accept any salary for public work.
4. Not to do any public work with borrowed money.
5. Carefully kept accounts are *sine qua non* for any organization.
6. Service which is rendered without joy helps neither the worker nor the served.
7. It is not good to run public institutions on permanent funds. A permanent fund carries in itself the seed of the moral fall of the institution.

8. It is difficult to make friends and people to appreciate the beauty of self-help.
9. The voice of the people is the voice of God.
10. Public service has its own reward.
11. A public worker should not accept costly gifts.
12. For gifts a trust may be created by the public worker.
13. The work of public institutions must be properly rationalized and duties and responsibilities be distributed amongst various functionaries.
14. One most important way of carrying our public work is by personal example and discussion with searchers for knowledge.
15. A worker's reforming zeal ought not make him exceed his limits.
16. A worker should not make any distinction between relatives and strangers, countrymen and foreigners, white and coloured, Hindu or of other faiths—whether Mussalmans, Sikhs, Parsis, Christians, *Dalits* or Jews.
17. A worker's character should be as clear as crystal and courage that would shame a warrior.
18. A worker knows neither day nor night in toiling for the cause.
19. If a worker's heart is pure, calamity brings in its train men and measures to fight it.
20. A worker's constant presence with people when they are in a terrible fright is a real consolation to them.
21. A public worker should not make statements without getting proof of their authenticity.
22. In order that worker(s) concentrate on work they must be made free from financial responsibility.
23. Worker may commence work from one's familiar place.
24. Service without humility is selfishness.
25. Trust in management and good work will bring money.
26. Worker should aim at work and not at name, substance and shadow.
27. A worker—specially an outsider—must have capacity to identify with people.

28. A worker(s) should not worry about thin attendance in meetings.

SECTION II

Education

1. Physical and mental training should have equal importance in the curriculum.
2. Good hand-writing is a necessary part of education.
3. Children should first be taught the art of drawing before learning how to write.
4. Every Hindu boy and girl should possess sound knowledge of Sanskrit language.
5. In all India curricula of higher education there should be place for Hindi, Sanskrit, Persian, Arabic and English, besides of course, the vernacular.
6. Don't lose patience with pupils.
7. The education that children imbibe in a well ordered household is impossible to obtain in hostel(s).
8. The education of the child begins with conception.
9. One should not remain under the impression that the child has nothing to learn during the first five years of its life. On the contrary, the fact is that the child never learns in after life what it does in its first five years.
10. Character building is the proper foundation for the education of children. If the foundation is firmly laid, the children could and would learn all other things themselves or with the assistance of friends.
11. Building body should not be underrated as such, physical labour (education) should become an integral part of education system.
12. Every youngster must learn at least some useful vocation.
13. As a rule the youngsters should not be asked to do what the teachers cannot do.
14. As far as possible mornings should be devoted to physical work and domestic duties, so school hours must be kept after the mid-day meals.

15. One should never attempt to disguise one's ignorance from one's pupils.
16. It is not necessary to load the boys and girls with the quantities of books.
17. The true text-book for the pupil is his/her teacher.
18. Children learn or take in much more without labour through their ears than through their eyes. Reading is a task for them, but listening is pleasure.
19. All training without culture of the spirit is of no use and may be even harmful.
20. The training of the spirit is a thing by itself.
21. To develop the spirit is to build character and to enable one to work towards a knowledge of God and Self-realization.
22. It is not through books that one can impart training of the spirit. Just as physical training is to be done through physical exercise, the intellectual through intellectual exercise, even so the training of the spirit is possible only through the exercise of the spirit. And the exercise of the spirit entirely depends on the life and character of the teacher. It is possible for a teacher situated miles away to affect the spirit of the pupils by his way of living. A teacher has to be an eternal object-lesson to the boys and girls.
23. It is true that when boys and girls of all kinds of upbringing are kept and taught together, the parents and teachers are put to the severest test. They have constantly to be on the alert.
24. It is very difficult to bring up and educate boys and girls in the right way. If one wants to be their real teacher and guardian, one must touch their hearts. One must share their joys and sorrows, one must help them to solve their problems that faced them, and must take along the right channel the surging aspirations of their youth.
25. The teacher or guardian is responsible, to some extent at least for the lapse of his pupil or ward.

26. Where there is no true love between the teacher and the pupils, where the pupils' delinquency has not touched the very being of the teacher and where the pupils have no respect for the teacher, fasting is out of place and may even be harmful.
27. Don't entrust children to commonplace teachers. Their literacy qualification is not so essential as their moral fibre.
28. Teacher is expected to teach the children not grammar and the three Rs so much as good manner and cleanliness.
29. In order to involve villagers and to get their active participation in education they must provide teachers with board and lodging.
30. Education system must meet the needs of the society, family, pupil and teacher.

SECTION III

Legal Profession and Practice

1. Lawyers should have a long tongue.
2. If the word of Lawyer is not to be trusted, where is the use of possessing a certificate in the matter.
3. Latin is very useful to lawyers.
4. The curriculum of study to the bar is easy. (Jokingly barristers are called 'dinner barristers'! Everyone knew that examination has no value.)
5. It is easy to read the law, but it is difficult to practise at the Bar.
6. A lawyer should know, human nature. He should be able to read a man's character from his face. And every lawyer ought to know Indian history.
7. Honesty and industry are enough to become a successful lawyer.
8. The barrister's profession is a bad job—much show and little knowledge.
9. For a barrister to vegetate for five to seven years is not unusual.

10. Don't compromise principle by any means.
11. Selfishness is blind.
12. Facts are three-fourths of the law.
13. If we take care of the facts of a case the law will take care of itself.
14. Facts mean Truth, and once we adhere to Truth, the law comes to our aid naturally.
15. True functioning of a lawyer is to unite parties.
16. The very intellect of a lawyer sometimes becomes an abomination to one inasmuch as it could be prostituted for screening crime.
17. The value of lawyers' work is the same as that of the barber's, inasmuch as all have the same right of earning their livelihood from their work.
18. It is generally believed that the lawyer's profession is a liar's profession.
19. It is important to practice law without compromising truth.
20. One's devotion to truth enhances one's reputation among the members of the legal profession as well as in clients.

SECTION IV

Parents

1. Character building is the bounden duty of every parent.
2. Children inherit the qualities of the parents no less than their physical features. Environment does play an important part, but the original capital on which a child starts in life is inherited from its ancestors.
3. The Indian parents who train children to think and talk in English from their infancy betray their children and their country. They deprive them of the spiritual and social heritage of the nation and render them to that extent unfit for the service of the country.
4. Under ideal conditions, 'true education' can be imparted only by parents and that there should be the minimum of outside help.

5. Education must encompass relationship between the school and the society, and between the teachers and the parents.
6. Unless parents step forward and regularly interact with teachers, the end-product—the development of the child as a citizen—would be pretty lopsided.

4

MORAL INTEGRATION
Plea for a Peaceful Society in the Twenty-first Century

The Tribute

Among the tributes received in New Delhi within hours of Mahatma Gandhi's assassination on 30 January 1948 was one from Sarojini Naidu who said: "May the soul of my master, my leader, my father, rest not in peace. Not in peace—my father—do not rest. Keep us to our pledge. Give us strength to fulfil our promises—to our heirs, your descendants, guardians of your dreams, fulfillers of India's destiny."

The force of her words reminds us that we should not rest till we are able to internalize in ourselves the twin principles of Truth and Nonviolence in our thought and action. We should be optimistic and hope that we would be able to overcome the present crises facing the world.

This chapter has been divided into six sections. The first deals with the present malaise in the international community. The second is devoted to the Gandhian concept of human behaviour. The third is devoted to the Indian scenario related to some of the specific cases of moral degeneration. Though only one section has been devoted to India, the chapter as a whole mostly draws from the Indian situation. The fourth section examines some of the problems of communal harmony and integration. The fifth gives a multiple-factor theory of integration to bring unity in diversity.

And the sixth section critically evaluates the politician's role which he can play in moving his own self from the 'ego-centre' to the 'decentre' level in order to make him feel concern for others and to develop an ideal society to keep peace and tranquillity in the, national and international community.

Contemporary Social Data

The contemporary social data of the international community indicates increasingly a decline in its ability to hold and maintain its order and stability. The charismatic nonviolent integrative clan of the founding fathers of modern society, which had remarkably succeeded in welding varieties of heterogeneous groups, communities and ethnic groups together into a single humanity of indifferent countries, is under a serious process of erosion. The unifying moral imperatives of social and cultural values are being replaced by division and disintegrative forces in almost all countries of the world. Something vital is missing today.

There seems to have emerged a great divide within social settings such as family, village, town, ethnic groups, and communities, creating splits in them despite liberalization and globalization of economy. Collectivities are being individualized, and jointness and communal values are getting broken and privatised. Such a social divide tends to place individual against individual, group against group. Such horizontal and vertical cleavages are further enhanced and accentuated by the monopoly of all the resources enjoyed by the so-called 'elite' who show a tendency to amass wealth and power at the cost of ethics and morality. A thinker once said that truth is a scare commodity but its supply has always outstripped its demand. While truth does not seem to be triumphing all around us—somehow, somewhere, someway, something is working which is bringing the human race to say about truth and nonviolence: "Truth alone will endure, all the rest will be swept away before the tide of Time. Nonviolence is the law of our species, as violence is the law of the brute. Nonviolence is the greatest force at the disposal of mankind. It is mightier than the mightiest weapon of destruction devised by man."

The present political and development processes are acting as a catalyst of a collective decadence. A society, which lays emphasis more on the accumulation of power than on the restraints, on wealth than on morality, on knowledge than on humanism, and on demagogy rather than on authentic sharing and participation in the process of change and development, is bound to pay a heavy price for its lack of collective wisdom.

The disturbing social data of violence all over the world do not make the earth worth living despite man's ability to conquer space. The recent assassination of the Sri Lankan former President, Rupasinghe Premadasa, and the recent suicide committed by the former Prime Minister of France, Mr. Pierre Beregovo who felt anguished by an attack on his integrity and propriety over an interest free loan taken from the friend businessman and the consequent collapse of his socialist party in the general election are no insignificant developments. The aftermath of the developments in Ayodhya on 6 December 1992 engulfed the whole country in communal riots. The country also witnessed an unprecedented series of brutal blasts in March 1993 in Bombay. Godhara Carnage—Gujarat communal riots.

These series of violence and unrest show decadence of higher moral and ethical values. The lack of spirit, of trust, faith, and interpersonal and inter-group involvement and concerns for each other is suggestive of the fact that the tested path of tolerance, justice, morality, and trusteeship shown by the former leaders has been forsaken by the present leaders all over the world.

According to Gandhi, real democracy should have meaning not for a few but for all including the poorest and even for the maimed, the blind, and the deaf. He did not believe in mere lip sympathy for the ideal which comes so easily to most present day politicians and leaders. The entire social order should be such that this ideal should be achieved in practice. A genuine democracy calls for a higher degree of seriousness of purpose and a sense of urgency. Gandhi realized that once people are awakened, they would become a revolutionary force. Their minimum expectations would have to be satisfied, otherwise they would explode. This explosion could take many unpleasant and ugly forms.

Today one of the basic questions is whether the rulers and political parties have a high level of seriousness or a sense of urgency. The answer is obviously "no". Despite many laws, the whole electoral process and system in India is becoming less and less an honest mirror of public opinion. [Sadiq Ali, "A Gandhian Approach to Current Problems," *Gandhi Marg*, Vol. 14, No. 4, January-March 1993, p. 550.]

This is true of all other parts of the world as well. Even criminals are acquiring political respectability. This power is assuming more and more credible forms. The situation in other countries is not bright either. The voters are bribed and often elections are rigged. The candidates are merchandised rather than elected. One of the saddest aspects of election times is that politics overrides all human considerations.

Of course, in order to come out of the present malaise and dilemma, the only remedy lies is in adopting Gandhian path to resolve conflicts. Arnold Toynbee has rightly observed: "At this supremely dangerous moment in human history, the only way of salvation for mankind is the Indian way—Emperor Ashok's and Mahatma Gandhi's principles of nonviolence and Sri Ramakrishna's testimony to the harmony of religions. Here we have an attitude and spirit that can make it possible for the human race to grow together into a single family—and in the Atomic age this is the only alternative to destroying ourselves." [Arnold Toynbee, Quoted by N.A. Palkhivala in his book, *We the People*, Bombay: Strand Book Stall, 1986.]

Nonviolent Behaviour

The nonviolent behaviour on the part of humanity requires the highest form of civilization. Civilization is an act of the spirit. Ancient India was far more civilized than Modern India with its satellites in space. The recurrent looting of banks in broad daylight arouses as little public attention as the going down of the sun in the evening. Our legal system has made life too easy for criminals and too difficult for law-abiding citizens. The country has forgotten that crime is not a problem to be handled by the police only but by the whole society. The two basic lessons which we are to learn from Indian history and from the Gita are: (i) Indian people have always taken their moral standards from their rulers and people have risen to great heights whenever they have followed in the glow of noble kings or leaders; and (ii) regions and kingdoms have been destroyed not by adversity but by abasement, and corruption is the greatest solvent of public institutions, and poverty poses a far smaller threat. [*Ibid.*, pp. 45-50.]

Politicians in India, instead of giving moral leadership for which people are yearning and waiting, are only occupied in maintaining a system which is poisoned by collective bad faith and polluted by individual self-interest. People are served by deception and craftiness instead of by vision and imagination. The duty of a citizen is not merely to vote but to vote wisely. He must be guided by reason and by reason alone. He must vote for the best man, irrespective of any other consideration and irrespective of the party label. The right man in the wrong party is any day preferable to the wrong man in the right party. Time has gone when 'Congress' was a word to conjure with. [*Ibid.*, pp. 51-52.]

Late N.G. Goray, a socialist leader, was fond of saying that reason was more important to him than emotion and action more important than thought. That is why he considered Shivaji greater than Ramdas, Jyotibai Phule greater than Justice Ranade, and Mother Teresa greater than J. Krishnamurti. [Vidyadhar Date, "N.G. Goray: A True Humanist's Obituary", *The Sunday Times*, New Delhi, 2 May, 1993, p. 2.]

Indians by and large, are "low arousal" people. They tolerate injustice and unfairness with feudalistic servility and fatalistic resignation. On 15 August, 1947 India achieved Independence. But Gandhi was not present in New Delhi. At that time, he was working among the poor people of Bengal. The reason for his absence was simple. He had two dreams in his life. The first dream was liberation of India from the British rule, while the second was liberation of Indians from oppression and injustice, from inequity from oppression and injustice, from inequity and inequality, from discord and disharmony. [N.A. Palkhivala, *We People*, p. 268.]

To quote his own words: "I shall work for an India in which the poorest shall feel that it is their country in whose making they have an effective voice, an India in which there should be no rich class and no poor class of people, and an India in which all communities shall live in perfect harmony. This is the India of my dream." [*Ibid.*, p. 268.]

His first dream was fulfilled but the second was not. According to the Mahatma, the true time for celebration would be when the second dream is fulfilled.

Gandhi was a leader of his people, unsupported by any authority; a politician whose success rested, not upon craft or guile, but simply upon the moral grandeur of his soul; a fighter who pushed back the mightiest empire on earth without the use of force; a spirit of profound wisdom and captivating humility, armed with only an iron will and inflexible resolve; and a frail man who confronted the brutality of military strength with the dignity of a simple human being. [*Ibid.*, p. 269.] To the Mahatma, Truth was God and non-violence was religion. At his memorable trial for sedition in 1922, he said: "Nonviolence is the first article of my faith. It is also, the last article of my creed. In nonviolence bravery consists of dying, not in killing." His compassion and humanity were as boundless as the universe. "Gather together," he said, "under one banner all men from all religions and races of India and infuse into them the spirit of solidarity and oneness to the utter exclusion of all communal and parochial sentiments." And again: "My Hinduism is not secularism. It includes all that I know to the best of Islam, Christianity, Buddhism, and Zoroastrainism. Truth is my religion and *Ahimsa* (the principle of nonviolence) is the only of its realization." [*Ibid.*, p. 270.]

Gandhi held the view that the life of a good citizen was the life of *Karma*—action in the service of the country. "My writings should be cremated with my body," he said. "What I have done will endure, not what I have said or written." [*Ibid.*, p. 271.]

The hatred and fanaticism which consumed the body of the Mahatma did not touch his great soul. Indian systems and ideologies may be relevant at one time and irrelevant at others. But teaching of this great and benign lamp of wisdom and humanity are for endless time. He gave us the priceless gift of self-respect and the sense of dignity as a nation. [*Ibid.*, p. 272.]

The last interview which the Mahatma gave was in the early afternoon of 30 January, 1948 to Margaret Bourke—an Amerian from the *Life Magazine*. She asked him whether he would persist in his theory of nonviolence in the event of a nuclear attack on a city. The Mahatma's reply was that if the defenceless citizens died in a spirit of nonviolence, their sacrifice would not go in vain. They might well pray for the soul of the pilot who thoughtlessly sprayed death on the city. This was his last message of compassion to mankind. [*Ibid.*, p. 275.]

He completely identified himself with the Indian masses. He observed: "We must first come in living touch with them by working with them and in their midst, we must share their sorrows, understand their difficulties and anticipate their wants. With the pariahs we must be pariahs and see how we feel to clean the closets of the upper classes and have the remains of theirs to be thrown at us. We must see how we like being in the boxes, miscalled houses, of the labourers of Bombay. We must identify with the villagers who toil under the hot sun beating on their bent back and see how we would like to drink water from the pool in which the villagers bathe, wash their clothes and pots, and in which their cattle drink and roll. Then and not till then shall we truly represent the masses and they will, as surely as I am writing this, respond to every call." [*Ibid.*, p. 278.]

The Indian masses responded to the Mahatma's call in a spirit of total surrender. He said to them that "real Swaraj will come not by the acquisition of authority by a few but by the acquisition of the capacity by all to resist authority when it is abused." [*Ibid.*, p. 279.]

He repeatedly used to mention that through realization of freedom for India, we would try to carry on and fulfil the mission of the universal brotherhood. He was really involved in achieving the broadest good of humanity at large.

Indeed in India

Indeed in India, the manner in which intolerance has begun to manifest itself is obvious. Disagreement is no longer reflected in a mere angry letter to the editor or a cross-table debate, violence has become the fashionable way to settle "disputes" and "conflicts". So, Narmada Bachao Andolan activists are beaten up in Gujarat, B.D. Sharma (a retired IAS officer, who was Commissioner of Scheduled Castes and Scheduled Tribes and Vice-Chancellor of a Indian University as well as Secretary in the Government of Madhya Pradesh) is assaulted in Madhya Pradesh, theatres are stormed and journalists are attacked all over the country. The ruthless constriction of the liberal temper and its replacement by authoritarianism has not occurred overnight. It is apparent that with the euphoria guaranteed by religious mobilization of the majority community, a more violent of physical and psychological intimidation is upon us. [Rajdeep Sardesai, "The New Vigilants Breed Intolerance," *The Times of India*, 5 May, 1993.]

The rising tide of tolerance has forced even those committed to free speech to look over their shoulders every time they say or write anything. The intolerant streak is not confined to the Hindus as is evident from a recent incident in which an attempt was made to burn down the office of a newspaper, *Urdu Times*, because it had carried an article critical of a few local Muslim leaders.

The nation appears gripped by the worst cynicism when the nexus between criminals and politicians is dismissed as a global phenomenon. The Union and the State governments are not called upon to account for communal carnage nor do voter exercise their right to recall defecting politicians. A Member of Parliament splitting a party with alleged forged signature and hoodwinking the anti-defection law receives the indirect blessings of the highest placed people. Hypocrisy, the hated sign of a morally drained society, is still the trademark of India's political parties. [*Ibid.*]

Insincerity and sycophancy are the hallmark of Indian politics. Is there any political party which can claim steadfastness to its politics.

The Basic Difficulty

The basic difficulty has been that people have not yet integrated themselves with either local, regional, or international community. The ruthless competition and globalisation has made everybody compete with each other rather than cooperate. This has often led to violence to eliminate the competitor rather than to improve over his technology, goods and services or skills.

Communal harmony and community integration are essentially two aspects of the same process to develop among each member love and affection for each other. These two essential aspects of working together at various levels are inseparable parts of one and the same process—in fact, one can say that only when these aspects are interlocked and merged with one process/we will have a community at various levels which ultimately must become a global community to resolve conflicts, not by violence but by peaceful methods.

This, however, does not mean that it is a community in which all norms, beliefs, values, and ways of life are standardized. What it means is that community should be viewed as "common life" of some kind and that there is value in identifying oneself with and sharing in this common life. Implicit in this has also been the assumption that association with, and feeling 'part of', the common life is not an experience. It provides the individual certain psychological security. It gives his life certain meaning which it might not otherwise have. It makes a community capable of dealing common problems which, if they were not solved, would lead to deterioration of physical or social community or both. It may be well to stress that this process should not lead to eradication of differences among sub-groups and sub-cultures in the community. What is important is an understanding of these differences, acceptance of them by all in the community, but at the same time, development of common frame of reference within which all can work, together for common ends. This is very much evident from the "concern" of the Union of Concerned Scientists, comprising about 1,600 scientists including a majority of Nobel Laureates who recently signed a "Global Warning to Humanity" which describes the damage done to the Earth as "too great if warnings go unheeded in which case no nation can escape injury." Continued environmental and economic instabilities would cause mass migration that would be unsustainable.

In fact, there is no single factor which, by itself, makes for a community. It is a complex whole, all parts of which are related, interact, and influence one another. To select one part of this whole and to identify it as the primary cause of integration or disintegration is not possible. The greater the mixture of races, ethnic groups, and nationalities, the more difficult is the task of integration. The economic factor is unimportant for integration. The mobility score increases as the integration score falls. Social problems tend to multiply not only absolutely but relatively, with the size of the community increasing all the time. We have to recognize that while there are many factors which make for or prevent community integration, we can only generalize loosely about these and can say only in specific situations, and after careful study, which of the forces in a given situation at local, regional, national, international level is more important than another. There are clusters of factors that interlock and reinforce one another and influence the degree of community integration.

Thus, an economic system may stimulate great differences in terms of rigid class and caste structure. A particular kind of educational system may also cause disparity amongst members of a community. It is difficult to separate linked factors in a community. All these factors are so inextricably linked together that change in one will affect the other. [*Ibid.*]

The problem of identifying forces which will work for community integration at the global level is one of considerable complexity. The global community divided into developed and underdeveloped communities must learn to live together on the principle of interdependence.

There are many Third World countries which are in no position to pursue an independent path of development. They do not have the necessary capital and skills nor for that matter, the appropriate political environment. Many are already involved in debt trap. Quite a few have been ruined by civil wars. The poor can never hope to catch up. The technological lag grows higher every year. The poor are expected to provide sites for polluting industries, markets for surplus goods and arms.

The Present Problems

The present problems, according to former Prime Minister P.V. Narasimha Rao, can be traced to a single source: the near complete alienation between the political establishment the bureaucracy, and the money elite on the one hand and civil society on the other. The former seeks self-aggrandizement: the politician through the electoral system and the bureaucrat through manipulating rules, regulations and procedures, and the moneyed elite, thanks to a promiscuous relationship it built up with former in the exploitative system.

Citizens find the state has progressively abandoned its writ to goons and hoodlums. The district collector, the cooperator, the MLA, the MP, and the minister no longer command the respect they once did. In the eyes of the common citizen, courts and Parliament serve merely to lend a measure of legitimacy to fraud and crookedness and profligate wheeling-dealing. [Srilekha Bose, "Moral Dilemma," A Letter to Editor, *The Times of India*, 5 May 1993.]

The leaders of the ruling as well as of other parties, out of their self-interest, fail to understand the basic fact that no party in country can survive, let alone thrive, if politics is merely a matter of vote banks. In India the political situation has become so grave that politics has been criminalised to such an extent that crime is becoming politicized. [Robert C. Angele, "The Moral Integration of American Cities," *American Journal of Sociology*, Vol. 5, No.1, July 1951, pp. 15-21.]

There are three factors responsible which have distorted a rational development of citizenship in India. One is poverty, creating the need for economic security at any price and its corollary, the widening gap between the rich and the poor; the second is the galloping population growth; and the third is the conflict between ethnicity and the doctrine of unity. In reconciling the implications of these pressures upon the public psyche, a self-centred society has emerged. This society seems unable to look farther than narrow self-interest, self-promotion, and selfish ambition. This is the rule rather than the exception which leaves particularly a heavy burden on all disinterested citizens who are acutely aware that we shall have no nation worth the name in the near future unless we can do something to restore the confidence of the people in a life-style that shows concern for others. [Shamlal, "Life and Letters: Where do We Go from Here?" (a review article based on Social Register, 1992, edited by Leo Panitch, Marline Press, *Times of India*, 8 May, 1993.]

A moral person is one who is concerned with the welfare and happiness of his or her fellow beings. He subordinates his individual goals in the larger interest of society. He is expected to move from the ego-centric self to a decentering activity, leading to the formation of a harmonious and reciprocal relationship. These ideals and values are inculcated and transmitted into a individual by the society in which he lives. [Dileep Padgaonkar, "A Review About Rao: Knowing Where He Stops", *The Times of India*, 15 May, 1993.]

There is not a single one of us that is not enriched by our composite culture, whether it be in music, food, or dress, to take a few everyday examples. For example, the image of the unseen thread in the garland is an excellent metaphor for what nationality or internationality can be linked to. If the thread is cut at one point, the garland ceases to exist. How is the thread to be safeguarded? I suggest that we need to shift to a language of a different kind in order to answer this question. The nation of world can only survive if there is a new socio-economic order where the biggest gulf of all, that is, the one between the rich and poor, is removed to cease the yawning gap between one citizen and another, [*Ibid.* and see K.D. Gangrade, "Our Present Malaise" in P.C. Chatterjee (ed.), *Self-images: Identity and Nationality*, Indian Institute of Advance Study in Association with Allied Publishers, New Delhi, pp. 1-4 and p. 262.]

The defeat of the impeachment motion against former Mr. Justice Ramaswami not very long ago was the defeat of the last vestige of ethics in India's public life. We have systematically devalued and debased our noble Constitution. In fact, we have abused and debased it beyond recognition. The motion was lost because the Congress Party issued an oral whip that its members should abstain from voting. This amounted to a travesty of the Constitutional mandate, inasmuch as MPs were prevented from discharging their quasi-juridical function of adjudication. [Tara Ali Baig, "Essence of Citizenship: Social and Moral Values in India", in S.R. Gupta, Urs Schottli, and Jurgen Axer, *et al., Citizen Development Society* (Friedrich-Naumann Stiftung, Mandira, 1990), pp. 4-5.]

We must have moral courage to take action based on our individual and collective conscience. Peace, stability, and unity cannot be bought. They have to be nurtured by promoting a sensitivity to human needs and respect for the rights and opinions of others. And when attitudes have been allowed to harden to the point that otherness becomes a sufficient reason for nullifying person to be treated as a fellow human being, the tapering of modern civilization crumbles with a frightening speed. As the twentieth century draws to a close, it has become obvious that material yardsticks alone cannot serve as an adequate index of human well-being. [K.D. Gangrade, "Youth in Conflict with Society in Citizenship in India", in S.R. Gupta, *et al., Citizen Development Society*, p. 66.]

If, what happened in the Ramaswami case is repeated, it is clear that the politicians will find soon that they are living on a borrowed time. The venality of the political class is now so transparent that no attempt to camouflage it under high moral principles will work any more. [Margaret Chatterjee, "Epilogue", in P.C. Chatterjee, ed., *Self-Images: Identity and Nationality*, Simla: Indian Institute of Advanced Study, in association with Allied Publishers, New Delhi, 1989, p. 262.] The moral authority of most of the politicians has almost disappeared, since they are seen as opportunists, in league with criminals and crooked businessmen. It is, therefore, not possible for politicians to impose discipline in a society which sees them as examples of indiscipline. The common man is alarmed at the moral sickness that is enveloping the world and lowering our ethical standards. Money power seems to have an all pervasive effect. One hopes that we do not reach a level where indifference by contagion or where lassitude slowly engulfs the nation and after a certain point of conditioning violence becomes acceptable, scandal becomes routine, and militant resistance turns into a film script. Education must be shaped as a potent weapon to reverse the process from seeking pleasure, acquisition, and violence to self-control, sharing, and compassion. [Aung San Suu Kyi, "What Economies Cannot Provide: Light for a Troubled World", *The Times of India*, 20 May 1993.]

We Indians must first integrate ourselves to achieve our ultimate motto of *Vasudhaiva Kutumbakam* (the world is one family).

Political parties sought to work for the unity and integrity of India. Unfortunately, all parties with rare exception have used caste, religion and language to their electoral advantage. If the Congress fomented the Punjab problem, the BJP was responsible for large scale communal violence and V.P. Singh and his JD sowed the seeds of caste antagonism. The allocation of Rs. 5 million by V.P. Singh government for Jama Masjid was described by the BJP as Muslim appeasement. But a grant of Rs. 67 million to the Dargah of Ajmer by the BJP government in Rajasthan was hailed as proof of secularism. The administration should not be a monastic practice but a temporal exercise holding the scales even between all men to which ever persuasion they may belong.

Charles Krauthmamer quotes "statistics to show that since 1960 the incidence of single parenthood has more than tripled in America, and that almost more than 30 per cent of all American children are now born to unmarried mothers. We have become totally inured to levels of criminality that would have been considered intolerable years ago. In America, child abuse is nineteen times more prevalent today than it was 30 years ago. Forty-seven per cent of women are victims of rape [Krauthmamer, Charles, "Defining Deviancy Up: The New Assault on Bourgeois Life", in *The New Republic*, Vol. 209, p. 20, November 22, 1993. Quoted by Haldar Dipak in his article "Will Deviance Overgrow Development", *IASSI Quarterly*, Vol. 16, No. 1, July-September 1997, p. 154.]

Unfortunately, during the last five years or more, situation has emerged, particularly in India, wherein it is difficult to say whether a particular offence of misdemeanour is opposed or tolerated. The space of economic offenders and scamsters opposed now,—but the very fact that they had been allowed to accumulate over the years proves that they were not only tolerated but perhaps encouraged as well. [Haldar, Dipak in his article "Will Deviance Overgrow Development", *IASSI Quarterly,* Vol. 16, No. 1, July-September 1997, pp. 155-57.]

According to a study in South Africa, a woman is raped every 83 seconds and in the United States every three minutes. It is well known that a large number of such cases go unreported because of the social stigma associated with it and also threat to the victim's life. Furthermore, worse is the growing trend of child rape (paedophilia) in the country. An average of two such cases are reported everyday in the country. Child rape victims accounted for 5.4 per cent of the total rape victims in 1995. At the national level, the number of rape victims has soared from 10,425 to 13,774 between 1991-95. There has been 4.2 per cent growth over 1994 with 13,218 cases. About 7,752 victims of rape were in the age group of 16-30 years, accounting for 56.3 per cent of the total victims in 1995. [Shailendra, "Soaring Rape Graph, Blot on Human Dignity", *The Times of India*, 23 February, 1998.]

Though the problem of marital rape is serious in India as in many other countries in the world, there is no state law to protect women. In the 1990s, several countries had enacted legislations so that spousal and non-spousal rapes are differentiated. These states are Australia, Canada, Israel, Italy, Holland, the United States, New Zealand, Sweden, Switzerland and the United Kingdom. [*Ibid.*]

In West Bengal, which the leftists claim to be a bastion of peace and lawfulness, the following incidents occurred last June among many others, as reported by *The Statesman* on 6 June 1997.

1. In early June, woman and her child were murdered in Free School Street Hotel in Kolkata.
2. In the same week of June, four armed men robbed a New C.I.T. Road house in Kolkata of ornaments and cash amounting to Rs. 37 lakhs.

3. The same week, a 62 year-old woman was murdered at her Lansdown Terrace home.
4. In the middle of June, a girl was raped and strangled in an engineering college campus.
5. In the third week of June, passengers of a city minibus were robbed by armed men in the afternoon.
6. In the last week of June, a Maruti Car was stopped in Kolkata and Rs. 27 lakhs snatched.
7. On 30 June, a gang robbed an oil godown of almost Rs. 45,000.

In Kolkata again, on June 29, a young woman coming to join her new assignment was raped by her would be employer within her office itself at revolver point, in broad daylight. He has been arrested, of course, and has been medically examined. But does that deter future rapists?

These are only a few zonal incidents. Collected nationwide, their number as already stated is a hundred times or even thousand times more.

But what is the reason of the abnormal rise in the level of present-day crime and its tolerance. The reason is simple. It is the increase of population, coupled with the increase of wealth,—which reduces fellow-feeling and group-wise single-mindedness, as individual selfishness increases. In the present circumstances, there is no adequate remedy immediately visible, unless one goes in for drastic changes in the legal system, providing ways and means of certainly of detection and severity of punishment, or both, and removing the legal lacunae.

The other factor which is responsible for the malaise quite obviously is that of rapid economic growth which alters 'social equations'. When those close to the bottom of the social hierarchy benefit from the growth, they threatened those who dominated the traditional hierarchy. Once the conflict has broken out, it is easy to point fingers at politicians, particularly, since each of them is pointing a finger at the other. But the cynical politicians can only exploit opportunities that is presented to them.

The primary remedy lies in paying attention to "character building" in the education system and adopting Gandhian values of life.

Failed Social Order

We must understand that we have now reached the end of our resources in speech making, and it is not enough that our ears and eyes are feasted with these speeches and declarations but it is necessary that our hands and acts have got to move towards a society which will really feed, clothe and provide shelter to everybody and treat everybody in the world as equal and pave the way to live in peace. We should move towards a society where everyone will live in harmony with his neighbour, where everyone will be treated with equal respect, will feel secure, self-respect and self-confidence and feels he/she is wanted. Everyone realizes that it is the global peace that makes the human race feel safe and happy.

In the new social order human race will not be determined and divided by caste, class, religion, race, colour, and the rich and the poor. Towards that social order, we have to march through in a peaceful way without hating and without killing anybody. This society will then have sustainable economy. People will participate in planning and executing. It is from the bottom to the top and people to government, not top to bottom. This is the nonviolent approach to achieve a new social order.

This should be the cherished goal of International Community to march towards the twenty-first century.

Three Great Leaders

The twentieth century has seen three great leaders—Mahatma Gandhi of India in the East, Martin Luther King in the United States, and President Nelson Mandela in Africa—who advocated and followed the nonviolent method to attain freedom. Anything attained through nonviolent means will have permanency and will sustain for ever, not when attained through force. Strength does not come from physical capacity. It comes from an indomitable will. Possession of arms implies an element of fear, if not cowardice. Gandhi believed that nonviolence was not a resignation from all real fighting against wickedness. On the contrary nonviolence is more active and more real fight against wickedness or evil that retaliation whose very nature is to increase wickedness. It will not be a nonviolent approach if we merely love those who love us. It is nonviolent only when we love those who hate us. Nonviolence is not only a personal virtue but also a social virtue. Nonviolence is infinitely superior to violence. Nonviolence springs from love and it always suffers, whereas cowardice springs from hate and it always inflicts suffering. Love is synonymous with nonviolence, but the nonviolence is not the same as pacifism.

Gandhi was inspired by Thoreau's civil disobedience and King was inspired by Gandhi's action of civil disobedience which created a revolution in India without guns. By using love, the Indians did not defeat the British, instead, they changed them from their evil ways and saved them. Fighting hatred will make hatred stronger. We should never be bitter to our enemies. Nelson Mandela had to suffer in jail for almost twenty-seven years to get civil rights for the citizens of South Africa. This long suffering and nonviolent struggle could get them their rights as India did from British after a prolonged nonviolent struggle. King won the right of the African-American to sit anywhere in the bus, secured their right to vote, and to start and invest their own business through the civil rights movements. King's steps to nonviolent campaigns were: (i) collection of facts to determine whether injustice exists; (ii) negotiation; (iii) self-purification, and (iv) direct action.

Gandhi believed, as Ruskin has put in his book *Unto This Last*, that "good of the individual is contained in the good of all." The only real and dignified human doctrine is the greatest good of all and this can be achieved by uttermost self-sacrifice. Inequality is evil but to eradicate an evil from the human breast by force or violence does not bring permanent results. What is gained by the sword will also be lost by the sword. Means and ends are convertible. If he takes care of the means, the end will take care of itself. Trusteeship is the answer to the issue of classless society where the wealth of an individual is shared by all. He is a trustee to preserve the wealth and willing to share with others who need it.

'Million Men March'

This is exactly what was expressed by the young people of the United States who participated in the 'million men march'—a march towards the twenty-first century. They reaffirmed that the sense of materialism in the United States should be killed. A community living in a state of chronic poverty does itself no good lusting after a luxury car that families cannot afford. It is actually killing the people. We need to persuade each other not to put value into a pair of 125 sneakers as a measure of our worth. We need to think in new ways. If we think of a suit and see our brother sleeping in the open even without a blanket, then we have failed. We should not go for a second set of dress or costly suit until the day everyone can have a suit or dress to wear. Money spent on war anywhere in the globe should be spent to relieve poverty at home and elsewhere.

Scientists should realize their social responsibility. They should focus on the global issues threatening mankind like population explosion, the environment and control of biological, chemical and convention weapons, and should stop the race against human race. Peace does not mean absence of wars. To millions of people it means satisfaction of these basic needs: food, shelter, health, education, and a place to live. It means that there is justice, freedom of opportunity for education, employment, recreation. We need to have a dynamic, democratic leader who could guide the people towards this new social order. We need a living and vibrant leader who is fearless.

There is a story of a drowning boy and philosopher. When the philosopher was lecturing him the boy cried "take me out of the water first". Similarly our people and of the world cry: "We have had lectures enough, societies enough, papers and books enough where is the man who will lend us a hand to drag us out. Where is the man who really love us? Where is the man who has sympathy for us? Ah! that man is wanted.

To Sum Up

The generalizations which are examined in various sections of this chapter can be seen as diagnosis of conflict or of social peace. If conflict arises from divergence and opposition, accommodation and cooperation arise from complementary, balance of power, and consensus. Complementary means the possibility of mutual advantage and cooperative interdependence is likely to be highly advantageous. The more integrated into the society are the parties to conflict, the less likely will be the chances of conflict being violent. This is the Gandhian way to create a peaceful society.

Power can be political or economic in its nature, it may emerge from the sword or the pen, or from the common voice of a collective people. Power can also come out of faith, one's conviction that one's way is the right or righteous way. It is this belief in oneself that we see at work in the mission of Mahatma Gandhi, in his practice of *satyagraha—satyagraha* insistence on truth.

Ethical values, however sound they are, must have a backing of *samanthya,* power; otherwise they are like a bow and arrow without an archer to use them. The weapon has neither strength, nor accuracy, nor purpose by itself. A leader of the nation has the responsibility of uniting the people. He must constantly remind himself of his responsibilities as a ruler. He should not be engrossed in his own life and in the pursuit of self-gratification. He must not become an uncaring and callous leader towards citizens. He must turn power from a gratification into a responsibility. This is expected of all leaders from top to bottom, or bottom to top, to serve people and build the nation to achieve world peace.

At a Washington meeting some years ago, Peter Drucker, the Management Guru, was asked who would make an ideal Chief Executive Officer. Several possibilities had been suggested by earlier speakers. Why not an accountant, said one; and what about a marketing expert, asked another. What corporation needs is an efficient manager, said a third. Drucker disagreed with them all. His vote went for a Doctor of Divinity. A man such as that, argued Drucker, would stand for values.

We need a man of values at the head of a government. We need a philosopher king, whose head is clear and whose heart is in the right place.

The twenty-first century has come with this challenge before voter(s) and people of India. If right type of leaders or representatives come to power they will be able to accept the challenge and lead the nation. If India accepts the challenge as a nation to give a lead, it will emerge as a world leader of peace.

Gandhi had set for himself two objectives. First, proximate or immediate objective was to get political independence of India following the path of *ahimsa* and *satyagraha*. Second, ultimate or long-term objective was economic independence of teeming millions based on social, economic, environmental, equity and ethical considerations. While we have achieved the former in his life time, the latter is still a dream after 50 years of independence of the country.

Khoshoo, T.N. writes: "According to Gandhi the ethical commandments relating to human behaviour in relation to other humans and living creatures and non-living resources are the five:

1. Nonviolence (*ahimsa*) towards animals and inanimate creations;
2. Truth (*satya*);
3. Shunning the materials obtained by illegitimate means and avoiding destruction and vandalism (*asatya*);
4. Celibacy (*brahmacharya*) because human needs keep the numbers in check, otherwise demand or resources will increase; and
5. Not converting or amassing material and wealth beyond requirements (*aparigraha*). The five principles enunciated by him are self-based codes of conduct. These prescribe what a human being should do, and relate to cleanliness, sanitation (*shaucha*) of one's mind, body and the

surroundings. Human being is essentially a dirty animal which unlike other animals generates considerable waste and garbage, often non-biodegradable in character and as such pollutes the environment.

Shaucha also includes ridding oneself of undue lust including sexual desire (*kama*), anger (*krodha*), greed (*lobha*), undue attachment (*moh*), and conceit and vanity (*ahankar*). Gandhi believed that there is divinity in all life, and that there is thus fundamentals unity in diversity.

The Gandhian model envisaged that development and governance should be bottom-up and not top-down; goal should be self-defined and not stranger defined; production should be aimed at basic goods to fulfil basic needs with use values, and not at non-basic and greed-oriented luxury goods; the process of production should be by masses and not through mass production; and the whole approach should be holistic and not sectoral. The Nehruvian (Western) Model of industrial development is relevant primarily to the industrial economic sector. This model needs refinement and has to be made sustainable. The Gandhian Model in the words of J.C. Kumarappa, leads to decentralized economic planning and actually 'Economy of Permanence', while in the Nehruvian or Western Model of industrial economy there is the danger that the rich becomes richer, and poor becomes poorer.

India's success will be measured not by homogenizing a heterogeneous situation, but by the success with which diverse societies can be harmonized and co-exist and become mutually reinforcing and supportive; where traditions and modernity are appropriately blended, and where man-made capital does not become destructive of the natural capital. Both models have their specific constituencies in India. Thus, following a democratic path, there is a need for a creative synthesis of the Gandhian and the Nehruvian Models (see Table 4.1).

The leaders of the ruling as well as other parties, out of their self-interest, fail to understand that no party can survive, let alone, thrive, if politics is merely a matter of getting into the drivers seat and running after material wealth. The moral authority of most of the politicians has almost disappeared since they are seen as opportunists.

Table 4.1: The Two Models

The Gandhian Model	*The Nehruvian or Western Model*
1. Intensification and diversification of agriculture, animal husbandry and forestry, i.e., bio-mass production, processing and utilization, i.e., Renewable Resources.	1. Intensification and diversification of industrial development using mostly non-renewable resources.
2. Photosynthetic/Solar Model: Use of solar energy and some non-renewable energy.	2. Man-made Industrial Economic System: Use of non-renewable resources and energy. This model should not be accepted without Environmental Impact Assessment and Environmental Management Plan.
3. Labour intensive.	3. Labour Displacing.
4. Caters to over 76 per cent of the population.	4. Cover hardly 10 per cent of the population.
5. Poverty alleviation at subsistence level.	5. Gap between rich and poor widening: rich become richer and poor become poorer.
6. Governance at village level through Panchayat: Bottom-up Approach.	6. Government Centralization: Top-down Approach.
7. Economy of Permanence: Sustainable.	7. Economy of Impermanence: Unsustainable.
8. Rural Development.	8. Industrial Development.

Source: T.N. Khoshoo, "Gandhian Environmentalism—An Unfinished Task", *IASSI, Quarterly*, Vol. 16, July-Sept., 1997, pp. 1-16.

5

GANDHIAN PERSPECTIVE ON HUMAN RIGHTS AND SOCIAL WORK PRACTICE

I

Gandhi's Human Rights Mission (not commission) has been to build a social order in which man can live in peace and harmony. His vision was to consider the whole world as a single family. His goal was *Sarvodaya* (development of all). His approach to development was holistic and not segmental. His principles were truth and nonviolence. He said: "Nonviolence is the first article of my faith and also the last article of my creed". His methods were based on *Satyagraha* (insisting on truth). He wanted to inculcate in people values which have been aptly described by William Blake as: "To see the world in a grain of sand/and a heaven in a wild flower/hold infinity in the palm of your hand/eternity in an hour". Gandhi thought that this cherished goal could be achieved by combining scientific and spiritual aspects in our educational system. He subscribed to Buddha's last words, "Be lamp to yourselves", in word, deed and action.

II

Vinoba Bhave, spiritual heir of Gandhi, felt that human rights need unity of five powers. He symbolised these powers by five fingers of the palm. The little finger (*Kanistha*) represents government which is very weak. Ring finger (*Anamika*) represents wiseman or *Buddhiman*. But there are many *Buddhijivi* than

Buddhiman. Middle finger (*Madhya*) is longest. It represents politics, commerce and business. Index finger represents a gentleman. It is very difficult to find gentleman in today's world even with a lamp in day light. Last, thumb (*Angustha*) represents people and their power. No doubt people are sovereign, but they are being exploited by the other powers. In democracy, people must exercise their power of vote to elect their representatives who are honest men of integrity. All these powers may be coordinated so that policies and programmes are people-centred and not leader or self-centred.

III

There is a poster which says: "Free people are not equal (in income). Equal people are not free." It touches a deep truth. Democracy is not egalitarian.

In politics there is greater concentration of power than in business. Political dynasties can be more entrenched than business dynasties. Look at the Nehru-Indira-Gandhi family. Every politican promotes his relations rather than grassroots workers. An NGO, Loksatta, estimates that 10,000 political families monopolise two-thirds of all seats in legislatures. Many parties are personal fiefs: Mulayam Singh Yadav is the SP, Laloo Yadav is the RJD, Navin Patnaik is the BJD. There is nothing egalitarian about it.[1]

The Universal Declaration of Human Rights adopted by the UN in 1948 has not become people centric. They have been universally violated because five developed countries having veto power dominate the decision-making power and process in the UN.

In Gandhi's view, in order to make Human Rights people-oriented, all types of exploitations need to be eliminated. People are dominated and exploited by concentration of three powers—mind, money and muscle. An elite having any of the three powers should consider himself as Trustee of that power to be used for development of society and not self-aggrandisement. Gandhi said: "There is enough in this world to meet everybody's need but not for even a single man's greed." We all know the story of greed of

Midas. He was one who got a boon from God, with the capacity of creating gold out of his gentle touch. Very soon he was fed up with the boon because he could not eat his own food and touch his wife or daughter. Whatever he touched became gold idol and thus he lost his peace of mind. The abundance of gold did not bring him happiness. He ran to God to withdraw his boon. All became normal thereafter, and he then understood the meaning of life in a better way. It teaches us a lesson that contentment is very important in human life. We all want autonomy but not accountability. We must erase from our minds Greed, Hatred and Delusion (GHD) to achieve the aim of Universal Declaration. When people want to possess more and more of everything, a lot of stress and strain is generated. Desires for worldly possessions increase incessantly and finally, turn into a whirlpool of miseries. Real peace of mind is not possible without practising non-attachment. The human mind is like an unbridled horse, which runs amuck if not controlled properly. Our ambitions multiply our wants, thereby leading to unfulfilled desires. Controlling our mind is the most important first step in self-realization.

IV

To create demand and motivate consumers to purchase, Indian barons are discovering the power of local advertising to keep the cash registers ringing. In July 2001, Star's Radiocity was the first private radio station in Bangalore. Today more than 200 brand advertise it, each paying between Rs. 1,000-3,000 for a 10-second spot. Of the total revenue, 40 per cent comes from 125 local shops like Deepak Silks or Huzaifa Decor. Most of them are first-time advertisers. While some of them are busy tracking the Rs. 9,000 crore national advertising market, others tap local advertising which has grown up to Rs. 36,000 crore. What's more, over the past five years, it has been growing at 15 per cent year-on-year, unlike national advertising which has of late grown at 5-7 per cent. This has given rise to consumerism.[2]

The advertisers have not spared food—fast food and a variety of soft and hard drinks. One-third of Western European consumers are now over-weight and by 2006, this will increase much more.

Corruption in India is a direct index of consumerism. India is ranking 72 out of 91 countries in a study of the Perception Index of M/s Transparency International, Berlin, an NGO.

All the malpractices are adopted to acquire illusory happiness. Which is the happiest place in the world? According to a recent research led by the London School of Economics, the happiest place in the world is (Would you believe?) Bangladesh. Interestingly the United States got the 46th place in this world of happiness Survey, with Britain at 32nd mark, India came in fifth. The study reveals how, in general, happiness is inversely proportional to peaks of economic development. Thus, although the British have twice the amount of money they had 40 years ago, there perceived quality of life has not improved. In fact, it has decreased, the survey tells us.[3] Such a remark was also made by the caretaker of Rabindra Nath Tagore's Shanti Niketan to me: "Sir, money has come but love has gone".

V

Let us face the facts. It is time to look at one of the root causes for the ecological crisis, poverty and unequal distribution. The truth is that one-half of the world's three billion people actually exist on less than two dollars a day. At the same time, 20 per cent of the global population living in high-income countries, account for as much as 86 per cent of total private consumption expenditure. The poorest 20 per cent account for only 1.3 per cent.

In South Asia, the proportion of the poor people fell from 44 per cent in 1990 to 40 per cent in 1998. However, the number of people living in poverty is increasing. Though per capita GDP has grown in 1990s at almost four per cent per year poverty reduction has been very slow.

There is need to bring about change in the social structure. There cannot be a worst example of violation of human rights than rape of women. An 18-year old girl was gangraped in full public view, surrounded by male cheerleaders in village Meerwala, Multan, in Pakistan. Her crime was that her 11 year old brother was seen with a girl from the higher Mastoi tribe. In India Bhanwari

Devi was gang raped for 'daring to create awareness' against child marriage. Young lovers in the Hindi heartland are lynched or hanged to death sanctioned by village elders or community, often because they belong to different castes or communities (See *Hindustan Times*, New Delhi, Rape as Spectacle, 5 July, 2002).

The consumption in rural areas is growing in size because of penetration, population and income growth. With due increase in consumption per user, demand is being ramped up. For instance, toilet soaps have seen a 59 per cent increase in consumption in volume due to the income multiplier effect while the toilet powder segment is growing because of population growth.

Take four Ps of marketing—price, place, promotion and product—being in positioning and packaging, thrown in D&R (distribution and reach) and you have a quick fix punch. Of the 3.3 million outlets in the land, only 1.2 million are urban. In India the consuming class is 150 million. A new working segment which is emerging is called the climbers (275 million). Then there are the aspirants (275 million) and finally the destitute (210 million).

The focus on the civil and political rights in the Indian context is also very bleak. We have not been able to provide to all Indian people:

1. A square meal a day,
2. Potable drinking water,
3. Education,
4. Health Services, and
5. Roof over head and other basic necessities.

The benefits of development and other welfare programmes have reached only to 15-20 per cent of people.

National Development Report of India 2001 brought out by Planning Commission of India (March 2002), reports that poverty ratio has declined from 44 per cent in 1983 to 26 per cent in 2000, i.e. the decline in nineties has been faster than eighties.

During the Cold-War period the focus was on the civil and political rights in the Universal Declaration which emphasized more on them than the social and economic aspects. John Galtung has aptly observed that the 'propagation of human rights consequently is also the propagation of Western Civilization and partly intended as such'. All Human Rights are universal, indivisible, interdependent and inter-related. The international community must treat human rights globally in a fair and equal manner, on the same footing and with the same emphasis. This will settle the question as to which set of rights are superior—civil, political, or economic. Social and cultural rights have been given low priority by Western governments.[5]

The narrow conception of individualism has developed into a modern theory of rights over duties. "Where everybody wants rights", asked Gandhi, "who shall give them to whom?" Anthony Parel in his new edition of *Hind Swaraj* and other writings (OUP, 1997) sums up Gandhi's views on rights as based on *Satya* (Truth) and *Dharma* (the source of duty). Real rights flow from duty. Bhikhu Parekh's philosophical characterisation: ". . . not just in the casual sense that one person's rights create corresponding duties for others but in the deeper sense that they are two different ways of looking at the same thing. One has a duty to exercise one's rights and a right to discharge one' s duties. Rights, thus, are a noble burden and duties a redeeming privilege." Gandhiji put the entire thing anecdotally: "I have learnt from my illiterate but wise mother that all rights to be deserved and preserved come from duty well done. Thus every right to live accrues to us only when we do the duty of the citizenship of the world. . . . Every other right can be shown to be usurpation, hardly worth fighting for."[6]

VI

In other words, Gandhian approach to duties and responsibilities are interrelated. Gandhi's assertion was that 'the Ganges of rights flow from the Himalaya of duties.'

Two incidents—one in 1893 in South Africa and the second in 1956 in USA—that changed the course of history of civil rights movement for human rights in the world are: (1) The eviction of

Mohandas K. Gandhi from the train at Petermauritzburg for having dared to travel in a first class compartment, and (2) Mrs. Rosa Parks' stout refusal to vacate a seat she had occupied in a public bus in Montgomery and her readiness to be fined for the 'crime' she had committed. These two incidents reveal amazing similarity of nonviolent assertion of the individual's right of equality and the inalienable right of human beings not to be segregated on the basis of one's colour or race.

When Gandhi was ejected from the train in the cold wintry night, he paced up and down and conceived the idea and method of Nonviolent. Non-cooperation which reduced in simple terms, means: "I won't hate you, but I won't obey you when you are wrong. Do what you like. I will match my capacity to suffer against your capacity to inflict the suffering—my soul force against your physical or brute force. I will wear you down by goodwill."

Two things happened as Mahatma Gandhi paced that platform: First, the most expensive expulsion in human history. The expulsion of Gandhi from that compartment meant the expulsion of the White man from an overlordship of Asia and Africa. For it meant the birth of the modern uprising of the subject-people of the world—India got her freedom, thereafter Burma (Myanmar), Sri Lanka, Indonesia, Indo-China, and then it leaped over to Africa where 36 nations have found their freedom from outside domination. The overlord reaped what they sowed—they sowed expulsion and they reaped their own expulsion.

But something more important happened—the birth of moral equivalent of war. Nations in East and West had been accustomed to settling their difference by war. It was felt that war was an ingrained necessity—there was no alternative. It was fight or flee, or be subservient. Then Gandhi told India and the world that 'you need not adopt anyone of these three—you could match your soul force against physical force and wear the other down with goodwill. . . .'

Almost simultaneously two great forces emerged in the world—Atom force and *Atmic* force—one physical and the other spiritual.[7]

In contrast to Gandhi's nonviolence, Lenin in a bitter bloodbath destroyed the empire of the Czars and established the Union of Soviet Socialist Republic. The Communist regime has collapsed after 70 years. Das Kapital has become a Bible of millions. It is more often quoted and argued about than understood; it has brought to the world not peace but a sword. Gandhi with no weapons and no material power, as the world reckons it, exercised an influence that spread far beyond, the Indian subcontinent.

The second incident that relates to Mrs. Rosa Parks, who is today hailed as the *Mother of Human Rights* took place in 1956 in Montgomery. Mrs. Park, a Negro woman in her thirties boarded a city bus and sat on a front seat but she had no intention to break the law of segregation which was in vague in the state of Alabama. She was promptly ordered to vacate the seat and move to the back seat of the bus. She was neither a member of any group of civil rights activists nor was it a premeditated or political strategy. She preferred to be arrested and fined of her defiance rather than weakly submit to a practice that perpetrated violation of basic human rights. The now famous Montgomery bus strike and the subsequent massive nonviolent civil rights movement under the leadership of Dr. Martin Luther King opened up immense possibilities of the potential of every human being to stand up and fight for his or her freedom and rights.

The city of Mauritzburg, a hundred years later in 1994, posthumously conferred on Gandhi a Gold Medal and citation in recognition of Gandhi's fight for human rights and freedom. Mrs. Rosạ Park said: "The life of a Negro woman was anybody's guess in those days. Humiliation and denial of all basic freedoms and utter lack of direction made the life of every black American in those days to lose hope in life."[8]

VII

We can see considerable influence of Gandhi in the various articles of the Universal Declaration of Human Rights. In its 30 articles, the Universal declaration defines that those principles are intended to offer a common standard of achievement for all people and all nations.

The first three articles proclaim that all human beings are born free and equal in dignity and rights and are endowed with reason and conscience; should act towards one another in a spirit of brotherhood, and are entitled to all rights and freedom without any kind of distinction. Everyone has the right to life, liberty and security of person.

Articles 4 to 21 spell out various civil and political rights including those of freedom from slavery; from torture to cruel, inhuman or degrading treatment or punishment; the right to recognition as person before the law and to equal protection by the law against abuse of rights; to freedom from arbitrary arrest, detention or exile; the right to fair public hearing before an independent impartial tribunal and the right to be presumed innocent until proved guilty. . . . Finally, "the will of the people shall be the basis of the authority of the Government", which shall be expressed in periodic election by universal suffrage and secret of free voting procedures.

Article 22 introduces a second group of articles defining various economic, social and cultural rights—those to which everyone is entitled by virtue of his or her membership of society. The rights, comprised in articles 22 to 27, thus include the right to social security; to work under just and equitable conditions; to equal pay for equal work; to rest and leisure; to standard of life, adequate for health and well-being; and the right to education, under defined conditions, and to participate in the cultural life of the community.

The concluding articles (28 to 30) proclaim that everyone is entitled to social and international order in which the declaration of rights and freedom may be fully realized.

VIII

Thus, Mahatma Gandhi opened a new chapter in human history by offering a new set of thoughts and strategies steeped in human dignity. These are highly relevant for professional social workers in their theory and practical work. He taught us that any attempt to violate human rights is abominable and against natural justice.

Hence should be fought tooth and nail. His life and work for twenty-one years in South Africa and thirty years in India, championing the cause of the downtrodden and oppressed who were segregated and ill-treated in the name of dreaded apartheid inspired millions of freedom-loving citizens all over the world including the poets and social reformers.

He demonstrated the work through his novel methods that what the weak and the suppressed need is courage of conviction to stand up and fight any unjust system. He clarified with telling effect that the weapon of the weak in this noble fight for social justice and equal rights is not any external weapon but soul force which is more powerful than even the atom bomb, and which in turn will arm a nation or a person with the requisite courage to fight the forces which deny fellow human beings their right to live in dignity.

Social work as a profession is a process of developmental effort to bring about social change. It aims to build capacity in people to work together as a team to achieve their cherished goals. It also aims to create a sense of responsibility in people to enable them to take charge of their own future. Professional Social Workers would find Gandhi's thoughts and work highly relevant to understand Indian society and to work with people.

Late Professor Sugata Das Gupta, a Gandhian Scholar in his own right said: "Gandhi in his life consciously undertook experiments with truth and nonviolence to build moral-ethical-social order that would best promote social order and social justice. All those who seek to understand contemporary society in its various ramifications, to analyse its problems and to study the process of change and methods of social work that might help the pace of planned development can ill-afford to do without him (Gandhi)."[9]

Gandhi's unswerving focus on the welfare of all (*Sarvodaya*) and the uplift of the poor provide social work with the underpinnings of general practice theory. When looking at the purpose of human existence and the process of human and social development from a Gandhian perspective, the role of social worker moves closer to the spirit of practical idealism that ruled

Gandhi's life and produced so many dramatic opportunities for change. Gandhi's most important contribution to Indian thought is that of "self-control" and "self-realisation". This ought to lead simultaneously to the well-being of the nation as a whole. This is also Gandhi's distinct contribution to political and social theory. At the time of the writing of Hind Swaraj, he was painfully aware that those who care for the nation, such as the apostle of violence, did not care for the soul and those who cared for the soul did not care for the nation. Gandhi wanted to bridge the gap between these two forms of human striving.[10]

Gandhi is usually called a political leader and a social reformer. It is because in most of his life he was actively engaged in a struggle for independence of India from foreign rule and in crusades against some of the social evils, such as, untouchability, low status of women and so on.[11]

Ammu M. Muzumdar says: "In the course of many of his (Gandhi's) activities of a social welfare nature Gandhi had developed certain principles, practices, and procedures which harmonize remarkably with the principles and techniques of professional social case work as it has developed in the western world—settlement houses, social group work, social case work, community welfare organisation, social legislation, and social action."[12]

Gandhi being not a professional Social Worker as envisaged in the modern world but from his activities in the field of politics, social reforms and social welfare can be fruitfully distilled in social work spirit.

Frances M. Yasas has made a study of the question whether or not the professional social work values are compatible with Gandhian Values. Commenting on the study, S.K. Khinduka says: "She (Frances Yasas) finds that Gandhi's work is something of reaffirmation of the basic tenet of social work philosophy that 'man is an object of infinite worth'. Dr. Yasas does not lose sight of the few dissimilarities that exist between Gandhian values and social work values but . . . she shows the essential compatibility, and hence the similarity between the philosophy of Mahatma Gandhi and the values underlying social work."[13]

IX

The individual is central in Gandhian thought. Society and its institutions are useful only as instruments through which self-realization of the individual can occur. Throughout Gandhi's life, where social structure impeded the process of individual self-realization, he became an architect for change in that social order—a reformer.[14] Social work also focuses on the individual and individual well-being. Social work's emphasis, however, has been more on social functioning than on self-realization. The mission of social work has been largely the individual and family function within a given system. In this orientation social work often overlooks the social change and the spiritual dimensions of the individual's development. It fails to adequately criticise the social order and social system that may stifle self-realization.[15]

For Gandhi, self-realization evolves in tandem with moral responsibility. Individuals work on their own development as befits their nature, including voluntary suffering and denial. Social changes springs out of moral growth and socially responsible actions and energies of the individual come from the grassroots. Gandhi felt at odds with all the economic change systems—capitalism, socialism and communism. Each, he felt, place too much stress on change from without or above, rather than change from within and below.

Definitions of social work and/or social welfare needs have been limited. Social work is inclined to help individuals accept and take comfort in the welfare state. Gandhian thought based on responsibility and self-sufficiency would be uncomfortable with an expanding welfare structure. His philosophy pushes us to move beyond the remedial and social adjustment approaches and to explore the moral and spiritual development of the individual. By directing our energies to the client's total development, we gain a richer way of looking at the individual. Gandhi's views on suffering will help fill a void in the profession. Social work lacks a theory of suffering and tends to treat suffering like a disease.

Typically, the professional response is to eradicate both the cause of suffering and its consequences. For Gandhi suffering is not necessarily a negative experience. It is a part of the self-realization process. When voluntarily assumed as a step towards growth, suffering can be perceived as positive. Gandhi reminds us that since we cannot possibly know the absolute truth, we are "therefore not competent to punish"—a most essential reminder, since man when tempted to violence always parades as another's policeman, convincing himself that whatever he is doing to another, that other "has it coming to him". Whoever acts on such righteousness, however, implicates himself in a mixture of pride and guilt which undermines his position psychologically and ethically. Against this typical cycle, Gandhi claimed that only voluntary acceptance of self-suffering can reveal the truth latent in a conflict and in opponent.[16]

When Gandhi speaks of self-realization, he is obviously speaking about the realization of the "higher-self" which for him coincides with the ultimate reality, better known to him as Truth. He considers nonviolence as the manifestation of truth. Self-realization by implication is the attainment of perfect nonviolence. Violence is the brute force belonging to the "lower-self", which according to Gandhi, should be reduced to zero in order to realize the higher self. He realized that violence and untruth were the greatest obstacles to man's progress.[17]

Social work today is something more than a method. It is a social institution, as Witmer calls it, and it should be understood as such. This means that it should be understood in terms of present day needs and the social and cultural forces of the society as well as in terms of its purpose. Gandhi introduced basic changes in the mode of thinking and living of the people. He made people think fundamentally about many problems, that confront the country even today. He left a profound impact on the thoughts and actions of the people. It is, therefore, necessary to examine his contribution to the theory and practice of social work.[18]

Frances M. Yasas says, "Indian students could learn the basic values of professional social work more easily, if they could see them as different ways of saying some of the things that have been taught by their own philosophers, saints, social thinkers, and social reformers, especially a person of the stature of Mahatma Gandhi.[19]

Gandhi's constructive work signifies a programme that would lead to the reconstruction of both man and society. Narayanasamy says constructive programme is aimed at changing the very basic of the whole social and economic order. The constructive programme is not the same as traditional social work. Professional social work has been developed to help in solving problems of modern society. It is something like a curative approach, whereas the constructive programme acts as a preventive approach in social behaviour and with minimised wants leading to a healthy cooperative endeavour. It is based on nonviolence and quality, eliminating violence, domination, and inequality which are the causes of all the fundamental problems of mankind.

The following table as developed by Narayansamy distinctly compares differences between social work and constructive work. Social work will gain very much by pondering over the issue and to adopt or adapt best suited to these in handling and dealing with social problems.

Table

Social Work	*Constructive Work*
1. The relationship of social worker with client forms two separate entities.	1. Constructive worker is a member of same society.
2. Trained in professional practice but attached to no code of conduct.	2. Voluntary worker trained in nonviolence.
3. To help others to help themselves.	3. To help his own society to grow from strength to strength.
4. Expects aid from external agency.	4. Generates resources from within.
5. Mostly urban-oriented.	5. Focused mostly on rural development.
6. Provides a healing touch but does not provide a permanent solution.	6. Creates preventive measures so as to form a foundation of permanent solution against ills of society.

Source: See Narayansamy, "Gandhian Concept of Social Work," *Gandhi Marg*, Vol. XXII, No. 2, July-September, 2000, p. 212.

The objective of Gandhian work would be to find out the basic causes of and conditions out of which arise all social problems. The method of "Social Action" will be directed towards the removal of those causes and conditions so that truth, nonviolence, and social justice could be given a practical shape in the reconstruction of society. This would imply basic and fundamental changes in the institutional framework and the value system of society. Even those laws, which may be bad in themselves or obedience to which would be inconsistent with the self-respects of the individual or human dignity, the respect of which is the ultimate value of the professional social work will have to be opposed or disobeyed if necessary.[20]

Parmeshwari Dayal, therefore, says that aim of social action is to combat problems and their causes which require a group and collective effort and which are necessary to be resolved for the reconstruction of society. Whenever group and collective energies are directed towards combating certain problems for meeting certain emergency situation or for obtaining long term results, we have social action.[21]

A study of Gandhian movements, their organisation and strategies would be of great help to professional social workers.

X

Gisela Konopka in her book *Edward C. Lindeman and Social Work* has beautifully identified values and methods.[22] They to a great deal resemble Gandhian values and methods.

A social work student in a seminar raised the question whether it was right for social workers to advocate untouchability when a whole village community was for it? Was it not one of the basic principles of social work to accept the people as they are and therefore of social worker to accept the community feeling as a fact? Undoubtedly, the social worker must know, analyse and understand the facts of the community. Yet, he is not merely an "observer" who enters a situation for the purpose of study alone. His concern is first and foremost to safeguard the "dignity" of every human being, and the right of each individual to fulfil himself to the greatest possible extent—short of abridging the right of others to do so. Untouchability violates this major value. This is a complete endorsement of Gandhian values.

The facts presenting themselves to the social worker include values. He in turn influences those facts with his set of professional values. What are they? The two primary values of social work and Gandhians are the *dignity and the right of each individual* to full development of his capacities and *interdependence of individuals* and their consequent responsibility towards each other in the framework of their capacities. Controversy is often based on the confusion of the *origin* of acceptance of this value with the value itself. For those who base social work on religion, the value is derived from God; for those, the humanist, from ethical laws. Until now every attempt to prove the value component has failed. Those theories of social work which derive the moral law from God do not need and will not search for scientific proof of it. Those who base it on human ethical value will continue searching for it.

While social workers do agree on permanent or basic values that guide their work, they often disagree about the *secondary values.* For instance, should every woman stay at home and take care of her children or should she be allowed to work if she wants to? Is it possible to have groups composed of only members from the same caste, religion, or economic status or should they intermingle? Is the use of rewards compatible with good practice or does it lead to too much competition? They differ over secondary values because of the influence of four factors: (1) Their own cultural and family background; (2) The precepts and demands of given groups to which they belong—Temple or church, professional or social; (3) Personal experience—illness, abandonment by a significant person, death; and (4) Different scientific theories regarding human behaviour.

All four of these determinants of secondary values lie more in the field of insight and scientific endeavour than do the primary values. Thus, secondary values need not be accepted as axioms, but can be investigated. If social work accepts itself as a profession based on primary values which are axioms as well as a profession constantly guided by secondary values which must be investigated, many of the controversies will lose some of their religious fervour and social work will enter a period far more consonant with the calm and cooperative effort expected of human relations profession.

It may be useful to elaborate and discuss in some detail so as to enable us to move into an integrated attempt at theory of knowledge of social work.

1. *Cultural and family background:* We first incorporate the values of those with whom we identify usually, i.e. our parents. Since this happens early in life the influence of this identification is ordinarily the strongest and most lasting one. This is not to deny that the growing child and even an adult continues to modify these values and attitudes through: (i) identification with other persons, (ii) consideration of ideas encountered in reading, discussing, and the like, and (iii) insight into themselves.
2. *Precepts and demands of a given group:* Groups have a very strong influence on individuals. The strongest influences come from the primary group—the family. Secondary groups are friendship groups or any group to which individual belongs by virtue of his own decision or by tradition. As he grows older such groups become more and more important to him. The groups develop their own precepts and sub-cultures with which the individual must conform or leave the group. The ethical codes of professional organizations prescribe value-determined behaviour of members. Each religion has its code of ethics by means of which it aims to regulate the behaviour of its members. Every human being belongs to a number of groups. Secondary values derived from groups, associations cannot be taken lightly and are not always easy to reconcile. At times thinking through these values in relation to the primary ones might change their application.
3. *Personal Experience:* Life experience strongly influences the value system of every human being. The more diversified such experiences are, the more open the person usually becomes to accept people with differing value systems.

4. *Different Scientific Theories Regarding Human Behaviour:* This area shows the constant search for a more integrated theory derived from several disciplines and blended into one.

Some basic concepts of social work and Gandhians are same. For example:

(i) Capacity for growth and change;
(ii) The awareness of the individual as an interacting member of society and the importance of interaction, individually and in groups, for his development and for the development of society.

Goals of Gandhian and Social Work

1. To enable individuals, clients or group members or groups as a whole to move towards greater independence and capacity for self-help.
2. To use the scientific method to prepare for action: fact-finding (observation), analysis and diagnosis in relation to the individual, the group, the community and the social environment.
3. Form purposeful relationships, conscious focusing on the needs of the people.
4. Conscious use of self-knowledge and discipline in relationships, but without the loss of warmth and spontaneity.

A question generally asked is whether unlike Gandhian work is social work only palliative or is responsible also for changing the social institutions. The answer must be that social work is responsible for attempting both: to hold individuals in the framework of existing conditions as well as to help change social institutions. When we recognize the multiple causation of problems and realize that the causes lie neither exclusively in the individual nor in the social structure, it becomes clear that profession which works towards social justice in a wider sense must feel responsible for amelioration and social change.

To Sum Up

Social work is a profession that presents a unique constellation of values, knowledge and method. None of the three parts can be understood independent of the other two. Social work knowledge is based on many disciplines with a trend towards increased integration, more emphasis on all areas of knowledge and better understanding of dynamics and inter-relationships. Systems differ, but not basically; the differences concern researchable facts, not values. Social work methods have in common basic goals and values and principles derived from them. They differ in specific skills and intermediate goals. They must be evaluated in terms of their effectiveness as well as their consonance with the primary values. The more the three social work methods (social case work, social group work, community welfare organisation) are integrated, and the more individual social workers gain knowledge of all three of them, the more the profession will be able to translate into practice the individualisation and cooperation.

There is lot of communality between Gandhian and professional social work. Both can enrich each other and join together to build a new India.

XI

Gandhi had the knack to identify talented people and to assign them work for the community. Let me cite a case:

In 1934 Mahatma Gandhi visited Belgaum as part of his *Dalit* welfare programme. A couple went to attend the meeting. While talking to them Gandhiji asked the woman what she could do for *Dalit* children. She innocently replied that she had studied only up to fifth standard, hence did not know what she could do for them. The Mahatma asked her, "Do you know how to bathe children and comb their hair?" "Yes"' she replied instantly. Then Gandhi sent two children with her and asked her to take care of them. The lady who readily accepted Gandhiji's assignment was Nagamma Veeranagouda Patil, a veteran freedom fighter and founder of the Balikashram in 1934 in Hubli, the second ashram in the country to take care of *Dalit* children. Thereafter Nagamma never looked back and continued to work for the children and became a role model for those around her. She died at the age of 97 years leaving behind her a rich legacy of service, which could inspire others to work for the cause of the oppressed classes of society. I am not sure, how manly of us will emulate the example of Nagamma.[23]

XII

Gandhi in his fifty years of public life in three countries—India, Great Britain and South Africa—demonstrated the efficacy of the Buddhist teachings, i.e. respects for all living beings and human dignity which is impossible without *compassion*. And Gandhi emerged as the voice of the voiceless and inspired social reformers, political leaders and thinkers, and fighters for individual liberty all over the world.

Among the notable streams of thought that influenced Gandhi are that of Thoreau and Emerson. From Martin Luther King and Khan Abdul Gaffar Khan to Julius Nyrere, Hochi Minh, Bishop Desmond Tutu, Petra Kelly and Nelson Mandela, there is a galaxy of men and women in different parts of the world who took a leaf from Gandhi to fashion their initiatives for ensuring justice and fight discrimination in the name of colour and race. And with Gandhi the fight for Human Rights took a new turn. From violent methods the movement turned to nonviolent tactics which Gandhi believed would be the weapon of strong and not that of the weak.

Will the professional social workers rise from their comfortable 'system maintenance jobs' to change the system? By and large there are no innovative leaders with the exception of Medha Patkar to accept the challenge.

Professional social workers should make Human Rights as an integral part of their training programme and take the responsibility to:

1. Make Human Rights a reality world-wide.
2. Prevent Human Rights violations.

3. Build a Global partnership for Human Rights.
4. Make Human Rights along with Peace, Democracy, and Development, the guiding principle of the 21st century.

Our Gandhian legacy and professional work obligate us to drive humanity towards this alternative vision of the world order in which man can live in peace and harmony.

The biggest challenge for social work is understanding the requirement of the client system (child, women, people in general). The whole exercise is like peeling an onion. You discover more when you start peeling. It requires a tremendous understanding of the problem of your client before you set out to look for the right solution. It is very important for us to have an excellent research back up.

In most instances, one finds that individuals lack the ability to take the initiative even though they have the intelligence and capability to take on challenges. The general feeling is why should one do that when there is no recognition of sincere efforts. I think it is very important to look beyond the assigned roles. If one keeps doing things, the results will follow. One may not get immediate returns for the initiatives, but they will definitely come. The futurists say that a child born in the mid-1990 will live for about 130 years and when it dies, a back-up of its mind would be available on a network. Its natural death will not be a trauma for the children, they will be able to upload their moms mind on a robot. Social workers will have to cope with and be ready to change their training programmes in order to meet the modern emerging needs.

XIII

In India, if we have any respect for Gandhi, we must have professional social work with social and human aspect at the base and economics at the apex. We have accepted globalisation with human face. However, we should remember that in these days of modern cosmetics, face can be human and yet the soul and heart can be cruel. In the present world which is full of hatred, bitterness, cruelty, racial discrimination, communal tension, inequalities, human degradation and erosion of values, Gandhi is more relevant than at any other time. In the present situation there is an imperative need to recapture the spirit of human touch of Gandhi.

On the first Independence Day in 1947, Gandhi was not in Delhi. He was in Calcutta giving the healing touch to the society that was torn by Hindu-Muslim riots. Delhi was glittering with lights, loud slogans and poetic assertion of the late Pandit Jawaharlal Nehru, who said, "At the stroke of midnight hour, when the world sleeps, India will awake to life and freedom and a soul of nation long suppressed will find utterance."

A few weeks prior to Independence Day of 1947, an emissary of Pandit Nehru and Sardar Patel was sent to Gandhi at Calcutta. The emissary reached at midnight and said, "I have brought an important letter for you from Pandit Nehru and Sardar Patel." "Have you taken your food?" asked Gandhi. When the emissary said 'No', gandhi served him food. And after he had his food, Gandhi opened the letter which said: "Bapu you are the Father of the Nation. 15th August will be the First Independence Day in 1947 and we want you to come to Delhi and give us your blessings." Gandhi reacted: "How stupid! When Bengal is burning, Hindus and Muslims are killing each other and I hear the cries of their agony in the darkness of Calcutta, how can I go to Delhi with the glittering lights?" These are the heart breaking words of Gandhi. He further said, "I have to live here for the establishment of peace in Bengal and if need be, I have to give up my life for ensuring that there is harmony and peace." The emissary started for his return journey in the morning. It was a moving sight, full of human touch. Gandhi gave the emissary a send off. He was standing below a tree. A dry leaf fell from the tree. Gandhi picked it up and put it on the palm of his hand and said, "My friend, you are going back to Delhi . . . give to Pandit Nehru and Sardar Patel as my first Independence Day "gift". "And while he was saying this, tears came from the eyes of the emissary. Gandhi humorously said, "How great is God! He did not want Gandhi to send that dry leaf. He made it wet." 'Carry this leaf as a gift full of your tears', added Gandhiji. That was Gandhi's human touch![24]

The question is as to how many among us would adhere to such a priority and commitment to work with strife-stricken people to avoid glittering Delhi?

XIV

Though significant indigenous literature is now available on social work produced by Schools of social work, yet by and large, most of the Indians dismiss Gandhi as totally irrelevant to the practice of social work. Gandhi was a great social activist but our social work practitioners do not find any material of relevance in Gandhi's writings and work that could enrich the methods of the profession. "Gandhi was one of the most outstanding activists of our time," quoted exhaustively by Prof. Alinisky of America, to draw sanction for his theory of methods. His (Gandhi) dismissal in India is ironical.[25]

The profession shows a great deal of impertinence and immorality as many a times it has refused to draw from Gandhian methods of individual, group and community help as well as social action, while building up its methods. The situation becomes worse when we find that we are all trying in vain to cling to a type of professionalism borrowed from the USA.

There is only one instance when a long dialogue was held with the participation of 'professional social work educators' and 'Gandhian constructive workers' for over two years under the leadership of late Jayaprakash Narayan. It is advisable that similar dialogue may be held again to learn from each other's experiences.

Gandhi's timeless teaching was that man's true progress is to be judged by moral and spiritual standards, and not by material or physical standards. Sacrifice was far more important than success and renunciation was regarded as the crowning achievement. The citizen ranked in society, not according to wealth or power, but according to the standards of learning, virtue and character which he had attained. This should be the foundation of professional social work's code of ethics.

The Mahatma has gone the way all saints have. But his spirit will live among us as long as India survives.

Social work as a profession has found that it can teach its methods by constantly analysing them and by exercising them in practice. Schools of social work must offer thoughtful, free and conscious investigation into philosophy in general and Gandhian philosophy in particular related to social work. Social worker has to become something more than a skilled craftsman and something more than a well-meaning idealist.

The Human Rights are not a luxury intended merely for the elite and the affluent and that our people, poor and downtrodden, are as intensely committed to the free way of life as the richest under the sun.

XV

Let us evaluate our performance to raise our future generation. India had set for itself a goal to reduce the infant mortality rate (IMR) by one-third by the year 2000 but was only able to lower it from 80 to 60 per 1,000 live births. Maternal mortality rate was to be halved but it actually went up from 437 to 540 per 1,00,000 live births. Again malnutrition among children under five years age was to be halved but came down from 53.4 to only 47 per cent. India will now have to meet these targets by 2015 as laid down in the UN Declaration. A child born in 1990 cannot benefit from the government's programme as he/she is either dead or too old now.

We should not forget that the life-span of man has increased from around 20 years in the 19th century to 80 years today. This has been largely on account of advances in agriculture and medicine. No fixed laws can be made regarding scientific advances because science keeps changing, as do our cultural mores. The professional worker must maintain equilibrium between the two.

The recently-appointed Commission on Human Rights has begun its enquiry in human rights violations in East Timor, Indonesian occupation. Closer home, the repeated allegations of rights abuse by forces in Kashmir and the police in Gujarat demand a fresh review of the agencies and laws enacted to protect the rights of citizens. No longer is it viable to silence critics as western hegemonists are trying to enforce universal moral code and undermining the independence and sovereignty of developing countries.[26]

If there is one universal political value that has been accepted all over the world—liberal or communist, democratic or totalitarian developed or underdeveloped—it is the necessity of the modern state as the central and key institution around which the political and social life of a community is to be organised. Thus, the state as the most formidable universalising agent is on weak grounds to argue for cultural relativism.[27]

Rights, as we see them today, took form in the context of the modern state. The discourse on the modern state has been simultaneous with the one on rights concerned with individual's status within the political arrangement of the modern state and its instruments. This reflects a realisation on the part of the proponents of the state about the dangers of giving absolute powers to the state. The state was not something that could be trusted for a humane treatment of its subjects. Its inception was surrounded by feelings of optimism as well as doubts, possibilities as well as perils, hope as well as ambivalence towards an institution that was considered by some as Frankenstein's monster. Thinkers such as Rousseau, Godwin, Proudhon, Burke and Marx considered the state as an instrument of oppression and morally illegitimate.[28]

These apprehensions did not prove to be entirely baseless. Last century was especially replete with instances of gross violations of human rights by the state and its various instruments. The state, exercising monopoly over the legitimate use of coercive power threatens individual freedom and dignity under the guise upholding the common good, public morality, peace and order. In this contexts, rights serve the purpose of a safety valve, rescuing individuals if the state exceeds its boundaries. Rights, especially civil and political rights, are thus guarantees extended to the individual from the state.[29]

The modern state is unique in its overriding claim over the loyalty of its subjects. In traditional societies, the absence of neatly demarcated boundaries and overlapping sovereignty meant that most of the conflicts being waged today in the defence of the nation state were non-existent. "Today, the worst cases of human catastrophe, be it Kashmir or Kosovo or East Timor, are results of the state's attempts to keep its boundaries intact. This leads us to the conclusion that though human rights may not be universal in the sense of rational principles that could be derived by logical reasoning, as a set of values inherently embedded in the modern state, they have universal presence, because the state itself is a universal phenomenon today. Thus, any scepticism about the universality of human rights has to begin with a criticism of the modern state. Such a discourse will reject the notion of progress, western epistemology and its emphasis on reason as the sole way to acquire knowledge. This also implies a rejection of history and the historical facts and calls for an alternative worldview based on indigenous resources of culture and community as suggested by some Gandhian thinkers.

Those who argue for a different system of human rights today on the basis of cultural differences between the West, where the modern conception of rights took shape, and their own societies, do so while ignoring that they have comfortably adopted a whole set of values including the modern state, market, science and technology from the West. Is the violence committed in the name of the state or development compatible with Asian values? If the nation-state system is taken as the unenviable signpost in the universal march of history, human rights are our inalienable companions during this journey. Denial of these rights is practically, politically as well as ethically incorrect within the existing world order.[30]

XVI

Vinoba Bhave had founded Acharyakul (Teachers Association) to give a positive and better humanistic direction to the present day political systems. Regarding teachers qualifications, he said: "Teachers should be fearless, non-partisan and unenvious. . . ." The actual Sanskrit words that Vinobaji used were: "*Nirbhaya, Nispaksha* and *Nirvair*".[31] These are the qualifications which a social work educator must possess to guide and instruct students.

Explaining the goals of education, Vinobaji had said that education should be based on three pillars of "*Yoga, Udyoga* and *Sahyoga*". What is *Yoga*? It is an education process of bringing harmony between mind and soul.[32]

What is *udyoga*? It is the process of producing the basic necessities of life based on simple and locally suitable technologies without violent exploitation of the fellow human beings as well as of the Mother Nature. What is *Sahyoga*? It is life of complementarity and spirit of voluntarism contrary to the present cult of cut-throat competition which breeds exploitation, leading to individual group or community violence. These can be gainfully considered as basic guidelines for construction of Professional Social Work Education curriculum at all levels.

Once a political leader went to meet Vinobaji at his Pawnar Ashram near Wardha, India. During the course of his discussion he expressed his deep concern over the high rate of illiteracy in the country. Vinobaji answered in a satirical way: "The real danger to our country is not from the illiterate masses but from the literate classes." Peace, value and human rights education is possible in schools and other institutions of learning.

Some of the institutions are following the Gandhian concept of Basic Education which lays emphasis on human dignity and dignity of labour. This concept is working in the educational institutions run by Rudolf Steiner. He is a well-known educationist and an original thinker from the West. Senior Schools in the US, UK and Europe have been practicing the idea of Basic Education in their curriculum as advocated by Gandhiji. The students that come out of these schools do make a difference when they enter into social life. For example, in the Steiner educational institutions, self-sufficiency is the key principle of community life. There is no competition among the students in their schools. This experiment was started in Scotland in 1939-40. It has now got spread in more than 20 countries around the world. Another such experiment is of the communities (institutions) of the Ark in South France. The Italian born, well-known artist and philosopher Lauza Delvsoto, initiated this model of Basic Education. Lauza came to India in 1934. He was in search of Jesus Christ. Someone told him that if he wants to see living Christ, he must go to India and look for a man called Mahatma Gandhi. Lauza walked all the way from France to Sevagram, Wardha. He stayed with Gandhi for a couple of months and went on a pilgrimage tour of India on foot. He was deeply impressed by Gandhi's approach to life. On getting back to France, he started the first Community of the Ark on the principles of Gandhi's idea of Basic Education. At present there are seven such communities successfully functioning in France, Italy, UK, Canada and Israel. The Twind School in Denmark is a unique revolutionary experiment in peace and value education. In the early sixties the whole of West had been protesting against the use of nuclear power, not even for peaceful purposes. A group of young thinking minds had initiated an experiment to find out positive alternative means to produce electricity with the use of wind power which was available in abundance on the shore of North sea. These young activists had been able to develop successfully ever built biggest windmill in the world. It has since been generating electricity for the needs of the entire population of the area. This Twind School has grown into an independent university.

An experiment of Basic Education has been successfully running in UK in the name of "Small School". It was initiated by a Indian born Gandhian activist, Satish Kumar, who has settled in UK with the inspiration of Schumacher. This school is being successfully run without the help of State. It is totally managed by teachers, students, parents and the local community.

In India as a follow up on the Gandhi Centenary celebrations (1969), a small experiment at Rajghat School of Nonviolence was started in 1970-71. The goal of the school was to create a spirit of positivism in the young generation, which has not seen Gandhi.

No school of Social Work has embarked on such an innovative experimental project. The examples cited above should be studied and some lessons may be drawn for teaching and practice of social work to make Human Rights a "reality".

We should philosophically remind ourselves that life's pleasures are like the dewdrops that evaporate with the first hint of warm rays of the sun. Pleasure vanishes like a transient bubble while possessions are evergrowing and therefore self-defeating. Human Rights require sacrifice and shrine so that people who are in the outer circle or marginalised get their legitimate rights. The social worker must involve family, educational, political and religious institutions to make people conscious of their duties, responsibilities and rights. He should also know to effectively use print and electronic media for this purpose.

REFERENCES

1. Swaminathan S. Anklesari Aiyar, "Democracy is not Egalitarian", *Times of India*, Bangalore edition, June 2, 2002, p. 12.
2. Vanita Kohli's cover story, "The Rise of the Locals", *Business World*, Vol. 27, 13-19 May, 2002, pp. 28-33.
3. Mukunanda Goswami, "Statistics don't Lie, Money can't Buy Happiness", *The Hindustan Times*, May 18, 2002, New Delhi, p. 2.

4(a). See *Life Magazine*, June 3, 2002, and the *Hindu Business Line*, Chennai, p. 1.

4(b). Madhu Dandavate, "Social Roots of Adult Injustice", *Indian Journal of Adult Education*, Vol. 63, No. 2, April-June 2002, p. 9.

5. Rabi Ray, Foreword to the book, *Perspectives on Human Rights*, ed. by Anil Dutta Mishra, Radha Publications, 2002, pp. v to xv.
6. Pandav Nayak, "Gandhi an Individual: A Human Rights Perspective" in *Perspectives on Human Rights*, see p. 145.
7. Stanley, E. Jones, "My Conversion to Nonviolent Non-Cooperation" in *Mahatma Gandhi: 100 Years*, Gandhi Peace Foundation, 1968, New Delhi, pp. 171-79.
8. N. Radhakrishnan, *The Gandhian Initiatives for Human Rights and Their Relevance Today*, International Centre of Gandhian Studies, 1999.
9. Dasgupta Sujata, A Symposium paper in T.K. Mahadevan's (ed.), *Truth and Nonviolence*, a UNESCO Symposium on Gandhi, Gandhi Peace Foundation, New Delhi, 1970, pp. 325-48.
10. Anthony Parel, "Gandhi's Idea of Nation in Hind Swaraj", *Gandhi Marg*, Vol. XX, No. 3, October-December, 1991, pp. 261-81.
11. Narayanasamy, S., "Gandhian Concept of Social Work", *Gandhi Marg*, Vol. XXI, No. 2, July-September, 2000, pp. 207, 209, 218.
12. Muzumdar Ammum, *Social Welfare in India: Mahatma Gandhi's Contribution*, Asia Publishing House, Mumbai, 1964, p. 158. Cited by Narayanaswamy in "Gandhi Concept of Social Work", *Gandhi Marg*, Vol. XXII, No. 2, July-September, 2000, p. 209.
13. Khinduka, S.K., *Social Work in India*, Kitab Mahal Pvt. Ltd., Allahabad, 1965.

14. Thomas Walz and Satish Sharma, Celesta Biannam, University of Illinois, Programme of International and Cross-Cultural Social Welfare, *School of Social Work Occasional Paper Series*, Manuscript No. I, Winter, 1990, pp. 11-35.
15. *Ibid.*, pp. 17-18.
16. Erickson, E.H., *Origin of Militant Nonviolence*, W.W. Norton & Co., Inc., New York, 1969, pp. 412-13.
17. Narayanasamy, p. 210.
18. *Ibid.*
19. Francis M. Yasas, "Gandhian Values and Professional Social Work Values", in Khinduka's *Social Work in India*, Kitab Mahal Pvt. Ltd., Allahabad, 1965, pp. 75-76.
20. Narayanasamy, S., p. 209.
21. Dayal Parmeshwari, *Gandhian Approach to Social Work*, Gujarat Vidyapith, Ahmedabad, 1986, p. 45.
22. Konopka Gisela Edward C. Lindeman, *Social Work Philosophy*, The University of Minnesota Press Minneapolis, 1958, pp. viii-220. See *Integration of Value, Method and Knowledge*, pp. 174-202.
23. Shyam Sunder Valtam, "In Gandhiji's Footsteps", *Deccan Herald*, Friday, May 31, 2002, September, p. II.
24. Madhu Dandavate, "Gandhi's Human Touch", in *Gandhi in Action*, Vol. IV and V, 1997-1998, pp. 99-100.
25. K.D. Gangrade, *Social Networks and Social Work*, Northern Book Centre, New Delhi, 1985.
26. Ravindra Rathee, "Universal Charter—Inevitably Tied to Modern State", *The Times of India*, June, 2002, Bangalore, p. 10.
27. *Ibid.*
28. *Ibid.*
29. *Ibid.*
30. *Ibid.*
31. Arya Bhushan Bhardwaj, "Peace and Value Education: A Gandhian View Point", *Gandhi-in-Action*, New Delhi, 1997-98, pp. 2-8.
32. Soli S. Sorabji, *Times of India*, June 23, 2002, New Delhi, p. 8.

APPENDIX I

IMPLEMENTATION OF HUMAN RIGHTS

To implement Human Rights everywhere, in June 1993 the 4th World Conference on Human Rights at Vienna (Austria) recommended as follows: "States should strive to eradicate illiteracy and should direct education towards the full development of the human personality and to the strengthening of respects for human rights and fundamental freedoms; the World Conference calls on all States and Institutions to include Human Rights, Humanitarian Law, Democracy and Rule of Law as subjects in the curricula of all learning institutions."

To ensure strict adherence to Human Rights as envisaged in UDHR, ICCPR, etc., the UN General Assembly through World Conference Recommendation proclaimed in 1994 that 1995-2003 is to be observed as United National Decade for Human Rights Education (1995-2004). The UN Assembly issued appeals to all governments and even to contribute in the implementation of a global Plan of Action for this purpose. This plan of Action has five objectives: (1) Assess needs and formulate strategies for furtherance of human rights education; (2) Build and strengthen programmes and capacities for Human Rights education at international, regional, national and local levels; (3) Coordinate development of effective Human Rights education materials; (4) Strengthen the role and capacity of mass media in the furtherance of Human Rights education; and (5) Disseminate globally the UDHR information.

As a result of all these efforts under the UN, action has been initiated at all levels. However, creating proper awareness for Human Rights in nations like India, which are infested with high level of illiteracy is a very tough job. Prevalence of illiteracy here poses multiple problems as a result of which serious doubts crop up in realising the goals of Human Rights Education Decade (HRED) during the UN Decade earmarked for this purpose which is scheduled to conclude in 2004, i.e. only after two years.

However, to pursue objective of the HRED, the World Council for Curriculum and Instruction's India Chapter (WCCI-India) launched 100 Schools Project for this purpose. An Asian Institute of Human Rights Education (AIHRE) was also set up at Bhopal in January. Later on, in December 1995, a WCCI Conference was also held at Amritsar (Punjab). With the interest growing in this area, today a network for Human Rights education has been developed in 50 districts of 10 Indian States. A team of 500 knowledgeable resource persons has been evolved to serve the cause of spreading Human Rights Education.

[See Review of the book by Harry Dhand, *Teaching Human Rights: A Handbook for Teacher Education,* New Delhi, 2002, pp. 261, *Indian Journal of Adult Education*, Vol. 63, No. 1, Jan.-March, 2002, pp. 68-70.]

6

ROLE OF SHANTI SAINIKS (PROFESSIONAL) IN THE GLOBAL RACE FOR ARMAMENTS

A Gandhian Approach

I

Introduction

"This is the best of the times and the worst of the times"—Charles Dickens.

This quote holds true in existing turbulent times. The globe seems to be wriggling in the jaws of nuclear age and terrorism. The message of Gandhi was that without getting bogged down by challenges, the *Shanti Sainik* should be prepared to walk into the valley of death all the time without compromising on ethics.

The last interview which Mahatma gave in the early afternoon on 30th January, 1948 was to Margaret Bourke White, who came to interview him for *LIFE Magazine*. She asked him a question: 'Would he persist in his theory of nonviolence in the event of nuclear attack on the city'? Mahatma's reply was that if the defenceless citizens die in a spirit of nonviolence, their sacrifice would not be in vain; they might well pray for the soul of the pilot who thoughtlessly sprayed death on the city. This was his last message of compassion to mankind.[1]

Mahatma's ideas about Truth and nonviolence have changed the course of human history. While Truth does not seem to be triumphing all-around us—but somehow, somewhere, in some way, something is bringing the human race closer to Truth. Mahatma said about Truth and Nonviolence:

— "I may be a despicable person but when Truth speaks through me, I am invincible."
— "Truth alone will endure. All the rest will be swept away before the tide of time."
— "Nonviolence is the law of our species, as violence is the law of brute."
— "Nonviolence is the greatest force at the disposal of mankind. It is mightier than the mightiest weapon of destruction devised by the ingenuity of man."
— "I do not believe in short cuts which involve violence. However much we sympathize with and admire worthy motives, I am an uncompromising opponent of violent methods even to serve the noblest cause. There is, therefore, really no meeting arrived between the school of violence and myself."
— "To me God is Truth and Love; God is Ethics and Morality; God is fearlessness; God is the source of Light and Life, and yet he is above and beyond all these. He is even the atheism of the atheist; He transcends speech and reason."
— "Indeed religion should pervade each one of our actions. Here religion does not mean sectarianism. It means a belief in ordered moral government of the universe. It is not less real because it is unseen. This religion transcends Hinduism, Islam, Christianity, etc. It does not supersede them. It harmonizes them and gives them reality."

The Mahatma dealt with problems which are timeless and universal, because they spring from enduring weaknesses of human nature and human society. Since the solutions he found for them were based on eternal verities, his influence and his relevance are also timeless and universal.[2]

The two primary values of Gandhians are dignity and the right of each individual to full development of his capacities and interdependence of individuals and their consequent responsibility towards each other in the framework of their capacities. This philosophy is a basis of general democracy and has been translated into political systems. For Gandhians, the acceptance of these primary values means constant use of daily practice. All practice must be judged in terms of the fulfilment of these values.

There is universal agreement and acceptance to adhere to the primary values of the dignity of the human beings and human interdependence. But there is difference over secondary values because of the influence of four factors: (1) their own cultural and family background; (2) the precepts and demands of given groups to which they belong—religion, church, professional or social; (3) personal experience—illness, abandonment by a significant person, death; and (4) different scientific theories regarding human behaviour.

All four of these determinants of secondary values lie more in the field of insight and scientific endeavour than in the primary values. The secondary values need not be accepted as anxioms, but can be investigated.

Commenting on the towering personality of Mahatma Gandhi, who often made impossible seem possible, Nobel Laureate Albert Einstein remarked that future generations would find it hard to believe that such a man existed.

Views of 16th and 17th Centuries Scientists

The great scientists of the sixteenth and seventeenth centuries, Gilbert, Galileo, Kepler and Harvey thought it was wrong to resort to practical verification of destructive weapons. Gilbert and Newton did not test by experimentation the theories they expounded about projects or the composition of the gunpowder. If, as Prof. Andrande, his teacher at the Newton's centenary celebrations, has asserted, Newton had an inkling of atomic power, but his reluctance to probe further into it suggests that it was because he feared the destructive powers it would unleash. Similarly Boyle was certain that it was not the scientist's business to discover "hellish machines of war" and made it also his duty to persuade others not to devote themselves to the invention of "destructive artifices". At the same time, there have been few other scientists who had greater sense than Boyle, of the science in promoting material welfare. Scientists of the modern age have lost that social and moral responsibility which Newton and Boyle had.

A scientist does not function in a vacuum. He has obligations towards his fellow men and the world he lives in.

There have been, in recent years several meetings and discussions of atomic scientists. Some noble laureates, opinion makers and Gandhians do condemn nuclear research and the development of superior weapons for destructive purpose.

Satchidananda Murthy in his book "*The Quest for Peace*" writes: "The divorce of scientists from social responsibility and their exclusive concentration on research and burrowing of scholars deeper and deeper into narrowed fields have been the cause of the growth of technocracy, civilisation without culture and politics without responsibility. If there was a sense of responsibility among scientists for what they invent and among scholars for how they interpret facts, totalitarian states would not have become realities in the modern world."[3]

One of the fundamental assumptions of modern science has been that the value-realm and facts-realm are completely disjointed and mutually exclusive so that knowledge and virtue belong to disjointed realms and science bears no intrinsic relation to justice. But this position has been contended on a grand scale by many thinkers. Mahatma Gandhi was forthright in ruling out the dichotomy of science and values. For him science made sense only when it stood in intrinsic relation with human values. That is, a scientific description of the world had to be value-laden because the world consists as much of values as of fact. Those holding such view go so far as questioning the very objective of modern science which excludes such an important and essential ingredient of reality from its purview.[4]

Prof. Radhakamal Mukherjee emphasized: "To discover values, whether intrinsic and ultimate or instrumental and immediate, as historical and workable theories, pragmatically and programmatically; to appreciate the continuity between the intrinsic and the instrumental values in all means-end-scheme; and to clarify, harmonize and adjust values, the laws or uniformities in the social cosmos—as dynamic expressions of the richness and uniqueness of the human personality and of social integration and harmony—are essential features of new outlook in sociology. This will bring about a Copernican revolution in the field of social science, shifting the stress from the method of Aristotle to Galileo with reference to social phenomenon; the former dealing with the properties of objects to the whole sociological situation. Like man's own nature, dispositions and possibilities; like his ever changing and enlarging social values change, extend and coordinate themselves as dynamic inter-relations in a functional on-going whole—the social order."[5]

He is further of the opinion that we should see the individual, society and values—the wick, the oil and the flame—a piece, in an indivisible unity of the inner and the outer, of the microcosm and the macrocosm. In a multi-dimensional environment, man develops values and symbols which are synthetic products of the human mind that enhance, elevate, and refine social relations and processes and bind men together in ever-expanding, ever-deepening participation and communication.[6]

According to Mukherjee, "Values may be defined as socially approved desires and goals that are internalized through the process of conditioning, learning for socialization and that become subjective preference, standards and aspirations. The result is that man orients himself to his desires and goals in a set pattern solving inner tensions or conflicts of imperious biological drives on the one hand and achieving harmonious social relations with fellowmen, on the other. Simultaneously the approval and restraint, reward and punishment of society develops compatible attitudes and dispositions. Thus values operate below as well as above the conscious level. Goals, values and norms are different stages and levels of value insight and experience gained in the social milieu. The concept 'value' cuts across desires, goals, ideals and norms. All social functions and structures are seats of values that keep society as a continuum process. Society, then, is an organisation and accumulation of values.[7]

The ultimate ground in which the unity of values is established is "Self" or Being. Human values and "Being" are not only interrelated but identical. Thus, ultimate value of all scientific discoveries and inventions has to be to achieve world peace to live in harmony and not to be dominate one over the other.

Need for Peace Education

The nations of the world today, instead of living in harmony are engaged in a race for armaments supremacy. what is the principal purpose of this race? To prevent one-nation-one-part of humanity from dominating or destroying another.

Much intelligence and much energy are going into this effort. India and Pakistan have also joined the exclusive club of nuclear age. Yet it seems more important than ever that even greater efforts should be made to achieve positive and mutually helpful relations (MHA) rather than mutually assured destruction (MAD).

This cannot be accomplished by harnessing technical forces, but only through man himself, working with other man. In this effort professionals can play a very vital and important role.

Nuclear Age

Some scholars have said: "The nuclear age could be dated as having begun at the end of 1938, when at the Kaiser Wilhelm Institute for Chemistry in Berlin, Otto Hahn and Fritz Strassman conducted an experiment on uranium. It disclosed a new type of nuclear reaction—fission. Just seven years later in the desert at Alamagordo, New Mexico, the first atomic explosion was conducted. It led one observer to exclaim "Brighter than thousand suns". Later nuclear weapons were detonated over Hiroshima and Nagasaki. It was no longer an experiment.[8]

In the view of Richard Butler, the nuclear age has been marked by three underlying characteristics: (1) Transformation, (2) Anxiety, and (3) Obscurantism.[9]

(1) The Transformation was from that of a fantastically exciting journey of purely scientific discovery into the desperate struggle to defeat Hitler, than to bring to an end the war with Japan in the Pacific. When one reads the record of scientific discourse and experiment on the atom during the 1930s, what is

revealed is a journey into the unknown. Totally absent from that intellectual journey was what came to be known as nuclear arms race, with all the terrible threat that it has since posed to human kind. The research for knowledge was taken over by politics and its attendant military pressures.

It is more than coincidental that a number of the leading scientists involved in the basic research were Jewish and had to flee from Germany to America as Hitler came to power. It is significant that a key source of the transformation of their work was the desperate race to get to the bomb before Hitler did. *The main lesson to be drawn from this transformation is the lesson of peace.* War has devastating effects, but they extend far beyond the battlefield into the fabric of human society as a whole.

Following the first detonations of nuclear weapons, it seems that almost diabolical clock work was set in motion, leading to today's situation of the world more heavily armed than ever before.

(2) The development of the nuclear age has brought with it an underlying and palpable sense of anxiety. Underlying fears of our survivability and associated expressions of the shortness or brutality of life have been evident in our literature and in all forms of art. A particular tragic expression of this anxiety and pessimism is readily detected in surveys of the opinions, feelings and expectations of young people all over the world. Simply, our children have become less than sure that there will be a future.

(3) The most insidious aspect of nuclear age has been the degree of obscurantism it has come to involve. While an underlying sense of anxiety has become widespread, it is plainly true that there also exists in the nuclear age, a chasm like gap between what the nuclear and military cognoscente knows about nuclear weapons and what the ordinary person knows about these machines of mutually assured destruction (MAD). Richard Butler further says: "War in this age is unthinkable. Peace is today as important as air we breathe, without it we die."[10]

The Gandhian perspective is being adopted throughout the world, slowly and steadily. Gandhi's India has a special role to play in identifying not merely the causes of conflict and conditions of harmony but also the instruments of peace.

Meaning of Peace Education

As far as the meaning of peace education is concerned, one can hardly improve upon the definition given by Lennart Virens and Robert Asperlaugh who opined: "Peace education includes development of knowledge, insights and skills as well as the building up of opinions and attitudes, deriving from norms and values embedded in peace and directed to the realization of peaceful human world." According to Mitsuo Okumoto, on the other hand, "Peace education means any education which handles the problem of the elimination of violence and as such there can be hardly any education that is not peace education. These two definitions of peace education, as also some other definitions given by other experts, have much in common." The most important point of commonness being the assumption that demand of our contemporary world society necessitate the liberation of peace education from all the traditional notions about it. Thus, Lennart Virens and Robert Asperlaugh Laureate focused on the knowledge of war and peace with a view to prevent a nuclear war and tended to legitimize the prevalent socio-economic injustice. They have introduced the concept of "crucial peace research" which asserts that our concern should not be merely to take care of the problem of positive peace but also to tackle social and economic conditions which produce violence. Obviously this idea of critical peace research is equally important and relevant to peace education.[11]

Okamoto refers to four types of education. The first type is 'peace education as a criticism of war'. This type of education is related to humanitarian or religious phenomenon manifested in the activities of various societies and groups. Some people think that the second type of education is called peace education as it may lead to liberation. among the most important concerns of this kind of education have been the promotion of human rights, fulfilment of human needs and the problems of social poverty, political repression, racial discrimination, malnutrition, illiteracy and disease. It is implied here that war is the foremost source of turmoil within developing countries. Thirdly, peace education can also be seen as a learning process which emphasizes the learning process in a given educational environment and seeks to help individual in acquiring qualities of tolerance and creativity. Finally, the fourth type of peace education is a life-style movement. This type of education emphasizes that the life-style of people has to be changed in many respects so that peace can be brought about in the international society. The argument behind this contention is that preparation for war is ultimately bound to lead to denial of the minimum necessities of life to poor people and that all the wealth and power that the West has acquired at the expense of poor and the underdeveloped (Third World countries) nations goes a long way in contributing to conflict and peacelessness. Therefore, peace education as a life-style movement emphasizes the need for a 'critical awareness' of this situation and stresses simplicity of life so that human survival can be guaranteed against the ills of over-industrialization and over-consumption.

The fourfold usage of the term 'peace education' reminds us of the Gandhian world-view which is based upon the 'spiritual unity of mankind and which implies that we have to work not only for the material welfare but also for the spiritual advancement of everybody everywhere. Gandhi had warned us that any effort for the more material welfare of an individual or a society to the neglect of other individuals or societies or any effort for the mere economic development to the neglect of spiritual development would be of no avail. For, it would be too much of a fallacy to pretend that 'one is too busy solving one's own problems to be able to deal with the problems of "Third World".' Such an attitude would mean a lingering dependence on the colonial mentality and exploitation of poor people. Peace education demands that such attitudes should be abandoned and efforts should be made to build a new politico-economic order.

There is a need for a meaningful interaction between the highly industrialized nations and the developing countries. This interaction can take place at two levels. First, the peace educators of the West can warn the countries of the Third World that if they try to imitate the development models of the western countries, they are bound to be confronted with the same problems with which the western countries themselves face today. After all, as we know, the industrial countries themselves have been misguided in a disastrous way and their prodigal life-style has already brought the world to the brink of a catastrophe. Secondly, the West should also learn from the values implied in limited consumerism and the technique of nonviolent resistance of which Gandhi has been the greatest experimentalist and innovator. Both these constituents of East and West interaction are clearly Gandhian. For Gandhi not only attacked the Western materialism but also cautioned the East against imitating the West. He held the view that a real East-West harmony is possible only if the West embraces the Eastern values and that if the East embraces the Western values, it would be nothing short of a disaster. In other words, economic development minus social and spiritual development is no development.

Apparently the question of East-West interaction as the basis of widening the base of peace education means either a mere fusion of Western peace education and Eastern peace education or a mere dependence of one on the other. What is important is that the East and the West both should develop their own models of peace education, keeping in view not only their own peculiarities and problems but also the global problems of human survival.

Modern man has to live in a global context and access to knowledge is an important tool of man's ability to adjust himself to newer vision of development and better living. This is particularly relevant to Africa and some of the Asian countries. Because most of the people living in all the Third World countries are suffering from abject poverty, illiteracy, oppression and socio-economic injustice. I feel the problem of peace education is not so much as how to further dramatize the danger of nuclear weapons as it is to encourage people to translate their real thoughts about comprehensive peace into action. Therefore, it becomes clear that a simultaneous attack on both the arms race and the development race constitutes an important component of holistic approach to peace education.

During the struggle for freedom under the leadership of Mahatma Gandhi, peace and human rights were the overriding national concerns. The emergence of Gandhi on the Indian national scene with his faith in nonviolence and *Satyagraha* gave boost to all that was regarded anti-war movements. A significant contribution of Gandhi was to give peace education and the peace movement a peculiarly Indian ethos and cleanse it of alien symbols and imageries. However, in post-independence India the intellectuals and elites have failed to disassociate themselves with cultural legacy of colonialism with the result that steady movement for peace, education and human rights has not developed in the country. The disintegration of the harmonious family structure and also of the concept of *Satyagraha* have contributed to India's failure on this front. Hence, there is a need for revival of these twin ideals.

II

Future

If we can accurately recognize some of the major trends and currents in the past and the present, we can make an educated guess about where we are heading. And if human beings do not like the direction in which the world is heading, they can examine their individual behaviour and government policies to determine if they should be changed so that they contribute to a more desired future. Late Rene Dubos, well-known bacteriologist helped coin the phrase 'think globally, act locally'. This is the way, according to Dubos, individuals can help bring about a desired future.

Of the many possible futures the human race faces on earth, three look most likely at present: (i) Doom, (ii) Growth, and (iii) Steady state. Some kind of catastrophe such as the savage terrorist attack in New York and Washington, on 11th September, 2001 might lead to the death of hundreds of millions of people; economic growth might continue into the future; or the world might achieve an equilibrium in its population growth, use of resources and production of goods. There could, of course, be a combination of two of these or all of all three. For example, one part of the world might experience a harsher life in the future while another part continue to expand economically, one part of the world could reach a steady state while another part continue to grow.[14]

However, we should be very careful about our short-term *versus* long-term goals and benefits. Garrett Hardin, a biologist, has coined the phrase "the tragedy of the commons" to describe what can happen when short-term interests and long-term interests of people are in conflict.[15]

Hardin shows (by giving an example) how it is rational in the short-term interest of each herdsman in a village to increase the number of cattle grazing on the "commons", the commonly owned and in the village. The cost of the overgrazing will be shared by all the herdsmen using the 'commons', while the individual herdsman will reap the profit which comes from selling additional cattle. Also, if the individual herdsman does not increase his cattle but others increase theirs, he loses out since the overgrazing harms his cattle. Thus, the tragedy occurs when each herdsman acting rationally and in his own best short-term interest increases his stock in the commons. Soon there is so much overgrazing that the grass dies and thereafter the cattle.

The global 'commons' today are those parts of the planet which are used by many or all nations: the oceans, the international river systems, the sea bed, the atmosphere and outer space. Technology can give some nations an advantage over others in exploiting these commons and it is clearly in their short-term interest to do so.

Doom

There are a number of scholars and research studies giving warning that if humankind does not change its ways, some kind of disaster will occur in the future. Thus, these works are not really predictions of what future will be like, but rather of what is could be like if present trend continues. The most frequently discussed disasters are those caused by nuclear war, food shortages, pollution, over population and the depletion of non-renewable resources.

Nuclear War

Jonathan Schell in the '*Fate of the Earth*'[16] argues that the nation-state system, with its competition among big nations armed with nuclear weapons and with the proliferation of nuclear weapons to Third World nations, is leading the world to a nuclear war. He argues that if such a war had to happen it would bring about the extinction of the human life on our planet.

Growth

Natural resources are not infinite in any real economic sense. It is true that the more developed an economy becomes, the more pollution it produces, but overall we live in a healthier environment than ever before. The best indicator of the level of pollution is length of life, indicated by the average life expectancy of the population. Life expectancy is rising around the world. Although a rising income in a country often means more pollution, it also means a greater desire to clean up the pollution and an increased capacity to pay for cleaning it up. Families have become fewer in the past century.

The most important question to be asked when considering population is as to what value is to be given to human life? Who is to say that the life of a poor person is not of value? Who is to say that a country of 50 million people with a yearly per capita income of $4000 is better than country with 100 million people and a per capita income of $3000? The best resource we have on earth is the human mind. The human mind is the source of knowledge. The more human minds we have, the more knowledge we will have to solve the problems we face.

Steady State

Lester Brown, Head of the Worldwatch Institute, a research group established to analyze global problems, says that the world can and must achieve a sustainable or steady-state society in the future. Brown maintains that economic growth is undermining the carrying capacity of the earth to support life. He is apprehensive that population growth cannot be allowed to continue indefinitely on a finite planet. He wants the nations of the world to strive to achieve relatively stable population of about 6 billion by the year 2020 instead of letting the world reach the world's population to 10 billion which the UN and the World Bank now projects.[17]

In a steady state society the population will not be concentrated in huge urban centres as it is now but will be widely dispersed in relatively smaller communities which are near renewable energy resources. These communities as well as individuals and nations will achieve greater self-reliance; they will be less dependent on others for their prosperity than is the case today.

Globally, the fund spent for Research and Development are now dominated by military expenditure. This has to be changed if a steady-state society is to be established. Funds for energy-related projects, population stabilization programmes, soil conservation and reforestation will be needed.

For the affluent, materialism—the search for happiness by continually acquiring new material goods—will be replaced with a new ethnic of voluntary simplicity, which will limit the acquisition of goods only to satisfy basic needs. The focus of life will be placed on personal and community development which include improving "human relations" and achieving intellectual and spiritual growth. The ultimate goal should be the quest for worth spiritual growth rather than the pursuit of material success.[18]

Gandhi strongly advocated this type of change for the survival of human race.

Role of Shanti Sainik

Theoretical and practical training of Shanti Sainik is to be much more rigorous than that of a military soldier. He must be well versed with KAP, i.e. knowledge, attitude and practice. He should be able to perform efficiently and effectively atleast four roles: (i) As a Guide, (ii) As an Enabler, (iii) As an Expert, and (iv) As a Therapist.

The Role of Guide

The primary role of the Sainik as a guide is that he helps the

Society (national or international) establish and find means (using communication and other methods) of achieving its own goals to have a nonviolent and no-poverty society. The role of a guide connotes here a person devoted to helping the society move effectively in the direction it chooses to move. The guide has some responsibility to help the society to choose this direction (not harm others) intelligently with due consideration of human factors of which (perhaps) he (the guide) may be aware because of his expert knowledge. However, he does not manipulate people as a politician often does. The Sainik must learn to interpret his role so that it is understood in the right spirit in the society.

The Enabler Role

In general terms, the role of the enabler is simply to facilitate the work by awakening and making them conscious of impending disaster. His task is to help people to verbalize their discontent (not personal). For one person, these discontent are so deeply buried that a good deal of skill and patience is required to facilitate expression, for another verbalization of discontent will bring a flood of hostility directed at some groups, for others the problems revealed with those which generally come under the heading of "personal problems". He must permit the flood of negative and hostile expressions of feeling (which is often pre-requisite to more positive expressions. He is a person who helps people to look at themselves to look below the surface and probe their deepest feelings about community life. He encourages verbalization of these feelings. He helps people see the "communality" of their feelings and nourishes the hope that something can be done "collectively" about these.

In many societies and communities it is easy to move towards organisation. "Apathy" is a socially patterned defect in societies or communities and passivity is often the norm. The Sainik must be prepared to recognize the nonviolent process of work as one which is often painfully slow.

The Expert Role

As an expert the Sainik's role is to provide data and direct advice in a number of areas about which he may speak with authority. He provides research data, technical experience, resource material advice on methods which the association or society may need and require in its operation. He may serve as an "expert" in problem analysis and diagnosis. He has to be skilled in research methods and able to carry on studies on his own.

The Social Therapy Role

This is a specialised function. It implies diagnosis and treatment of the community (society) as a whole. Jayaprakash Narayan was so much disenchanted with present methods that he advocated "Total Revolution". Obviously such treatments must be carried on through representative groups or leaders, but it may require leaders with the help of the professional input of the Sainik to face many of the underlying forces, the taboo ideas, the traditional attitudes which create tensions and which separate groups in the community.

These roles will open up new frontiers of human fulfilment. As Gandhi said: "A small body of determined spirits (Sainiks) fired by a unquenchable thirst in their mission can alter the course of history." The Sainik must develop capacity himself and in his group to involve actively in getting their participation of other professional personnel to make people aware and conscious of proliferation of nuclear weapons and their consequences on humanity. I shall like to give importance and significance to some of the selcted professionals as members of team in this humanitarian task.

III

Involving Professionals

Psychologists

Since it is human behaviour that will precipitate or avoid nuclear war, psychologists should be making an attempt to analyse what is maintaining such a mal-adaptive and self-destructive behaviour pattern and how this can be changed. Four major areas where psychology may have something to offer are: (i) The first area involves trying to understand the psychological reactions of the public and world leaders to the nuclear threat. (ii) The second area concerns the psychological effects of living with the threat of nuclear war. (iii) A third area relates to how manly error or distortions in the decision-making process could lead to a nuclear war. Psychologists have studied the sources of human fallibility as well as decision-making under crisis conditions. (iv) The fourth area involves the study of conflict and the development of methods for dispute resolution which lead to conflict management without recourse to violence.

One of the strengths of professional groups has been the application of their professional expertise and knowledge to their concern about the nuclear threat. Defining a professional group in terms of professional concerns rather than merely a peace group for one's profession provides "expert power" and legitimacy as basis of one's effort.[20]

Artists

Errel O'Neil does not subscribe to the position that the ideal political position for artists is neutrality. He feels theatre workers can become involved, through their work in tangible constructive action to inform people about issues of peace and war and spread a sense of empowerment of "ordinary" (common) people.[21]

Activating Politics

Jo Vallentine from her experience as parliamentarian gives personal account of her time on the path towards peace via the parliamentary process—the underpinning of which was her commitment to the 300 years old Quaker Peace Testimony. The Quaker Peace Testimony presents a firm belief in the strength of nonviolence, in the need for reconciliation of opposing forces and the overwhelming power of love as a source of spiritual energy. As a parliamentarian one can contribute directly to the disarmament debate through groups such as the Parliamentary

Disarmament Group, and the Joint Foreign Affairs, Defence and Trade Committees. And, of course, one can carry the message of peace directly through meetings, both formal and informal with politicians, from across the political spectrum. However, she reminds us that the hope for our world lies in our own hearts and hands. For too long, we have the State to make our decisions for us. We must reclaim our rights. Whichever path we may choose in our struggle for a just participatory and sustainable society, the truth is evident—the importance of power of nonviolence. It means being sure of our moral ground and sticking to it through principled and disciplined, yet peaceful direction. Secondly, the underlying concept of both nonviolence and civil-disobedience has to be love. Without it our action will be empty. We are seeming nothing short of transformation of ourselves and our world.[22]

The Medical Profession

A preventive approach was the only logical response of a physician facing the possibility of destruction due to nuclear war. The horror of nuclear war became part of common rhetoric. The Soviet leader Khrushchev was quoted saying after a nuclear war, "The living would envy the dead". The medical profession continues to concentrate on the message: "There is no cure of the disease, there is no hiding place from it. We are involved and the only treatment is prevention."[23]

Music

Judy Small feels music and peace are connected. She thinks both from a Church and a political point of view. The music itself, because of the way it can make people feel, as well as the way it can make people think, is important in sustaining the grassroots of the peace movement.[24]

The Teaching Profession

Education for peace is a perspective which should inform all elements of the education process. The aim is to ensure that within the general curriculum and policies of an institution, there should be a clear policy on the role of the Institution in education for peace. We need a professional association of teachers committed to peace education.[25]

Scientists

According to Robert J. Hunter, *Scientists Against Nuclear Arms* (SANA) is an Australian organization of (national) scientists and others, united in common bond of opposition to the enormous build up of nuclear arsenals by the nuclear nations and particularly the Superpowers. We must find some alternative way of looking at the world's defence problems. There is a heartening development in some of the countries such as the development of idea of Mutually Assured Security (MAS). This should be adopted by all the countries and a resolution in the UN may be passed to this effect.[26]

Lawyers

Peter Le Guay says that lawyers are required not only to "act locally, but also to act globally". Lawyers, whether international or domestic, have a role to play in advancing nuclear disarmament and preventing nuclear war. Like other professions, their standing in the community enables them to form effective pressure groups, capable of changing the direction of government policy. Their skills make them particularly suited to conflict resolution; while their legal know-how provide an invaluable source of reference for determining the legal issues pertaining to nuclear weapons and those effected by them.[27]

Profession of Social Work

Social workers see peace as a community responsibility rather than as a specific social work concern. It would be better if social workers join with other professions on the issue of peace because social work does not have high profile. Social work traditionally being pathetic towards social action and work in the area of peace is no exception. Social work and peace may not yet make happy bed fellows, but there seems to be no necessary impediments to their union. Although there is a lot more we need to understand about social work and peace, there is also a lot of work we can begin to do. We can challenge our professional perceptions and misperceptions of peace work, re-order priorities, and put to work the skills we already possess.[28]

To sum up, Professions and Professionals have much to offer in creating a world where citizens and world leaders alike share sense of learned resourcefulness rather than learned helplessness.

Wars do bind people to the nation-state. But that hegemony has never been complete. People's History contains fascinating stories of soldiers in various wars, disturbed by the futile death and destruction, disobeying order to fight. Thousands of others have refused compulsory military draft. The have all been part of a large anti-war movement led by innumerable students, workers, women and teachers throughout the 20th century and extraordinarily people such as the socialist Eugene Defs, who was charged during World War I with "obstructing" recruitment. Aged 64 at that time, she was to spend 32 months in jail. She refused to defend herself, but addressed the jury before being sentenced: "I have been accused of obstructing the war. I admit it. Gentlemen, I abhor war. . . , I have sympathy with suffering, struggling people everywhere. It does not make any difference under what flag they were born or where they live."[29]

This is the spirit all professionals must imbibe to work for peace and harmony on the planet.

Power of Self-confidence

The Shanti Sainik must have full self-confidence in himself. Let me give an example of Nelson who was one of the very able commanders of England's fleet of war ships. The battle of river Nile was going to start. Nelson was explaining the strategy to his officers who had some fear and doubts in their minds. Captain Berry who was standing by the side of Neslon said, "If we win, the whole world will be surprised at victory." Nelson was vexed on hearing Berry's words. He pulled up the Captain and said: "Forget the language of 'ifs' and 'buts'. We will certainly win." Still frightened, Captain Berry dared to say: "The enemy is stronger than we. We are naught before the enemy in terms of numbers, equipment and facilities they have. Our victory in this case will depend on our luck." Nelson, who was very unhappy on hearing the depressing words of Berry, said in a very serious tone: "Captain, our success has nothing to do with luck. We shall win on the strength of our bravery, confidence and courage and not because of luck. We may all die, but win we shall." These words of Nelson acted as a catalyst and lifted the morals of the officers. Not depending on their luck, but on their "will" to act and their confidence, they faced the enemy head on and achieved a great victory.[30]

Shanti Sainiks should draw a lesson from this case and never fell depressed.

Alertness—Essence of Success

Alertness is one of the essential qualities Shanti Sainik must possess. Let us take an example of Napoleon.

It was midnight. Napoleon was fast asleep in his camp. His bodyguard woke him up and said, "Sir, the commander wants to see you right now". "What business has he?" asked Napoleon, turning his side. "The enemy has launched an attack from South. The Commander wants to know what is to be done?" said the bodyguard. Maintaining his cool, Napoleon said, "Hand him over plan No. 34, kept in the chest lying in the corner of the room and ask him to send the information about the attack tomorrow morning."

Plan No. 34 contained information as to what was to be done if the enemy attacked from the South. The Commander was surprised as to how Napoleon could make available so soon as plan which would require hours to be prepared. The battle was fought according to plan No. 34. The news of victory was conveyed to Napoleon by the Commander who asked Napoleon, "How could you prepare the plan so quickly, Sir? Do you have some divine power?" "Yes, planning and foresight are my watchwords. These have taught to me that a man should always remain alert and cautious about future eventualities", replied Napoleon.

IV

Conclusion

Loaves of Gold

Once Alexander mounted an attack on a town inhabited only by hapless women and children. The menfolk had already been killed in the battle. Alexander could not decide whether he should or should not attack the unarmed women. At noon Alexander felt hungry. He stopped before a house. After many knocks at the door of the house, an old woman supported by a stick came out. Alexander commanded: "Get me food that you have, I am extremely hungry". The old woman went inside and brought a covered plate which she presented to Alexander. On removing the cover from the plate Alexander found that it contained some old jewellery. He was greatly irritated and was red with rage. In a fit of anger he said, "You old wretch, what have you brought? Shall I eat this jewellery? I had asked for food." The old woman coolly retorted: "Are not you Alexander the Great? I have heard a great deal about you. I am glad I could have a look at you today. I learn that your food consists of gold and in search of this food you have been wandering, plundering gold and wealth and killing innocent people mercilessly. If ordinary loaves could satiate your hunger, did not you have enough in your own country? Otherwise why should you need to snatch other people's loaves?" Alexander was stunned on hearing the old woman. His pride was shattered to pieces. The old woman then served him with great affection.[31]

Happiness

Happiness does not come cheap and easily. Unless there is a spiritual dimension to pleasure, we would never realize contentment. Pharmaceutical companies advertise dozens of tablets as cures for depression. These firms spend billions to sell their products to eager public. Happiness is what we all want. If only we could just take "happily pills" that worked. A recent survey by London School of Economics found that the happiest place in the world was Bangladesh. India was fifth. The affluent US and UK did not fare very well coming in at 46th and 32nd place respectively. The moral we have before us is that money can't buy happiness.[32]

The same is the opinion of German Philosopher Schopenhaur. He says that we measure the happiness of a man by considering how many of his desires for happiness, out of the total possible desires for happiness, are satisfied. If the enjoyment of happiness falls short of the desires for happiness, we say that the man is to that extent unhappy. If the ratio has to be explained mathematically we have to divide the enjoyment of happiness by the desire for happiness and show it in the form of a fraction, thus:

$$\frac{\text{Enjoyment of Happiness}}{\text{Desire for Happiness}}$$

But this is such a queer fraction that its denominator, namely the desire for happiness, is always increasing in a greater number than the numerator, namely the enjoyment of happiness, so that if this fraction in the beginning is 1/2, it becomes later 3/10, that is to say, if the numerator increases three times; the denominator increases five times, and the fraction becomes more and more incomplete. Thus, it is futile to entertain the hope of a man becoming fully happy.[33]

New Ideology

Some years ago, human beings were still conscious enough to pay heed to the spiritual side of their growth. In India most people are proud of being a part of a spiritual legacy, which goes back beyond the Vedic times. The emergence of industrial and consumerist societies throughout the world brought along with it a new wave of thought and ideology of wealth and the means for its acquisition. Today, at the height of world's industrial and material glory we see that there is neither an end of poverty nor any contentment in those who have been a part of this growth. In fact, the new society based on the ideology of wealth and ever-widening gap between the rich and poor is one of the root cause of war (race for development of sophisticated nuclear weapons) and terrorism that have plagued the entire world.[34]

Way out

Then, what is the way out to achieve peace of mind in today's times? It is necessary for a human being to find his or her place in the scheme of things in this universe. The Buddha said about 25 centuries ago that all life was a transitory phenomenon. He said: "Life is like a flash of lightening". We, as human beings, have such a short life that it is useless to waste it in fighting each other and also dispelling out energies in only acquiring material possessions. Therefore it is of great value to follow the path of self-inquiry to attain peace and achieve happiness which is our birth right.

Double Standard

Most of us follow policy of double standards. Countries like the US and Israel always preach to other nations to maintain peace and solve the problem of terrorism through negotiations but when they receive the smallest blow, they go on rampage. We have seen the US doing in Afghanistan and Iraq and now the Israelis are doing the same thing. These so called superpowers must rise above their double standards and find a serious solution to the problem of terrorism to achieve world peace.

Gandhian Way

Gandhian vision was and is that the whole world is a single family. His goal was *Sarvodaya* (Development of all). His principles were Truth and Nonviolence. His method was *Satyagraha*. His idea was to develop man of character.

In his Ashram somebody committed a theft. Gandhiji asked them to bring the thief after he was served breakfast. Expressing surprise, the inmates said, "Breakfast to a thief!" Gandhiji strictly instructed that the thief should first be made to take his breakfast and then brought to him. When his orders were carried out, he said, "The thief is also a human being. He also feels hungry. Then he is in our captivity it is our obligation to feed him. Why did it not occur to you? How could I, on the other hand, ignore it?" Then Gandhi advised the thief, "Brother you should not steal. Stealing is a sin. If you had to steal because of penury, I can get you work in this Ashram."

3. *Bapu's Generosity*

In Sevagram, there was a *goshala* (a place where cows are kept and cared for). For managing it, Gandhiji had appointed a young boy. It was winter. The boy had only one sheet to cover himself. Early morning Gandhiji would reach the *goshala*, have a look at the cows and calves. One day he asked the boy, "Son you sleep in the open at night. Don't you feel cold?" The boy, while looking at the ground, stood silently. Gandhiji understood. He returned to his tent and said to Ba (his wife) that if she had some old *saris* (cloth to cover the women's body) she should bring them out. Ba did as desired by Gandhiji. Both of them filled the *saris* with cotton and then stitched it into a quilt. In the evening, Bapu called that boy and handing over the quilt to him said: "My boy, take this quilt to cover yourself at night. You must be feeling cold." Next day when Gandhiji reached the *goshala*, the boy fondly approached him and thankfully said: "Bapuji, yesterday night, for the first time this winter, I had deeper sleep." Bapuji just smiled.

Gandhi was not only a legend but also one of the greatest men born on the earth.

Name Removed and Restored

Strange indeed are the quirks of history. Gandhiji was a member of Inner Temple. His name was removed from its rolls because of his subversive activities during India's Independence struggle. It was subsequently restored. Gandhiji's bust now decorates the coffee room of the Inner Temple and his statue has been installed in its lawns.

Recently, University College of London has proudly claimed Gandhiji as one of its 19th century alumni. The alumni department dug back its archives and found an old card index box containing a small yellowing index card in which his hand-written Gandhiji's name and dates of attendance. It is now established that Gandhiji from 1888-1889 was enrolled in a course on Indian Law and Jurisprudence. This indeed is the University College London's discovery on Gandhi.[35]

Gandhian Order of Society

To Gandhiji, the future of world society should be made up of "ever-widening, never ascending circles" of communities. He wrote: "It (the world society of men and women) will be an oceanic circle whose centre will be the individual, always ready to perish for the village, the latter ready to perish for the circle of villages, till at last the whole world becomes one life composed of individuals, never aggressive in their arrogance, but ever humble, sharing the majesty of the oceanic circle of which they are integral units." Aware, that this concept might be brushed aside as utopian, he added: "I may be taunted that this is all utopian and therefore not worth a single thought. Euclid's point, though incapable of being drawn by any human agency, has a imperishable value."

Jayaprakash Narayan said, "If Gandhi's moral solution of the problem of individual *versus* society is rejected as impractical, there cannot be any other solution possible. Perhaps a complete solution will never be possible. The key to solution lies in Gandhi's method of social change and reconstruction through truth and nonviolence, of his political, economic and social ideas, the key to his attitude towards the question of power, organisation of work and community. He believed that the human and social ends he had set before himself could be achieved in a nonviolent society in which there is a thorough-going decentralisation of power and production and control of wealth, and which is composed of comparatively small autonomous communities, willingly federated and cooperating together.

For Gandhi, nonviolence was a means and not an end. Man was the end—his material, mental and moral growth. The supreme consideration is man. The end to be sought is human happiness combined with full mental and moral growth. The pursuit of truth and steadfast adherence to it were not prior values but were conceived as essential being for the fulfilment of the cherished goal. Happiness and moral growth of the individual were not possible without freedom and equal opportunity for all. This was ideally possible only if both man and society were nonviolent.

Having placed man at the centre of society, how did Gandhi conceive of inter-relationships? This is the problem that neither individualism of the West nor the Collectivism of the East has yet been able to resolve. Gandhi tried to resolve it by introducing a moral solvent, by assigning mutual moral responsibilities to both. While the well-being of the individual was a social aim, the well-being of society too was to be attained.

In his view, "unrestricted individualism" was "the law of the beast of the jungle". While the individual is entitled to complete freedom, he must learn to discipline himself so as not only not to infringe the freedom of others, but also to be of service and benefit to his fellowmen and the community at large. "Willing submission to social restraint for the sake of the well-being of the whole society enriches both the individual and the society of which one is a member." Society, on the other hand, must work ceaselessly for the well-being of the individual, fully respecting his human rights and treating him as a human being.

Gandhi was against centralisation. He felt: "Centralisation as a system is inconsistent with the nonviolent structure of society." Because, "Centralisation cannot be sustained and defended without force." He said: "The State represents violence in a concentrated and organised form. The individual has a soul but the state is a soulless machine, it can never be weaned away from violence to which it owes its very existence." Naturally, the ideal society according to Gandhi, is a stateless democracy where social life is so developed as to have become self-regulated. He wrote, "political power means capacity to regulate national life through national representatives. If national life becomes so perfect as to become self-regulated, no representation is necessary."

Gandhi refused to draw any blue print for the future. He wrote in 1929: "We do not know our distant goal. It will be determined not by our definitions but by our acts, voluntary and involuntary. If we are wise, we will take care of the present and the future will take care of itself." Again, "I cannot say in advance what the government based wholly on nonviolence will be like."

He was realistic to admit that the complete nonviolent and stateless society might never be established because everyone in society might not reach the requisite level of moral development. Therefore, he conceded that government cannot succeed in becoming entirely nonviolent because it represents all the people. "I do not conceive of such a golden age. But I do believe in the possibility of a predominantly nonviolent society."

To save society from degeneration, we should practice the three Indian qualities: *Data* or giving; *Dayadharm* or sympathy and *Damyatta* or control. That is, Truth, Nonviolence and Love are the trinity for the solutions of all problems confronting the human race.

In a devastating tragedy, a man lost everything he had—his family, friends, wealth and estates. As a result, however, he became aware of something exhilarating and uplifting. "I lost everything", he reflected excitedly, "but I have found my self!" The divine soul, self-residing in our ephemeral bodies has been buried beneath umpteen shrouds of vanity, money, fame, status, power, the opposite sex, friends, colleagues, enemies, foods, drink, addictions, make-up, jewellery, clothes, cars, computers—even the stars in the sky—in fact everything in the universe we attach ourselves to. In 1998, 94,700 female and 99,000 males in the US underwent cosmetic surgery in a bid to improve their appearance. In the same year 234 billion dollars were spent on cosmetic products world-wide. But the farther we wander in these outer wrappings, the more we lose contact with our centre, our essence. As a consequence we experience heightened levels of anxiety, anguish and emptiness. One meets with melancholy, dejection and hopelessness. It is no surprise that 200,000 people in the US alone and millions more in other parts of the world attempt suicide every year.[36]

"Like as in Aladdin's Cave, there are rocks and dust near the mouth but deep within there lies priceless treasure . . . anchor your lives in your soul, and anchor your soul in God."

For real empowerment the strength of the inner self has to be tapped. Once a man achieves his inner higher self, nothing can harm him.

This knowledge and light must dawn upon us. Knowledge of self is always an asset and ignorance is never a bliss. This knowledge must radiate. Psychiatrists are essential today because we have ceased to respect elders and listen to our teachers and parents. Psychiatrists have only replaced 'Gurus'.

Even though apparently awake, one is still asleep if one sees multiplicity. "Wake up from this dream of ignorance and see one self. Self alone is real. This world today is, tomorrow is not-empty as a dream, shifting like a circle of fire. There is but one consciousness, pure, transcendental, though it appears as a multiple in form." Gandhi said, "Man has learnt to fly like a bird and swim like a fish but has to learnt to walk with dignity on earth." He further said: "an eye for an eye only ends up in making the whole world blind."

George Bernard Shaw had aptly said, "Life is a flame that is always burning itself, but it catches fire again every time a child is born." Thus, the Shanti Sainik has to continuously work as a river, which if does not flow its water will get stagnated and soon become polluted.

Today's world is torn by strife, threatened by various tyrannies and blackmailed by nuclear weapons. The current social milieu, in my view, based on inequality has made upper class materialistic, vulgarised the middle class and brutalised the lower class. Gandhiji said: "There can be no rule of God in the present state inequitous inequalities in which a few roll in riches and the masses do not get enough to eat."

A well trained and groomed Shanti Sainik as a professional have much to offer in creating a world where citizens and world leaders alike share a sense of learned resourcefulness rather than learned helplessness. A better understanding of the factors that lead to both conflict escalation and de-escalation may be critically analyzed in our society in the sense that it is not currently in the political agenda of any major power brokers in our society. No political party as peace as one of their objectives in their manifestoes. A Shanti Sainik has to be self-less and not to run for name, fame or rewards for his work. "His spirituality is not about preaching." He has to make himself a better person. As Goethe said, "a building needs three things: that it stands on the right spot; that it is securely founded; and that it is successfully executed."

In one sentence we can say that the main aim of Gandhian ideas is to awaken the sleeping power of the soul. Shanti Sainik should remain humble and polite. He does not have to be high and mighty like a plain tree. As wise Sant Kabir of India puts it:

> What is the use of merely being
> high and mighty?
> Like the upright date palm?
> For weary and hungry passers by,
> Its branches and leaves afford
> No shade,
> And for fruits they are too high
> to be plucked and savoured.

An institution which wants to train and prepare Shanti Sainiks needs to have three basic freedoms—(i) freedom to decide what to teach, (ii) whom to teach, and (iii) who will teach.

The main aim of Gandhi's education system was to quicken man's spirit of service. How would it matter if people knew everything, but did not know how to live in brotherliness with their neighbours. In his scheme he envisioned that the acquisition of true education is priority through participation in a particular patterns of life in a community and not merely through formal schools. Schools are to prepare citizens for a new society—a nonviolent society and teach children to live on the basis of cooperation, truth and *Ahimsa*.

REFERENCES

1. Singhvi, L.M., Rai M.R. and S. Ramakrishnan, *Nani Palkhivala—Selected Writings*, Viking Bhavan's Book University, 1999, New Delhi, pp. 240-41.
2. *Ibid.*, pp. 242-43.
3. Quoted by Raja Ram Shastri, in the Foreword to the book, *Society and Culture*, edited by R.M. Loomba and G.R. Madan, Allied Publishers, New Delhi, 1987, pp. v and vi.
4. *Ibid.*, p. v.
5. Dubey, Sarla, "Dimensions of Values" in *Society and Culture*, edited by R.M. Loomba and G.R. Madan, Allied Publications Pvt. Ltd., 1987, New Delhi, pp. 62-63.
6. *Ibid.*, p. 64.
7. *Ibid.*
8. Butler Richard, Foreword to the book, *Professions in the Nuclear Age*, edited by Sewell Sandra, Kelly Anthony and Daws Leonie, Boolarong Publications, Brisbane, Australia, 1988, pp. ix and x.
9. *Ibid.*
10. *Ibid.*, p. xi.
11. Agrawal Mahendra, "Peace Education in the Context of Global Crisis", *Gandhi Marg*, Vol. VI, Nos. 4 & 5, July-August, 1984, pp. 199-216, especially page 202-203.
12. *Ibid.*, p. 202.
13. Rene Debos, cited by Seitz L. John, *The Politics of Development*, Popular Prakashan, Mumbai, 1988, p. 171.
14. Seitz, L. John, *The Politics of Development*, Popular Prakashan, Mumbai, 1988, pp. 171-72.
15. Garret Hardin, *The Tragedy of the Common's Science*, Vol. 2, December 13, 1968, pp. 1243-48, in Seitz L. John, p. 150.
16. Jonathan Schell, *The Fate of the Earth*, Avon Books, New York, 1982.
17. Lester Brown, *Building a Sustainable Society*, WW Norton, New York, 1981.
18. Alexander Solzhenitoyn, "Men Have Forgotten God", *National Review*, July 22, 1983, p. 876.
19. Murray, G. Ross, *Community Organisation: Theory and Principles*, Harper & Brothers Publishers, New York, 1955, pp. 200-28.
20. Connie Peck, "Overcoming Our Helplessness about the Nuclear Threat", in *Professions in the Nuclear Age*, edited by Sandra Sewell, Anthony Kelly, Lonie Daws, published by Boolarong Publications, Brisbane, Australia, pp. 3-16.
21. Earrol O'Neil, "Fires, Dreams and Nightmares", in *Professions in Nuclear Age*, pp. 18-22.
22. Jo Vallentine, "Activating Politics for Peace", in *Profession in Nuclear Age*, pp. 23-33.

23. Ian Maddocks, "The Medical", in *Profession in Nuclear Age*, pp. 36-214.
24. Judy Small, "Singing for Our Lives", in *Profession in Nuclear Age*, pp. 45-55.
25. Brain Gagen, "The Teaching Profession and Peace Education", in *Profession in Nuclear Age*, pp. 57-64.
26. Robert J. Hunter, "Scientists Against Nuclear Arms (SANA)", in *Profession in Nuclear Age*, pp. 73-85.
27. Peter Lee Guay, "Law, Lawyers and Nuclear Disarmament", in *Profession in Nuclear Age*, pp. 105-17.
28. Sandra Sewell and Anthony Kelly, "Social Work and Peace", in *Profession in Nuclear Age*, pp. 173-90.
29. Vagraj Adve, "True History, Zindabad", *The Hindustan Times*, December 9, 2001, New Delhi, p. 10.
30. N.D. Kapoor, *Fragrance of Life*, Vishwa Jagriti Mission, New Delhi, 1995, p. 50.
31. *Ibid.*, pp. 78-79.
32. Mukunda Goswami, "The Key to True Happiness Lies in Gita", *The Hindustan Times*, December 10, 2001, New Delhi, p. 2.
33. Bal Gangadhar Tilak, *Srimad Bhagvad Gita Rahasya*, Published for the Tilak Brothers by D. Tilak, S. Tilak, Pune, 1995, pp. 144-45.
34. Prasoon Pant, "Find Peace through Awareness of Self", *The Times of India*, December 10, 2001, New Delhi, p. 1.
35. Soli J. Sorabjee, "Gandhiji", *The Sunday Times of India*, Oct. 28, 2001, Mumbai, p. 10.
36. Aslam M., "Getting Purified through Roza", *The Times of India*, December 5, 2001, New Delhi, p. 12.

7

RESOLUTION OF CONFLICT
A Gandhian Way

A question is generally asked as to what would have been the response of Gandhi to the September 11, 2001 attack in America on its World Trade Centres and Pentagon; December 13, 2001 attack on Indian Parliament and rioting in Gujarat in 2002. Let me cite an interview which the Mahatma gave in the early afternoon on 30th January, 1948, to Margaret Bourke White. She had come to interview him for *LIFE Magazine*. She asked Gandhi whether he would persist in his theory of nonviolence in the event of a nuclear attack on a city? The Mahatma's reply was that if the defenceless citizens died in a spirit of nonviolence, their sacrifice would not be in vain; they might all pray for the soul of the pilot who had thoughtlessly sprayed death on the city. This was his last message of compassion to mankind. He said: "Nonviolence is the greatest force at the disposal of mankind. It is mightier than the mightiest weapon of destruction devised by the ingenuity of man."

Gandhi further said: "I do not believe in shortcuts which involve violence. However much I sympathize with and admire worthy motives, I am an uncompromising opponent of violent methods even to serve the noblest causes. There is, therefore, really no meeting ground between the school of violence and myself."

The heart that bled at the sight of the misery of others was bled to death on 30th January, 1948 with three-death-dealing slugs buried deep in it. The Mahatma has gone the way of all saints. His spirit lives and that spirit will continue to live among us, as long as India survives.

Swami Vivekananda, speaking in New York had said: "Since death is inevitable, let it go in a noble conquest, and what conquest is nobler than the conquest of the lower instinct of man? Unless we are prepared to pay the price to achieve mastery over our lower self, the highest self cannot be unfolded and revealed to us. The goal of human life is to manifest the divinity which is within us. Arise, wake and stop not till the goal is reached. For centuries, we have seen change. From the Unreal lead me to Real; From Darkness lead me to Light; From Death lead me to Immortality."

With the modern day inventions we are able to fly like birds faster than the speed of sound, swim faster than fishes and remain alive under water. Man has walked even on the surface of the Moon. But as human beings we are not at peace with ourselves nor with the world around us.

In fact we are under tremendous stress in the present times On the one hand the world talks about globalization and aims at a borderless world. On the other, we worry about petty personal gains. The only solution to this problem is that we need to work towards changing our mind-sets. We must wage a war against anger, hunger and illiteracy.

There is a common notion that violence is essential for demonstrating the strength of our response—an idea we have absorbed for too long from angry people around us. But are they the ones who inspire our deepest respect? Violence is a response of frustration and weakness when we are at our creative worst. We should ask ourselves and call upon our people to come up in their ingenuity and compassion with solutions that will match a Gandhi, a Buddha, a Ashoka, and Akbar and other great people of our land. Were they weak people? The nation's leaders are merely our reflection and reflection of present society.

The only answer is that every Indian (or people of the world) should introspect and remove the seeds of hatred he has within for other communities, nations, people of a different religion, caste or colour. There is need to focus not on the differences but what makes us alike, a common humanity. Let us first kill the hatred and anger within us and prepare for a future of genuine good, future for the whole continent and the world.

In his (Gandhi's) view, cult of violence had to be rejected at all costs and at all places. He taught us that Indian way to resolve conflict is not to struggle over values and claims to scarce resources and power in which the opponent or enemy is either neutralized or eliminated. But that our aim should be to develop harmonious relationships between different communities, castes, religions and other groups and to replace hatred with love and affection. The contemporary world situation which is ridden with violence should steer the whole international community to examine the value system the world intends to follow.

In competitive politics, the political parties are engaged in a race for political supremacy. What is the principal purpose of the race? To gain political power either to build or to destroy the nation for personal or party gain or both. Much intelligence and energy are going into this effort. Yet it seems more important than ever that an even grater effort is made to achieve positive and mutually helpful human relations. This cannot be done by mere political forces. Among several others, political parties and leaders, instead of creating harmonious relations, have created hatred, and men have become thirsty for the blood of other men.

The world and specially India in today's scenario has not become a better place to live in despite more than five decades of independence. No doubt, we have many spectacular achievements in science and technology and other fields to our credit. But, in the development process adopted by us, we have alienated man from man.

The time has come now for rethinking on the issue. Mahatma Gandhi's decision to march to Dandi was a message "so simple that it reached everyone". Through the march, Gandhi tried to provide means for the lowliest to undertake the change of self and take part in the change of society. The purity of means is an end in itself. Gandhiji, in his scheme, put the people at the centre. His policies and programmes were designed to secure full support and participation of the people and to develop capacities in them to work as members of one world community. The people felt that he was talking to them directly rather than through impersonal means of communication. He emphasized self-discipline, truth, *satyagraha* and nonviolence as some of the methods to achieve the goal set by the leaders through active involvement of the people. He said, "I am endeavouring to see God through service to humanity." One important corollary following from this is that loving and serving mankind is also part of Gandhian ideal. This reminds me the story of Abu-Bin-Adam he one night saw in his dream a luminous angel writing something. Being asked by Abu, the angel told him that he was sent by God to find out the devotees of God and prepare a list of their names. Abu said, "Why then have you come to me? I am not a devotee of God. But if God asks you to prepare a list of those who love their fellowmen, then of course you can include my name." The angel did not say anything and disappeared leaving back the list he had prepared. Abu-Bin-Adam's name was on the top.

In fact, the basic Gandhian principle in working with people is to lead them from conflict of interests to a community of interests. Gandhi's goal was to bring about a community of interests by holding it up as the common good, by making *Sarvodaya* the motivation of all individual action. It is a process of the right discernment of the context for the sake of right action which would help to take it from conflict to harmony without sacrificing any value to that harmony. Gandhi as the father of the Indian Nation and as an effective national leader, succeeded in uniting the people of India as he was able to integrate different dimensions—the people's task, behaviour and socio-economic behaviour—and did not utilize one at the expense of the other.

Mahatma Gandhi won commitment from his followers and he had the skill to get them involved. He had a keen understanding of people and set of principles for dealing with their motivation, emotion, pain, trust and loyalty. India suffers from ethnic differences and economic backwardness. Indian politics consists of both the politics of group identity and the politics of resource allocation. The political conflicts would be minimised if the politicians do not interfere in the formation of group identities or allocation of resources. Gandhi maintained that the basic human need was to rise above animal nature and transcend it so that man could be creative. He did not think that love and hate are antithetical drives: They are both answers to man's need to transcend his animal nature.

Mahatma Gandhi had a holistic view of life. Accordingly, his development philosophy revolved around man, his society and environment (nature) and their respective and simultaneous development. He believed that instead of man exploiting the society and both exploiting nature, there was a symbolic way of life in which they were in harmony with each other. In his frame of reference for development, man is the centre of attention. The objective is the moral and spiritual development of man.

Man is primarily his consciousness, his capacity to be self-conscious, and his built-in potentiality to judge between good and evil. Because that will help him in his evolution to higher levels of being rather than obstruct his path. This give him a leverage not only to aspire for higher levels but to endeavour to attain them.

Gandhi believed in this effort and the path he outlined lay through ethical, moral and spiritual disciplines. The keynote of his ethics is "love" which means a near identity of interest with every sentiment. This love has to be expressed in the form of service and sacrifice. His ethics in relation to material things and property consisted in his concept of Trusteeship. Every human being is a trustee not only of his faculties and attainments but of everything he comes by, and trusteeship consists not only in using his powers and goods properly but in using them selflessly and for the well-being of others.

Most of the present breed of leaders have taken to politics as their main source of income or livelihood. In the Gandhian era, particularly the Indian leaders gave up their lucrative professions and took to politics not as a means of livelihood but to join the struggle for India's freedom from foreign rule and to build a new India. They did not expect anything in return. Their values must be revived to build the nation and maintain its unity and peace.

The decline of virtues to live together (coming together is beginning, keeping together is progress and working together is success) can be described in four stages from 1900 onwards till today. In the first period, the virtue is at its fullest. In the second, virtue diminishes somewhat. In the third, virtue diminishes further. And in the fourth, virtue is at its lowest. Gandhian way is the only way to reverse this process.

Sir Jayendra Saraswati, Sankaracharya of the Kanchi observed that there are two kinds of outside elements—direct and indirect—political pressure, money and so on. In the context of Gujarat, I will refer to a story. Once a King named Parikshit died of snake-bite. Overcome by grief, his son swore that he would avenge his father's death by wiping out the *sarp-vansh.* He would put to death all snakes. Friends advised him that one unfortunate incident could not justify violence on all snakes. It would serve no purpose and would certainly not bring back King Parikshit back to life. This is what is happening in Gujarat today. One mistake was committed at Godhra. If a few members of a particular community commit violent acts, we cannot hold the entire community at ransom. The see-saw violence in Gujarat must be brought to an end forthwith and peace should prevail (*The Times of India*, "Rule of Peace", April 27, 2002, New Delhi, p. 12). The brutality of the truth hits one in the stomach. This is a chilling reminder of times ahead. The State will make noises but not take concrete action to stop violence altogether.

That all men are equal like brothers, is a supreme moral truth. It is reinforced by modern science. However this is only in theory and the ethics of equality in practice remains no more than a pious dream, totally beyond man's reach unless both *Ahimsa* and Science find equally a place in our lives.

Man has to learn a lot from Nature. In Nature, harmony is the normal rule and conflict an exception. Members of the same species never kill one another. Their fights are either sports or ritual. There are a few species which deviate from the rule. And the greatest exception is human species which calls itself homosapiens—man the wise. Homosapiens torture and murder one another in war and peace with abandon, wantonness which has no parallel in Nature.

To conclude we may recall Einstein's statement (20th November, 1950) which is very inspiring and so relevant in the atomic age.

The most important human endeavour is the striving for morality in our action. Our inner balance and even our very existence depend on it. Only morality in our actions can give beauty and dignity to life. *To make this a living force and to bring it to clear consciousness is perhaps the foremost task of education, including adult education* (emphasis added). The foundation of morality should not be made dependent on myth or ties to any authority lest doubt about the myth or about the legitimacy of the authority should imperil the foundation of sound judgement and action.

The foremost task of education-character building must find a first place, above all, in the training of teachers and adult education workers.

No religion has ever been able to establish its superiority to all others. This truth has been expressed in the Rgveda: *Ekane Sat Vipraha Bahudha Vadanti* (the truth is one, the wise calls it by many names). Swami Vivekananda has rightly said: "If anybody dreams of the exclusive survival of his own religion and the destruction of the others, I pity him from the bottom of my heart and point out to him that on the banner of every religion will soon be written in spite of resistance: 'Help and not fight', 'Assimilation and not destruction', 'Harmony and peace and not dissension'. Ezkiel Isaac Malekar, 'True Religion is respect for life' (*The Hindustan Times*, May 1, 2002, New Delhi, p. 2).

Atomic Age: The Gandhian Way

In the Atomic age without *Ahimsa*, i.e. compassion and wisdom, there can be no survival of mankind. In his foreword to Swami Ghananda's book, *Sri Ramkrishna and His Unique Message* (1970), Arnold Toynbee, an historian of international repute says: "At this supremely dangerous moment in human history, the only way of salvation for mankind is the Indian way (Gandhian Way). In the Atomic Age, the whole of human race is based on utilitarian motive. This should be given up and the Gandhian way should be followed to achieve world peace and harmony. Gandhi, the greatest political genius of our times indicated the path to be taken to achieve the cherished goals.

In Gujarat each one of the 100,000 refugees in the relief camp is a wounded human being, burdened with memories too harrowing for words. "The death of a million people", said Lenin, "is statistics. But the death of a single human being is tragedy."

Jonathan Swift's words should resound in our ears: "We have just enough religion to make us hate each other but not enough religion to make us love each other."

Riot Fundamentalists

Few people understand the anatomy of communal riots better than the psychologist, Sudhir Kakkar, author of the "Colours of Violence: a Study of Hindu Muslim Conflict and Riots". Kakkar is a Senior Fellow at the Centre for Study of World Religions at Harvard University. I am reproducing some of the excerpts from his interview with Rashmi Sehgal. He provides psychological perspective to the events in Gujarat (see for details, *The Times of India*, Saturday, April 27, 2002, New Delhi, p. 12).

Why do risks occur, especially among communities which have a great deal of interdependence due to economic, historic and sociological reasons?

Possible Causes of Riots

Donald Horowitz has done the most comprehensive study of these riots all over the world. He concluded that for a riot to take place, there must be a long standing animosity between the groups, even if the degree of this enmity is vastly exaggerated in the time leading to the riot. The target group is perceived as aggressive and constitutes a political threat on one whose strength appears to be augmented by it extra-territorial affiliations.

Donald Horowitz has identified four indispensable elements which need to come together for a riot to occur:

1. A hostile relationship between the groups.
2. A response to events that engages in the emotions of outrage or wrath of one group.
3. A keenly felt justification for violence as punishment of the other group for wrong doing.
4. An Assessment by the rioters that violence carries little risk.

At the time of a riot, the version of eternal conflict between Hindus and Muslims gains ascendancy while in times of relative peace the focus shifts back to a history emphasizing commonalities and shared peace of the past.

Polarisation of Indian Society

Rajni Kothari says: ". . . this time it was not some stray happening in one area (Godhra) but a development that can lead to an increasingly growing conflict between Hindus and Muslims. Within India, human rights devotees see the growth of a dangerous onslaught against riot. It is not just one community but the whole secular and democratic ethos of the country. . . . The result is a dangerous polarization which goes beyond Gujarat and could take on national character. . . ." He further says, ". . . the polarization that is emerging is not just inter-communal. It is also urban *versus* rural, westernised *versus* indigenous, opposing segments on communal lines within diverse regions, as well as within institutions. Such a spread within educated people is perhaps the most disturbing aspect of this polarization. For it is from these professional classes that middle ground was found. . . . It is this shifting of the middle ground and the accentuation of polar positions that matters me and others." (See Rajni Kothari's article, *The Hindustan Times*, Wednesday, May 1, 2002, New Delhi, p. 8).

Social Harmony

Social harmony or social order is created when people need each other. If A needs B's help, he must gain and keep B's cooperation.

B's response in turn will be determined by how much he needs A or by the benefits he can derive from the association. Cooperation is always potentially unstable. Its attainment raises such questions as: Who needs whom? Who is dependent on whom/What resources do the parties have for social exchange? The dependence and reciprocity are key conditions that affect how much cooperation there will be and what form it will take. Cooperation has a positive dependency and exchange may have social importance and in understanding relationships.

Mahatma Gandhi gave to his autobiography the title: *The Story of My Experiments with Truth*. He wrote in 1926: "What I want to achieve, what I have been striving and pining to achieve these thirty years is self-realisation, to see God face-to face, to attain *Moksha* (salvation). I live, move and have my being in pursuit of this goal. . . . The experiments narrated are spiritual or rather moral, for the essence of religion is morality." And he further says: "I claim for them nothing more than does a scientist. . . . I have gone through deep self-introspection, searched myself through and through, and examined and analysed every psychological situation. Yet I am far from claiming any finality or infallibility about my conclusions. One claim I do indeed make and it is this. For me they appear to be absolutely correct, and seem for the time being to be final. . . . And so long as my acts satisfy my reason and my heart, I must firmly adhere to my original conclusions." In the concluding chapter of *The Story of My Experiments with Truth,* Gandhiji says: "My uniform experience has convinced me that there is no other God than Truth . . . and . . . the only means for the realization of Truth is *Ahimsa*. . . . After all, however sincere my strivings after *Ahimsa* may have been, they have still been imperfect and inadequate, as a result of all my experience, that a perfect vision of truth can only follow a complete realisation of *Ahimsa*." And he continues: "I must reduce myself to zero. So long as a man does not of his own free will put himself last among his fellow creatures, there is no salvation for him. *Ahimsa* is the farthest limit of humility."

There is a chapter with the title 'Face to Face with *Ahimsa*'. This refers to the first *Satyagraha* in India initiated by Gandhiji and after twenty-one years of "preparation" in South Africa. Writes Gandhiji about his meeting, early in 1917 with indigo cultivators at Champaran (Bihar): "It is no exaggeration, but the literal truth, to say that in this meeting with the peasants I was face-to-face with God, *Ahimsa* and Truth." Further, "I began to prize nonviolence only when I began to shed cowardice. . . . The path of true nonviolence requires much more courage than violence."

Gandhiji's "experiments" are moral-spiritual experiments. The basis of morality is self-control or self-conquest through self-suffering. And indeed declared the Mahatma in his book *Hind Swaraj:* "Swaraj is self-control." Einstein said: "Liberation from the bondage of the self constituted the only way towards a more satisfactory society."

Neighbourhood

Modern science and technology has produced neighbourhood, but not brotherhood or sisterhood. Geographical distance has decreased but people have become more distant. Man has got alienated from himself. With all the facilities of modern means of communication, man must learn to live and let live. Maulana Syed Athar Hussain Dehlvi says that in the Hadis it is mentioned that a person whose neighbour is hungry with him cannot be a Muslim. If the neighbour is not a Muslim, then according to the Prophet, "your responsibility is even greater to help him to trust your." The Prophet defined the neighbourhood as being 40 houses in the front, and back right and left. The 40 houses will also have a 40th house. So the Prophet made the entire world a neighbourhood. Religion begins with one's neighbour. To provocatively promote unity, we need to house Hindus and Muslims together. (*The Times of India*, Voice of Sanity, April 30th, 2002, New Delhi, p. 12).

We should be ashamed of resting or having square meal so long as there is even one Muslim or Hindu man or woman without food or work, the Mahatma emphasized. "Unless Hindus and Muslims learn to live together in peace and harmony, India as we know it, will cease to exist."

Self should be able to 'conquer' one self. It is of utmost importance to always remembers that real foe of man—ever present deadly and most difficult to conquer—is within himself. Others can help him or her in fighting the enemy outside but it is of little avail because it is important to fight the enemy within [Gita, 111 (3)]. The Buddha says: "I as a man conquers in a battle a thousand men, and if another conquers himself is a great conqueror." Self-control is the foundation of all human development and earnest seeking. As one great soul has said: "I sought my soul, I could not see. I sought my God, my God eluded me, I sought my brother or sister, I found all the three." This is the profound lesson we should learn to live in peace and harmony. We should realize that a computer has no choice of its own; the choice belongs its programmer (i.e., men or women). This is the fundamental distinction between a computer and its programmer. That is to say, *Kingdom of God is Within Us* and we have to search it in our selves.

One must understand that religion is a searchlight for inner self, while politics is for running of the country. The voters should elect leader who would stand up of the people's right without worrying whether it would fetch them votes. Moreover, the voters must bring forth individuals (politicians) who are upright and have strong ethical and moral conviction.

Mahesh Bhatt writes: "A couple of years ago a senior assistant of Jayaprakash Narayan came to meet my philosopher friend, U.G. Krishnamurthy. "Jayaprakash has succeeded in persuading 600 dacoits to lay down their arms in North India", said the assistant with a flourish, hoping to make an impression on U.G. "All very well", relied U.G. and asked "But what is he going to do about those 600 dacoits whom we have put (chosen) into the Parliament. How is he going to save the people from their blood-thirsty games?" (*The Times of India*, May 5, 2002, p. 12).

In the *Brihadaranyaka Upanishad,* there is an episode of contemporary importance. God, men and demons lived with their father as students of sacred knowledge. On completion of their studies, God requested *Prajapati*, their father and principal teacher to give them benediction. *Prajapati* uttered the word '*da*' which all the three groups understood in three different ways. The Gods interpreted it as *Udamayatta*—on instruction to control themselves. Man took the word to be *datta*, i.e., to give. Men are by nature avaricious and hence not willing to distribute their wealth according to the best of their ability. The demons are generally cruel, hence the stress is on compassion. All the three evils mentioned are present within us. They must be overcome to achieve peace and harmony.

The Gandhian way is the only way and let us make an honest attempt towards this before it is too late. Let us go forward with the Gandhian alternative and let historians record that atleast an attempt was made in this direction.

We have failed to project the revolutionary Gandhi who offered a healthy vision of life based on self-respect, self-help, non-exploitation of man and nature, nonviolence, etc. All our arts, science and technology, and social sciences should be geared to this direction if we care and have concern for human survival.

The communal disturbances which were earlier confined to large cities and towns seem to have spread even to villages as is the case in Gujarat carnage of 2002. The traditional amity seems to have receded yielding ground to religious passions. Gandhi believed in three sources of integrative religion—the integration of personality which recounts the individual to his own nature, integration with his fellowmen, and integration with God, the supreme spirit. Gita refers to the triple process of integration—*Yoga, Dana, Tapas*—and exhorts everyone to practice the necessary discipline to build up personality to create a new social order based on equality and to establish God as the Creator of life. Gandhi put into practice meticulously spiritual programme of integrating all aspects of life.

The motto of the material world is "to kill or be killed." Whereas that of the Gandhi's spiritual world is "to live and let live." In life, everyone respects values, but these we want to see in others not in integrating ourselves. This process needs continuous effort and work on the part of all the institutions which socialize men. Family, education, religion and political heads of all these institutions must change themselves in order to achieve the cherished goal of integration. They need to see themselves as educators and learners. Rabindranath Tagore beautifully put it this way:

* A teacher (leader) can never truly teach unless he is learning himself.
* A flame can never light another lamp unless it continues to burn its own flame.

It is easy to renounce the material world but true renunciation is when one renounces from the heart. For such a person, everything flows effortlessly. A process of reconciliation and compromise is needed between the warring parties to avoid conflict.

There is strong tendency in human society to take shelter in scientists, loved ones, and leaders of political, religious, psychological and philosophical movements. We pattern our lives after our "role models" in these fields. The role models to be emulated have to be of certain stature to salvage India's position.

Mahatma Gandhi had said: "God is not a person. God is an eternal principle." Similarly, in Indian society all should realize that unity in diversity is there to bring social harmony among people of different religions.

We can atleast pray to God to bring sanity to man so that he does not become an enemy of another man or his religion. Prayer benefits us in many ways. "Our prayers should be for blessings in general", said Socrates, "for God knows best what is good for us". R.L. Stevenson was more specific: "Give us the strength to encounter that which is to come, that we may be brave in peril, constant in tribulations, temperate in wrath, and in all changes of fortune and down to the gates of death, loyal and loving one to another."

Marriages of children belonging to two different religions is one of the ways to bring integration, social harmony between two communities. This has received severe setback due to riots in Gujarat (See Harit Mehta's Article, Appendix I).

APPENDIX I

RELIGION KEEPS COUPLES APART

See Harit Mehta, *Times of India*, New Delhi p. 8, May 6, 2002, Ahmedabad.

Hanif Mohammad (name changed) has shelved his plans to marry Amrita (name changed) following threat calls days after their names were displayed on the notice board at the office of the Registrar of Marriages. "I received threats to my life and Amrita's father got threatening calls that her face would be disfigured if we went ahead with the marriage. There is no point in risking our lives, and therefore, we took a practical decision," he says.

Hussain Sheikh (name changed), around 20 years of age got married to Neha (name changed) last year under the, 'Special Marriage Act' in court. Now, Sheikh has been forced to send his wife to her parents place. "There are no security problems as such, but her parents feel that she is not safe in our mohalla. I'll bring her back when things calm down," says Sheikh, who owns a shop on Relief Road.

Inter-religious marriages are fewer now because of the riots. The communal divide has not only forced couples to shelve wedding plans but forced those already married to live apart, atleast temporarily, in their respective community-dominated areas. Two months ago, around 20 such marriages took place in a month at the Arya Samaj Mandir here. But not a single one has been reported in the past two months. If a Hindu boy wants to marry a Muslim girl, she has to first convert to Hinduism and only then the marriage can take place.

"However, in the past two months, we have not come across a single case like this," says Pandit Diwakar Shastri of the Arya Samaj Mandir. On an average, of the 350 marriages that take place at the Arya Samaj Mandir, over 20 are inter-religious marriages. Says Shabbir Alam Saheb of the Jama Masjid, "We used to have at least two cases every month, where a Muslim boy wanted to marry a Hindu girl. But there has not been a single such case since February 28." In fact, he says that there has been a steady decline in the number of Hindu-Muslim marriages since 1998-99. Since then there has been a concerted effort from both sides to pressurise people to desist from going in for inter-religious marriages.

According to sources in the office of the Registrar of Marriages, of the eight to ten marriage notices in a month, one or two were inter-religious marriages. "The figure has gone down by 50 per cent in March and April," says an official despite the fact that under the Special Marriage Act, neither party has to convert.

REFERENCES

1. Gangrade, K.D., *Eternal Relevance of Gandhi,* Gandhi Smriti and Darshan Samiti, 2002, New Delhi, pp. 31-34.
2. Gangrade, K.D., *Gandhi since 50 years of Azadi,* Gandhi Smriti and Darshan Samiti, New Delhi, 1999, pp. 14-20.
3. Ahmed, Feroz, (ed.), *Atom Self,* Collection of Lectures delivered by D.S. Kothari, New Age International Publishers, 2002, New Delhi, pp. 377-78.
4. Radhakrishnan, N., *Gandhi: The Quest for Tolerance and Survival,* Gandhi Smriti and Darshan Samiti and Gandhi Media Centre, New Delhi, 1995.

8

GANDHIAN WAY OF CONFLICT RESOLUTION
Three Case Studies

For Gandhi, the very act of struggle was enriching. The purpose of the three cases referred to in this chapter is to discuss the method of fighting: (1) Conflict in Priority: Case of Sunita, (2) River of Life Flows: Case of Maya, and (3) Born Rebellion: Case of Renu. What makes these cases different from others is the nature of the participants who were stubborn, or as Gandhi put it, ". . . they were able to speak out and stand up for their convictions" [*Harijan*, April 7, 1946]. They stood by the integrity of their positions and refused to accept a solution that did not adequately honour them. The support system available to them from within (kin-group) and outside (social worker, teacher or supervisor) also helped them to come out of their problems.

The man-woman ratio is gradually decreasing in every decennial census. This is due to preference of boy over girl. The Indian Society must change its social attitude towards the girl-child. She should be allowed to be born, survive and not be neglected. This in turn will give us a civic society worth living. There are a good number of people who feel that the girl child's life in India is a 'candle' in the wind which flickers for a moment to be extinguished for ever. Gandhi gave equal importance to women and actively involved them in the freedom struggle and development of society.

Swami Vivekananda, while referring to Manu's well-known dictum that "Gods are pleased where the women are happy (worshipped)," strongly pleaded for their equal partnership with men. "A bird with only one wing can't fly," he would say.

In Indian patriarchal society, women have been conditioned not only to silently accept men's authority and tolerate violence as part of their lives but also rationalise it.

The diktat of the *Manu Smriti* holds that only a direct male descendant can save a man's soul from the hell associated with the *pitra-lok* and assure his salvation. Women are traditionally kept away from death rituals. In the last week of the year 2001, the holly city of *Kashi* (Varanasi), considered to be one of the oldest living cities in the world, saw an important event in history. For the first time, a young girl, the youngest of the four sisters, publicly held the torch to cremate her father at the ancient burning ghats. This defies thousands of years of patriarchal male wisdom.

Khushwant Sing, still in mourning by the recent loss of his wife, Kanval, wrote how his daughter Mala had borne the entire responsibility in physically caring for her ailing mother. It was only natural as well as circumstantial that she performed the last rites, as her brother Rahul was out of town. These cases may sound as innocuous acts, but they indicate winds of change.

In the Ramayan, Sita sets a complex chain of events in motion when she steps outside the limits of the *Lakshman Rekha,* which is an imaginary line drawn by her brother-in-law. This *Lakshman-Rekha,* which is an intangible and defining moral code, is in vogue even today, sometimes for the better, but usually for the worse. Women are free, indeed encouraged, to earn, to have careers, to contribute to family income, but the onus of family sacrifice and identity withdrawal still falls squarely on them and them alone (See Namita Gokhale, "Passage of Rites for Death is Male Monopoly", *Delhi Times*, India, January 12, 2002).

I

Conflict in Priority: Case of Sunita

Indian Marriage System

In India, marriage is a calculated and traditional extension of kinship. A relation between two persons dominated by thoughts of each other is considered immoral. Evidence of social change may be found in some of the romantic suicides, which are protests against the control of the kin-group but these also show continuous power of community and kin. The individual has a life-long involvement with his relatives and this is true even among sophisticates.

Sacrament

The system is considered sacred, and the accepted scope of individualism does not provide for personal preferences in marriage. Previous acquaintance is usually of little concern to the practice involved. There is virtually no comprehension of the concept of romance and seldom even a hint of rebellion.

A survey conducted by Hyderabad based market research firm 'NFO-MBL' over five metros found 53 per cent of Delhi's youngsters saying religion was an important part of their lives. The survey covered those in the 15-19 age group and represented the top 60 per cent of the socio-economic strata (Sujata Dutta Sachdeva, "The Rebel is Dead, Long Live Nice Kids", *Times of India*, November 18, 2001, New Delhi, p. 1).

Teens Love Family and Religion

Priests of Delhi at the Sạí Baba Temple in Connaught Place and the Chattarpur Temple near Mehrauli corroborate these statistics. According to them there has been a definite increase in the number of young people visiting these places. Pandit Sudhir Sharma, the chief priest of Hanuman temple found an increase of 35-40 per cent over the last two years: "While girls come in groups, boys come with friends during the day and families in the evenings." This was evident in the queue outside the Sai Baba Temple.

Eighteen years old Sudhir Sharma, a student says, "I have been coming here regularly with my family for the past two years. Now, some of my friends too have joined me."

In Mumbai, there is the lowest religious orientation (21%) among youngsters. In Chennai, Calcutta (Kolkata) and Bangalore there is a respectable 30 per cent. Sociologist, Renuka Singh, observes that there is a positive correlation between religion and family ties. Religious orientation is something a child picks up from home. The family ties are so strong that they have a direct impact on beliefs. She writes: "While these go-getters are willing to surrender themselves to rituals, they are not willing to surrender themselves to fate."

The new age youth is however more goal-oriented, says the survey. Psychiatrist Dr. Achha Bhagat explains: "They have a surety of purpose and don't want red herrings in their lives." But conforming to traditions is important for all of them. While 80 per cent want more interactions with the opposite sex, 54 per cent say they would prefer an arranged marriage. Shivani Bhatnagar, an 18-year old student from Delhi says: "I have many boys as friends but I want my parents to choose the right boy for me."

Renuka Sing feels conformism has more to do with youngsters wanting to feel safe: "Indian kins are not individualised, they do not want to break way from family ties. They fear taking risks and responsibilities." Thus most of them want parents involvement in marriage. They feel the need for continuity in a fast changing society which is provided by arranged marriage and religion.

Death Penalty

There were some youngsters who did not follow the traditional system, especially in rural India and had to pay for their lives. For example, a gruesome tragedy that occurred in Muzaffarnagar district in the summer of 2001 was unpardonable. Teenage lovers were hanged to death as hundreds looked on. The newspaper covered the tragic story of a Jat girl and a Brahmin boy, who were neighbours and had been in love for months. Their families had tried to break the alliance because they were of different caste.

When boy's father caught the young lovers in a compromising position in a field nearby, he summoned the family and the village elders. They held an impromptu village meeting and ordered a 'death sentence'.

The next day the police arrested the family and other villagers who had taken part in the event. The parents, while consoling each other in jail, said without remorse, "We had to do it for the village honour." The police chief added, "They will be let of, of course, because witness won't come forward. This sort of thing is not uncommon around here." They recalled three such incidents during the past year (See Gurucharan Das, "The Ambiguous Village", *Times of India*, November 4, 2001, New Delhi, p. 18).

Criteria for Selection of Spouse

There is a potent and intricate interdependence of individual and kin. The arranged match is crucial and romantic marriage is abhorrent and socially disapproved. Rigid conditions are applied in spouse selection: (i) membership in the same ethnic community, (ii) identity of caste, (iii) bride younger than groom, (iv) bride, a virgin, and (v) horoscope of each closely matched. In addition, the dowry power of the girl's family; security and occupational prestige of the boy; and their status are considered in match-making.

A number of factors support familism and are inconsistent with the romantic angle. The greatest moral duty of a father is arranging a 'good' marriage for his daughter, and this duty falls on a son after the father's death. These are responsibilities of blood kins. Desire for family prestige may pressurize the father or brother towards almost impossible financial sacrifice.

In marriage the individual is both imprisoned and sheltered by his kinship group. The son helps in his sister's dowry. A challenge to an arranged match is not an easy task. The lineal family as a status bearing entity in the community plays its most critical role when the marriage approaches near. Every relative has his funds or status at stake, Romantic marriage is not consistent with the rigid dictates of caste, prestige and family honour. It threatens not merely the father's rightful authority but the honour of the generations, past and future, of which the father is the legitimate guardian.

The Hindu family is usually based on patrilineal descent, following the male line, and it is patrilocal which requires the couple to settle in the husband's village. A new marital unit is dominated by the husband's kin through their very proximity. The father-husband is the social authority. From early childhood the male is schooled in superiority. A family of many males is a "fortunate one" and that of many daughters is "burdened". To the father's position, services are due and deference is paid. There is a deep-seated belief that the wife must be completely loyal and subservient to her husband and his family. It is generally agreed that the husband owes his first allegiance to his own parents rather than his wife.

Case of Sunita

Sunita was born in a village with a silver spoon in her mouth. Her father was a big landlord, a richman and the Headman of the village. He was in favour of girl education. He admitted her into a girl's school and later in a women's college for education. The daughter followed the footsteps of her brother and joined the 'School of Social Work' for her post-graduate education.

Shock to the Father

The Headman (the father) in his enthusiasm allowed and encouraged his daughter to study. But when he came to know that the girl had been going on fieldwork along with a boy from her class in a slum and rehabilitation colony, it was a great headache to him. One day the girl innocently took the boy to her home. The father was shocked to see the boy as he felt that he did not measure to his (father's) social and economic status. He was also not a Jat. He was very apprehensive that his daughter might get entangled with the boy if they continued to work together. Moreover, as a Headman of the village, he had to set an example by following traditions and norms of society.

He, therefore, the very next day, asked the girl to leave the school. He wanted to marry her off as a very good proposal had come from the family of an MLA. But the girl was not interested in marriage at this stage without completing her studies.

Mother Favourable

Sunita's mother was not in favour of discontinuing her studies. She was aware and happy that her son who had completed the course in 'Social Work' had got a good job. She knew that professional qualification would be an excellent standby in need and tried to persuade her husband not to withdraw the daughter from the school. But her husband was firm on his stand.

Brother's Advice to the Father

Sunita's brother who had obtained a degree in 'Social Work', requested and appealed to the father to consult the teacher of the school who was her 'Field Work' supervisor. The father needed great persuasion to visit the school and meet the supervisor.

Father Visits the School

When the father visited the school, he was very much impressed by the environment and student-teacher relationship. The supervisor cordially received the father of the girl. He was informed about the good performance of the girl both in the class room as well as fieldwork. The father was happy to know this. But he told the supervisor that he was very apprehensive that she might get entangled with the boy who was her co-worker. He was informed that as a policy she was purposely sent with a boy to slum or rural areas so that he could provide security to her. Moreover it was desirable for a boy and a girl to work together as a team to understand the problem and needs of the community.

He was told that he should have confidence in his own child. The relationship between the two opposite sexes should not always be misconstrued that it would ultimately end up in marriage. As Post-graduate students they were mature enough to decide for themselves and parents should not interfere too much in their decision. "The completion of studies might help her to have a good career and a good job and also a good match", the teacher convinced the father.

Father Agrees to Continue Her Studies

The last advice convinced the father as his own son had got a good job due to his studies. Thus he allowed his daughter to continue with her studies. The girl did not disappoint the father and the family as she passed her final examination with flying colours. Her own confidence rose to new heights. Now, the father began to encourage her to prepare for *Indian Administrative Services* (IAS).

Successful in its Competition

She was selected in the IAS and became not only the proud child of the family but of the village and the region. She got married to a doctor belonging to her own community. Her father was very happy and thanked God that he listened to the sane advice of the supervisor of his daughter and allowed her to complete her studies.

She had now risen to the post of a Joint Secretary in the Central Ministry of the Government of India. She had two children and her ambition was to give them all possible facilities to pursue their studies in the field of their choice.

Analysis

The girl child in India is very rarely given free choice to either choose her academic career or life partner. Normally a father or other family members impose their choice in selecting field of study and also a life partner for a girl child without consulting her.

In this particular case the brother, mother and supervisor not only came to Sunita's rescue but provided her the much needed support system to remain firm on her choice for further studies. Though there was initially a conflict between the choice of the father and the daughter, it was amicably resolved with the intervention of the teacher.

II

River of Life Flows: Case of Maya

Girl's Birth Celebrated

Maya (not real name) was born in a family of farmer-cum-business community of rural India. Her birth was celebrated as her grandparents had four sons. Of the four sons, the second remained unmarried due to some physical deformity of nose. Maya was the apple of everybody's eye in the family. Her mother passed away leaving behind her young children. Maya under the care of her grandmother became very fond of her siblings. Though she was only 6-7 years old, the responsibility of taking care of her brother and sister fell on her tender shoulders.

Her father turned down many proposals to remarry despite pressure from the members of his family. His reasoning was that he was not very confident about having a stepmother for his children as he was witness to many cases where a stepmother became the cause of neglect of children and ruin of households.

Deprived of Education

Traditionally in the villages the girls were not sent to school. Maya's grandfather and father, both wanted to send her to school. But they were unable to do so because there was no exclusive school for girls in the village. They did not want to violate the norm of the village culture by sending her to boy's school.

Thus her grandfather took the responsibility of teaching her at home. Her life was sailing smoothly with the love and affection showered on her till she reached the age of twelve.

Social Exchange in Marriage

Maya's unmarried uncle during one of his business trips cast an eye on one of the girls of the village situated at a distance of five kms from the village. He conveyed this to the girl's family through a friend. The girl's family knew about the reputation of the boy's father as a highly respected man in the community. They were equally eager to give the hand of their daughter to an eligible and deserving bachelor. But they were unable to do so as they were very poor. As a result, they were finding it extremely difficult to get their daughter and younger son married.

The girl's family, therefore, put a condition that they would be ready to give their daughter in marriage in exchange of a daughter for their son. The condition was difficult but not insurmountable. The uncle felt that he would be able to prevail and persuade his parents to marry Maya in exchange. His parents as well as his younger brother were reluctant to accept the proposal. They were not willing to marry Maya in a poor family. However, the uncle did not lose hope and continued to press for his proposal. He suggested that he would support the family financially and would help them to come out of the poverty syndrome. He also brought the pressure of members of the community on the parents and younger brother to yield to the request. He promised to the younger brother that in any untoward event he would stand by the side of the girl. He gave guarantee to support her in need. The parents reluctantly agreed to the proposal. Maya was married off in exchange of an aunt for her uncle.

This type of custom known as social exchange was and is prevalent even now in some of the communities which were and are not able to afford to get their children married.

Life in In-Law's House

The young bride was excited to get new beautiful clothes and ornaments to wear. She was oblivious of married life. After the marriage the mother-in-law relieved herself from all the household chores and put all the burden on the shoulders of the young child. Her up-bringing was such that without any murmur she smilingly carried out her responsibilities. Her husband was loving and caring. He did odd work and had a small business to earn his livelihood.

The river of life was flowing. She was facing all the adverse circumstances cheerfully. By the age of 16-17 she was blessed with a beautiful girl child. She, her husband and mother-in-law concentrated all the attention on the girl. They started doing embroidery work to supplement the family income. As the designs and neat work were highly appreciated, orders began to pour in. They began to dream of a better and bright future.

Tragedy Fell on the Family

The couple hardly lived a happy life for a year when a tragedy fell on the family. An epidemic took away her mother-in-law and husband.

Maya had to face single-handed this tragedy. Her father came to console and share her sorrow. Her in-laws relatives also came. But as soon as death ceremonies and rituals were over, they left. While leaving they told that they had given substantial amount of money to her mother-in-law and husband. In lieu of that they would like the house to be transferred in their name. But when they were confronted to produce evidence in writing or witness, they failed to do so. They also knew that verbal transactions would not help them to even resort to the law court to get the amount. They unhappily reconciled to the situation.

Parental House

In the parental house her grandparents had died and the brothers had separated. Her younger brother had left the village to study in a nearby city. Her younger sister who was married also died and so did the husband leaving their only son to the care of their maternal grandfather. Destiny confronted her with all kinds of tragedies. She was finding it extremely difficult to cope with them.

A well meaning friend and a close relative met her who thoughtlessly asked: "Have you got over it now?" She was actually referring to her husband's death. The words although meant to be kind were probably unconsciously substituting for, "How are you? You look better." However, the question spoken in good faith, plunged her into a tunnel of thoughts which she had to deal with firmly in order to crawl out of darkness and back into the sunshine.

Philosophically, and in the Gandhian way, her reply was, "No matter how painful a loss is, life continues, the rivers keep flowing, the birds continue singing." Nature remains constant and balanced, which fortunately helps us maintain our equilibrium while we temporarily lose our way. Life demands and presumes that tragedy will eventually be accepted with grace and we shall continue with our lives and duties with a smile, suppressing suffering and personal losses. We have to pick up and force ourselves to continue.

In due course of time some of the edges of the pain are smoothened while the emotions and the agony change their form and eventually remain deep within the privacy of one's soul. A wall is erected through effort and determination to seek sympathy, which in any case should be temporary solace provided by friends and relations in the early stages of loss.

Both joy and sorrow go hand in hand. It is these experiences of life which arouse a turbulent storm of sensitive passions leading us to a greater maturity, by which we evolve into a total person with varying facets to our personality. All of us unfortunately have to suffer at some point in our lives and it is through suffering, no matter how painful, that we gain greater insight into our lives while cultivating the vital emotions of compassion (See Nina Sood, "River of Life Flows Despite Human Loss", *The Times of India*, Monday, November 19, 2001, New Delhi, p. 12).

She reconciled that she had no control over the destiny and she accepted the challenge and decided to rear her daughter. Now all her dreams were to live for her daughter's sake.

Uncle's Betrayal

Her uncle betrayed her and her father. All the promises made by him to get married in exchange of his niece fell on his deaf years. He among all his brothers was prospering in business and other commercial activities after break up of the joint family. Despite the fact that he had no issue of his own, he did not show any compassion towards his niece and her child. His wealth brought him good name and fame. But he was indifferent to the plight of his niece and brother whose business and farm did not yield sufficient to meet their needs. They (both father and daughter) thought of migrating to the city to try their luck there. She thought her skills in embroidery would be able to find good market in the urban city and also a good school for educating her daughter. Her brother who was already there in the city was a source of great encouragement.

Migration to the City

The brother rented a small hutment on a nominal rent in one of the slums of the city. Life commenced with a happy note as the father started a petty business and the embroidery work also began to get some monetary returns. The brother also contributed to the family kitty by earnings from his tuitions.

Contact with Social Worker

The embroidery work brought her into contact with a lady social worker who was working in the community. This lady helped her in getting some formal training in her work. She was able to obtain a certificate in teaching, tailoring and other crafts. This strengthened her confidence. She began to produce quality goods. The support available to her from her father, brother and social worker enabled her to get order and market the material. The demand of goods prepared by her increased substantially. She kept three assistants to cope with the orders. She brought more machines and rented an additional room exclusively for her work.

Bank Loan

Practice had made her embroidery work perfect. On the suggestion of the social worker, she applied for a bank loan for display of her works. She got the loan and her earnings began to soar and now she could manage her own life without the support of her father or brother.

Shock of Her Father's Death

Her life was moving smoothly. But one day when she went to give bed tea to her father, she found there was no response from him. The doctor was called and on examination he found that the father had died due to massive cardiac arrest. She was shocked and became inconsolable. He had been the guiding spirit and source of encouragement. He always advised her to follow the path shown by the social worker and Gandhi.

The members of the colony, both men and women rushed to her house. She had become very popular in the colony as 'Bahenji' (sister) of all—old, young and children. Her training in tailoring and embroidery to the daughters of the colony enabled their parents to find a better "match" for them.

The Social Worker also came and gave her emotional and much needed support. The brother, members of the colony, friends and relatives cremated the father. The brother performed all the ceremonies and rituals required in connection with the death of the father.

It is said: Time is the best healer. She was able to overcome despair and emotional shock and resumed her work with fresh energy and devotion.

Departure of Brother for Higher Studies

The brother was able to get scholarship for higher studies in a metropolitan city. However, he was not willing to avail the scholarship leaving sister and niece alone in the city. But the sister, the elders of the community and the social workers encouraged and convinced him not to lose the opportunity and persuaded him to proceed for higher studies. The members of the colony assured him not to worry about the sister as they promised to stand by her in the event of any need. They also felt that higher studies would open doors for better career in India or abroad and his achievements would raise the status of his family as well as of the colony.

He reluctantly agreed and with the blessings of the elders and the sister took their leave. His performance in his studies was excellent. He topped the list of successful candidates. The institution offered him a teaching position in the institute itself with an assurance to be sent to America for his doctoral work.

When he came back to the colony, all of them welcomed him and rejoiced his achievements. They were very proud about the fact that even a slum could produce a high quality intellectual. His sister's joy and happiness knew no bounds. He accepted the job and joined the institute as a teacher.

Disappointment with the Daughter

Maya was not happy with the educational attainment of her daughter which was below average. Her daughter was more interested in playing and embroidery work than school. The pressure tactics extended by the sister and brother and the elders of the community did not yield favourable results. She remained adamant not to go to school and with great difficulty was able to study only upto the 9th standard. Time passed so fast that the daughter reached marriageable age.

Finding Suitable Match for the Daughter

Maya got no help from any member of her caste or community to find a suitable boy for her daughter's marriage. She could not go in for an educated and well-placed boy in her own community because of low standard of education of the daughter. However, luck favoured her. One day father of a boy came to request her to give the hand of her daughter for his son. The boy was a graduate and was working as a Section Officer in one of the educational institutions of the city. She called her brother to see the boy. The brother approved the boy. He then along with his sister and one or two elder members of the colony visited the boy's family. The family had just two members—the father and the son. They were also living in one of the better served slums of the city having electricity, potable water, and flush latrines.

The visiting team found the boy good, loving and well behaved and therefore approved the boy. However, the ultimate choice was left on the boy and the girl. They met twice or thrice and agreed for the marriage. The brother in the capacity of maternal uncle had agreed to bear all the expenses for the marriage. The bridegroom's party was very happy with all the arrangements made by the maternal uncle. Except dowry he gave all the gifts as suggested by the elderly ladies of the colony.

The departure of the colony's girl was a touching scene as everybody had a mixed feeling of sorrow and happiness.

Fortune Smiled on Maya

The slum was acquired by the government for development purposes. Each inhabitant of the colony were given a plot of land and some money to build two room flat. Luckily Maya got a good plot which opened from all the four sides. She also got some compensation and money as heir of her in-laws house and land. She with the assistance of her son-in-laws build a double storied house of eight rooms.

Her son-in-law and daughter were doing very well. Her daughter gave birth to two sons and a daughter. The elder son became a lawyer and the younger one a businessman. Both of them got excellent partners from their own community belonging to very reputed and economically well off families. The daughter was also married into a good business house.

All of them are living a happy married life.

Maya Invites Daughter's Eldest Son to Live with Her

As she started growing old, she invited her daughter's eldest son along with his wife to live with her. They came to live with her and showered all their love and affection. The grandson and the granddaughter-in-law provided her with all the comforts needed by Maya in her old age.

Opened a Girls' Hostel

One day a girl from the university came to Maya's house and suggested to open a girls' hostel for the university students. The university was not able to accommodate all the girl students in its hostels due to limited seats. The proposal appealed the grandmother and the granddaughter-in-law. The other members of the family too agreed to the proposal. The girl students poured in and the house turned into a girls' hostel. She became *Nani* (Grandmother) of all the students. They began to enjoy homely life under the protected wings of their *Nani*.

Well Lived Life

Maya (*Nani*), who is now about 85 years is leading a fulfilled life, though initially it was full of struggles. She hopes to live for 100 years. Even at this advanced age she continues to surprise people with her energy and talent. Her major concern has been to provide facilities for girls.

She feels indebted to her father, brother and the social worker for providing congenial and conducive environment for her success in life.

Solutions to women's problems lie in raising their statuses inside the house and society. The example of Maya should inspire all of us. Women should emulate her and not run away from problems or commit suicide.

Analysis

Hardwork and self-reliance are twin tools in a woman's life to overcome all odds in life. These values gave Maya sufficient strength to fight back. Social worker's counselling too played an important role in her success, who often said: "Life can be as beautiful and as ugly as you make it. It's like a jigsaw puzzle in beautiful colours. All you have to do is to find the right place and match the colours. If you think beautiful, you will do beautiful, is the law of positive thinking." A positive frame of mind equips an individual with immense energy. To be born a girl child in our society is not exactly a blessing. She is tender like a flower and can be easily destroyed.

By accepting responsibility for our problems, we begin to learn to solve them for ourselves. We should not oscillate between the two poles—the real and the desirable—but should be ready to face situations as they come. Maya's case is the best example to be followed by women in distress.

III

Born Rebellion: Case of Renu

Patriarchy and conservatism are women's greatest enemies. A mother teaches her daughter that obedience is all important.

Parents, Social Background

Renu was a born rebel. Her father was a professor in a Technology Institute and mother a teacher in one of the schools of the city. She had a brother older than her who received all the attention and care. He was sent to a highly prestigious public school, while she was sent to an ordinary school. This created sibling rivalry between the two. The parents wanted the boy to become either an engineer or a doctor. But did not want to invest much on the education of their daughter. Their preference was to save money for her dowry than to spent on her education. Thus seeds of rebellion were sown by the discriminating behaviour of the parents. She remained a disciplined child but did not abide by the decision of her parents for her career.

Brilliant in Academics

She had a very brilliant academic career. She chose professional Social Work as her career. Her father wanted her to either go for Economics or Political Science. He did not want her to go in for training in social work which demanded too much time from students. Instead, he wanted her to help her mother in domestic chores, who was keeping bad health. She continued helping her mother in the kitchen in the morning and evening hours to lighten the drudgery of cooking. But she insisted on joining the school of Social Work against the wish of her father.

Good in Studies

Her intelligence and hard work was reflected in her excellent performance both in academic and fieldwork.

Relationship with the Teachers

Her relationship with the teachers were very cordial. She kept her supervisor informed about her personal problems and took his guidance. She was ambitious and wanted to demonstrate to her parents that she to could excel in her studies as her brother did.

Policy of the School

The school as a policy used to place students on two-month Block Fieldwork (Practical) at some agency (Voluntary organisation, Welfare Department of the Government, Industry), other than located in Delhi. Renu was eager to go to Mumbai to get away from over-protected and sheltered life of her house. She gave her choice to work in Bombay (Mumbai). All arrangements were made to send her to Mumbai. But her father was not willing to allow her to go out of Delhi.

Father Meets the Director of Fieldwork

Father told the Director that his daughter was needed to look after her mother who was suffering from heart problem. The Director told that let her attend to her mother and training would be arranged at a time when she was not needed at home. But this will delay her in completing the training. Prolonging the study period was not acceptable to the father as he was very keen to get her married as early as possible after completing her post-graduation.

Father Made Lame Excuse

The Director called the girl to know the exact status of her mother's health. She informed him that her mother was healthy and she had no heart ailment and her father had given false information to prevent her from going to Mumbai. She expressed her desire to go to Mumbai. The teacher was very happy to know that she had matured enough to take decisions for herself.

Fieldwork at Mumbai

Her performance at the Mumbai agency was very good. Over

there she came across prospectus of Hawaii University and applied for admission and scholarship. She got both but waited for her final results.

She communicated her results to the Hawaii University, USA. They were happy to know about her performance and extended her travel grant and exemption from fees.

Father's Happiness

Her father so far had a negative attitude towards her education. Now he was very proud father and he himself helped and paved the way for her to go to the USA for further studies.

Her stay in Mumbai created self-confidence in her due to which her father also realised her capabilities. He no longer wanted to become a stumbling block in her promising career.

Returned to India

She obtained 'A' grade in the USA and came back with the best testimonials from her American teacher. The father was not interested in early marriage for his daughter now. He permitted her to take up a job if she wanted. She applied to an International Rural Agency and got selected to the post of an Assistant Secretary. She rose to the position of Secretary. She got good name, fame and status in her field.

Destiny Snatched her Away

She worked for 5-6 years in the organisation and had hardly reached the age of 28-29 years when cruel hands of destiny snatched her away from this world in a road accident.

Her father became very depressed and felt very guilty for not supporting the bright young girl. It was her own effort and the supervisor's support when made her realise the immense potential and confidence within her which made her reach the pinnacle of her successful career.

9

GANDHIAN AGENDA FOR THE TWENTY-FIRST CENTURY

I

Don't Worry About Future: Live Like a Lotus

When we are consumed with remorse over the dead past and with sorrow concerning the unborn future, let us visualise Sri Krishna saying to us, "you are worrying unnecessarily."

Swami Vivekananda said, "When an event is past (Twentieth century), do not nurse its memory. Cremate it and forget it. Otherwise it will decompose in the mind and stink. Do not worry about the future (Twenty-first century), for tomorrow will bring its own problem and the problem will have its own solution, just as yesterday's and today's problems have have had."

There is a distinction between thinking and worrying. Thinking is essential, worrying is unnecessary as it actually prevents thinking. Constructive thought is the first step to contemplation and eventual cessation of divisible thinking. It is made possible only when the *inner* awareness is freed from past (which exits but as memory) and future (which exists as worry, a mixture of fear and hope). Only the present is. It is a present, a gift from God.[1]

A question is often asked: What is the purpose of life? If we recall the Biblical line that asks of what profit it is if a man gained the whole world and lost his soul. This concern about losing one's soul seems to be seriously troubling many of us. There remains, as Ashish Nandy writes, an irreducible element of spiritual concern which informs the toughest materialism in India. . . . The traditional concept of Ragarishi (leader) was a holistic one attempting to emphasise precisely the need for Kingliness encompassing managerial and administrative skills, directing and motivating and rishiness where *sakshi bhavana* or witness consciousness kept an eye on not letting the individual to be wholly absorbed in the whirlpool of name and fame; to constantly see everything from the wide range level of the spirit. In the modern information and technological age, while the prospects for some are alluring, there are those who are worried about the human cost. This was the concern of Gandhi. We can see restlessness, borne-out and a sense of futility creeping early in professional life. Senior managers are seeking help for 'monitoring' needs wanting to sit and share their confusion and fragmentation as well as wanting to know how to guide and facilitate their juniors rather than resorting to the old and increasingly irrelevant models of command and control. Many feel an unmistakable hollowness and unfulfilment in their lives. Though they are paid well, they feel they are not giving back to society and life as much they have taken from it.[2]

This state of disillusion and confusion is an indicator of hope. "If there were no confusions", says Chogyam Trungpa, "there would be no wisdom". With confusion, restlessness, fragmentation and constant busyness on the rise, the demand for "wisdom" is growing. A not so-good consequence in the arena is now wide open for all sorts of 'spiritual fast foods' that leave us "full" but hardly satiated. The Sanskrit word for health is *Svastha,* which is really *svastha,* a state of being centre in one's self. The challenge there for most of us who are *asvastha* is to find ways of shifting from our displacement. The real voyage of discovery would then consist not in looking for new landscapes but in looking for soul's real home, thereby ending the exile and claiming real *svastha.*[3]

The answer to some of these disillusions can be found in the Gandhian ideals and methods. The Gandhian path is the sure way to reach the cherished goal of harmony and peace.

Existence moves in polar opposites: action leads to inaction. Effort leads to effortlessness. Buddha has said: "Pass through a river, but don't let the water touch your feet". That's the meaning of the Eastern symbol of the lotus. A lotus is a flower that lives in water, and yet stays away. It's like being in the market place, but not allowing the market place to enter into your being. It's like living in the world and yet not being of the world which is what is meant by a witnessing consciousness".[4]

This is the basic teaching of Gandhi to be emulated by all. He held that the power of peace was greater than the power of violence. He and his followers successfully put this into practice in South Africa and India.

Maulana Wahiduddin Khan says that Prophet Mohammed was of the view that the concept of peace, as opposed to violence, influenced the course of events at the earlier times and continued to have an impact on later generations. In present times this thinking has assumed the status of 'permanent social philosophy'. Many prominent thinkers are its advocates. For instance, it was this principle of 'peaceful activism' on which Mahatma Gandhi based his movement of nonviolence, the freedom movement which successfully achieved its target. Then it was this same principle by which the South African leader, Nelson Mandela, became successful in his political movement in support of the black against the whites. This peaceful activism could have understood only by one whose vision was so profound as to enable him to penetrate appearance in order to see reality; one of the rare insights, able to penetrate the present and see the future. As we know in present times, the invention and use of the latest weapons of war have only increased the destructiveness of war or violence. On the other hand, advances in modern science and technology, for example today's communication systems, have to a hitherto unimaginable extent, proved strongly supportive of the peaceful method. These extraordinary possibilities which lay hidden in the darkness of future, fifteen hundred years ago, required an exceptional vision, which is exemplified by the life and prophethood of Prophet Mohammed, Gandhi and other saints of India.[5]

II

Spiritualised and Sanctified Politics: Charismatic Leader

Gandhi spiritualised and sanctified material world of politics.

Plato's concept of 'Philosopher King' was intellectual, while Gandhi's was the spiritual strength in the present complex alignment of economics and political forces. Before him, no saint even dared to enter the dirty world of politics. The more the dark forces of unjust oppression closed upon him and his people, the higher he rose in moral stature and brighter shone his spirit. When a person rises from "physical" to "metaphysical" level, his *selfishness* vanishes and his spirit expands as to encompass the whole *universe.* At that moment, all his physical and material sufferings and fears disappear and a divine experience of a paramount, permanent, and pervasive bliss results. This is why frail and fragile Gandhi could bear the brutal beating and bestial treatment by the colonial power. He imbibed the rich spiritual tradition of Harish Chandra, Shivji, Dadhichi, Ram, Gautam, Mahavir, Nanak and Kabir who renounced the physical comforts and worldly pleasure, which are all transient and temporary because of their dependence upon our limited sense-organs, and went for permanent and pervasive spiritual bliss which he experienced in the service of suffering humanity. Faith in deathlessness of spirit converts a chicken-hearted person into lion-hearted, one who never fears torture and death and stands up against the mightiest of the mighty for his rights. His spirituality makes the barriers of caste, creed, and religion fall, and all the discordant feelings of animosity and rancour disappear. Because of the pervasive property of the spirit, sympathies of a spiritualist become universalised. For him, Hindu, Muslim, Christian, Sikh, Jain etc. are only names of a single omniscient soul. He fears nothing and his fearlessness becomes infective. So people became brave and self-sacrificing under the leadership of the Mahatma. . . . He became their redeemer and emancipator. He became the repository of faith and fidelity for the masses.[6]

Gandhi had consciously identified himself with the starving masses of India. He was a charismatic leader. Deriving his understanding from Rudolph Sohn and more particularly from his study of the salvation, Max Weber defined charisma as a quality of the individual personality by virtue of which he is set apart from ordinary men and treated as endowed with supernatural, superhuman or at least specifically exceptional power and qualities often regarded as exemplary. Weber remarked: "Charisma shall be understood to refer to an extraordinary quality of a person, regardless of whether this quality is actual alleged, or presumed. Charismatic authority, hence, shall refer to rule over men, whether predominantly external or predominantly internal, to which the governed submit because of their belief in the extraordinary quality of the specific person.[7]

To him, charismatic authority is outside the realm of everyday routine and is sharply opposed to rational bureaucratic and traditional authority. The genuine prophet or true leader in pure type Weberian Charisma who imposes his own will and the member of the religious or party group responds to his call with wholehearted devotion through a blind, fanatical, unrestrained and uncritical faith. The concept is well expressed in Weber's account of Gladstone: "In 1886, his power was already so charismatically oriented to his person, that when the question of Home Rule was raised, the whole apparatus from top to bottom did not ask: 'Do we really stand on Gladstone's ground?' It simply on his word, fell in line with him and said: 'Right or wrong, we follow him'."[8]

Weber adds five more specifications to his basic definition: First, "Charisma" is the greatest revolutionary power in periods of established tradition. Secondly, it neglects considerations of economic efficiency and rationality. Thirdly, the charismatic leader and his followers constitute a congregation. This congregation consists of disciples who have no career or qualifications in the bureaucratic sense and no privileges. They are selected or chosen by the charismatic leader on his pre-emptory judgement of their charismatic gifts. He may dismiss them summarily when he feels that they have failed his trust in them. Fourth and the fifth specifications deal with the psychological and sociological components of charisma.

This charisma is a psychological quality in the sense that it is a 'gift of grace' to a person. However, this psychological quality must be socially recognized and validated. It is the recognition on the part of the followers which is crucial for charisma. . . . Indeed a genuine charismatic leader believes that it is the duty of his followers to recognize his quality and obey him. . . . If, on the other hand, the charismatic leader is unsuccessful for long and fails to benefit his followers, it is likely that his charismatic authority will disappear.[9]

Did Gandhi possess such a quality? The answer is an emphatic 'yes'.[10]

The conception of leadership expressed in preceding paras is essentially individualistic. Weber's leader is individualistic; the source of his actions lies in himself, in his own personal conditions, and not in his following or associates.[11]

Sociologists and Historians like Talcott Parson and Arthur Schlesinger Jr., among others, have noted that Weberian classification of traditional, rational, bureaucratic and charismatic authority does not apply to present day democracies. Parson finds that the individualistic emphasis in the Weberian treatment of the concept of charisma as a normative order is identical with the Durkheimian group-oriented concept of "collective sacred". The charismatic individual announced a break in the established normative order and declares such a break morally legitimate and thus sets himself in opposition to the established order.[12]

Schlesinger has theorized that the Weberian concept of charisma is basically incapable of dealing with the realities of democratic culture dominated by pressure groups, interest groups, personality appeals, and conscious organizations. Though at the time of crisis the rise of some heroic leadership is not ruled out in the elitism of Schlesinger, he finds that Weberian charisma is a pre-industrial concept, an mischievous innovation of Weber, a useless word which has become synonymous for heroic or "demagogic" or even just "popular". Schlesinger concedes that Weber's strict definition of charisma still applies to parts of Africa and Asia. But the advance of bureaucratic determinism and the methodical rationalization and routinization of life in modern industrial societies have proved the uselessness of the charisma as a concept for analyzing leadership.[13]

To Lucien Pye and others, the prevalence of charismatic leaders is an important characteristic of non-western political processes. They think that the cohesive force of the nationalist movement often requires charismatic leadership because the process of breaking from a traditional past results in loss of authority of the indigenous ruling houses and aristocracies. This authority was sanctioned by super natural beliefs. The slow spread of western education and the scarcity of mass media retard the development of a new consensus and the vacuum may be filled by charismatic leaders. According to them, "withering of the deep emotional roots of respect for traditional authority takes place and the free floating habits of obedience seek new attachment in charismatic authority.[14]

In Gandhism, the masses are not condemned to political passivity as in Weber. Gandhi was the first to switch the emphasis on political thought from the elite to the masses. He constructed theoretic justification for sustained political action for national emancipation, sustained social action against the religious orthodoxy on questions of untouchability, women's rights, a sustained economic action based on constructive programme for the betterment of living conditions of the rural poor, sustained moral action against addiction and other forms of moral deprivation, bad faith, non-adherence to truth, etc. All these actions were based on a sense of civic virtue, discipline, duty and spirit of self-sacrifice that lie behind the masses of ordinary people and the saints.[15]

Gandhi himself opposed the personality cult developing around him: "I lay claim to nothing exclusively divine in me. I do not claim prophetship. I am but a struggling erring humble servant of India and therefore of humanity. There is already enough superstition in our country. No effort should be spared to resist further addition in the shape of Gandhi worship."[16]

Again in 1927, he said: ". . . though a non-cooperator, I shall gladly subscribe to a bill to make it criminal for anybody to call me Mahatma and to touch my feet."[17]

Whenever Gandhi called off a national movement at different phases of its history, his critics charged him as a reactionary or as an agent of bourgeoisie among others. He took bouquets and brick-bats with his usual calmness. He said: "A servant of people should never fear or give way to bitterness if he finds himself a victim of misunderstanding, whether unintentional or wilful. The acts of men who have come out to serve or lead have always been misunderstood, and to stick to one's guns, come what might, is the essence of the gift of leadership. Misunderstandings have been my lot ever since I entered public life, and I have got inured to them."[18]

Gandhi is a monumental personality not because of the so-called Weberian charismatic qualities possessed by him, lending an individual complexion to the historical events of his time but because of the possession of personality traits which made him the most capable of serving his time's great social needs which had arisen under the influence of general and particular causes. Gandhian movement cannot be identified with the mesmerist movement of eighteenth century France. The term "mesmerism" is associated with Franz Anton Mesmer. He came to Paris in February 1778 in the hope of curing Parisian through Animal Magnetism. Mesmerists emphasized its general atmosphere of "harmony", the physical and moral accord of man and the laws of nature.[19]

Gandhi's superiority lay in his ability to recognize that the masses cannot liberate themselves without destroying all the human conditions of life of contemporary society, which exist in the people in a concentrated form. He was a hero, not in the sense that he could halt or change the course of historical development that was taking place in the on-going society, but in the sense that his activities were the conscious and free expression of that necessary and unconscious courses. Therein lay all his significance and power.[20]

Gandhi's concern was the future of humanity which was founded on the twin principles of Tagore's poetry: "Where the mind is without fear and the head is held high."

III

Future of Humanity

Gandhi humanized India's political struggle. Through his message of nonviolence, the nation developed that capacity to remove hatred towards the British people. Swami Ranganathan said: "The uniqueness of the mind of Mahatma Gandhi has to inspire the coming generations. Many of the incidents in India's freedom struggle will have no value after sometime, and even some of his theories, political or economic, may not have much value after sometime. But the very spirit, his very approach to human problems, collective human life, is something permanent. It is that which will influence the future of humanity. Violence has presented a serious problem in human relations. We have to get rid of it to make evolutionary process proceed in the right direction towards human fulfilment. It is here that what Gandhi was and what he has said become significant. If we listen to his teaching and get inspired by him, we can have a development in the future. If not, all sorts of problems will afflict human society.[21]

Bertrand Russell had said: "Unless men increased in wisdom as much as in knowledge, increase of knowledge shall increase sorrow". Knowledge must rise to wisdom. If we study Gandhi's life seriously, we will find knowledge rising into wisdom there. That wisdom cannot come until we know, not the world outside, but also the divine dimension of our own inner nature.[22]

There is some profound spiritual dimension within every human being. That is the dimension from which Gandhi lived and worked. That is being completely ignored today. In modern science and technology there is no mention at all of inner life of a human being. How to make mind calm and quiet? How to make it love people and not hate? How to check hatred. How to check evil? How to check violence? These things are not taught by the language of physical science. But Gandhi's language is full of this. This is what we need. Gandhiji was all *Sattva*. He raised his mind to that level which made him capable of remaining calm and without hatred when the police in South Africa roughly handled him.[23]

The Republic of South Africa, which has become free from racial discrimination today, has given Gandhi high honour because he began his great work of political and social change from the nonviolent and humanistic point of view from there. He was absolutely free from any anger and any kind of hatred. This kind of achievement cannot come from the study of physical science and technology but only from the science of spirituality.[24]

The human being must get this inner education. It is a scientific truth about human being. That is what *Vedanta* has given us—*Adhyatma Vidya*—the science of spirituality. Gandhi was immersed in this great science. This is not religion in the usual ethical sense of the term, with all sorts of intolerance and violence and some sort of ritual ceremony. No, it is human growth, development beyond the mental, beyond the rational or intellectual to the highest spiritual level. That spirituality found manifestation in Gandhi and became manifested as love and service, and human concern. The whole world needs today to evolve in this direction to guide humane evolution in this spiritual direction.[25]

We have become slaves of our professions. Our professions take up the whole of our lives and we give very little time to the cultivation of the understanding of the mind, which is what we call living. Our profession comes first, then living. We approach life from the point of view of our profession, our job, and spend our lives in it, and at the end of our lives, we turn to meditation or spirituality. Most of our lives are a series of connected and disconnected constant efforts and in the efforts the problem of ambition and contradiction brings about a certain exclusive process which we call concentration.[26]

Our intelligence, not merely the capacity to reason, but rather the capacity to perceive, to understand what is true and what is false, is being destroyed by the emphasis on authority, acceptance and imitation. All this implies an extraordinarily pliable mind, whereas mediation is the unfolding of the mind and through it, the act of seeing without restraint. The seeing without the limitation of thought, which in time requires a mind, is astonishingly quiet still.[27]

IV

Development of Body, Mind and Spirit

Education must address itself to the development of the whole man—body, mind and spirit—the head, the heart and the hand.

While the trinity is best developed in coordination, the most important is the heart. The basic thing for the "culture of heart" is to develop unswerving faith in God. This can be done through a life of austerity, purity and simplicity.[28]

So far as education is concerned, according to the Indian ideal, education is that which leads to liberation or that which aims at building up character and righteous conduct of man as laid down in the maxim of Mumbai University. According to this view, mere intellectual development without corresponding development of character, learning without piety, proficiency in the sacred lore and deficiency in its practice are bound to defeat the very purpose of education. Education should teach the students not merely to think correctly but also to feel nobly and to choose loftily through Gandhi's scheme of education, which stressed life-oriented learning against examination and lecture-oriented education.[29]

The English word 'education' etymologically means 'drawing out'. That means an endeavour to develop our latent talents. In this sense we cannot look upon knowledge of the alphabet as education. When we say that we develop a certain thing, it does not mean that we change its kind or quality, but that we bring out the qualities latent in it. Hence, education can also mean 'unfoldment'. True education is something different. Man is made of three constituents, the body, mind and spirit. Of them spirit is the one permanent element in man. The body and mind function on account to it. True education is that which reveals the qualities of spirit.[30]

The knowledge that is being imparted today may possibly develop the mind a little, but certainly does not develop the body and spirit. Gandhi had a doubt about the development of the mind too, because it does not mean that the mind has developed if we have filled it with a lot of information. We cannot therefore say that we have educated our mind. A well educated mind serves man in the desired manner. Our literate mind of today pulls us hither and thither. That is, what a wild horse does. Only when a wild horse is controlled, we can call it a trained horse. How many "educated" young men today are so trained?

Now let us examine our body. Are we supposed to cultivate our body by laying tennis, football or cricket for an hour everyday? It does certainly build up the body. Like a wild horse, however, the body will be strong but not trained. A trained body is healthy, vigorous and sinewy. The hands and feet can do any desired work. A pick-axe, a shovel, a hammer, etc. are like ornaments to a trained hand and it can wield them. That hand can ply the spinning wheel well as also the ring and the comb while the feet work at a loom. A well trained body does not get tired in trudging 30 miles. It can scale mountains without getting breathless. Does the student acquire such physical culture? We can assert that modern curricula do not impart physical education in this sense.

The less said about the spirit the better. Only a seer or a seeker can enlighten the soul. Who will awaken the dormant spiritual energy in us all? Teachers can be had through an advertisement. Is there a column for spiritual quest in the testimonials, which they have to produce? Even if there is one, what is its value? How can we get through advertisement teachers who are seekers of self-realisation? And education without such enlightenment is like a wall without a foundation or, to employ an English saying, like a whited sepulcher. Inside it there is a corpse eaten up or being eaten by insects.

Gandhi tried to work out a synthesis between physical labour, scientific knowledge and human sympathy or on educating of the heart and had along with the hand. Teachers hold the key to education system and development of child. Abraham Lincoln (President of United States of America) had beautifully summarized the duties of a teacher when he made this request to his teacher: "Teach him that for every enemy, there is a friend. . . . Teach him that it is far more honourable to fail than to cheat. . . . Teach him to have faith in his own ideas even if everyone tells him they are wrong."

It is said that once a group of farmers in the USA went to New York and stayed on the 80th floor in a posh hotel. One day when they went shopping and came back with heavy load of gift parcels, they found that the lift (elevator) was not working. So they had to climb up and decided that while climbing the stairs, each one will tell his tale of woes by turns. All of them did but the one whose turn was to tell the story while climbing the last 80th floor was a little hesitant. All his colleagues assure him that they were there to share his woes. He replied: "your are right, my tale of woe is not only mine! It is ours because you were good enough to trust me and hand over the bunch of our keys to me when we went out. Now, while climbing the 80th floor I realize that I have forgotten the keys on the ground floor."[31]

Hearing this, Vinoba Bhave (A leader of Bhoodan Movement) reported to have reacted thus: "By all means go ahead in making progress in science and technology. Go not only to the 80th floor but to the 800th floor, to the Moon and the Mars but do not forget that the key of 'moral progress' is on the ground floor, i.e. preserve our eternal and perennial values".[32]

When Vinoba was asked. 'What was Gandhi?' he said, 'science plus spiritual knowledge is equal to Gandhi (S + S = G)'. Prof. John Dewey of New York University observed: "Gandhi's system of education is, I am sure, one step ahead of other systems. It is full of immense potentialities and we all hope to learn much from India in the revolutionary educational efforts". Thus, Gandhian education system is highly relevant in the twenty-first century.

Gandhi emphatically said: "Compulsory education to children must be universally given in their respective mother tongues". The high water mark on his insistence was reached on 6 February, 1916, on the occasion of the opening of the Banares Hindu University, declaring that it was: a matter of deep humiliation and shame" for him that he was compelled to address his countrymen in that sacred city in a foreign language. He observes "Our language is the reflection of ourselves, and if you tell me that our languages are too poor to express the best thought, then I say that the sooner we are wiped out of existence, the better for us." He added further: "No paper contribution will give us self-government. No amount of speeches will ever make us fit for self-government. It is only our conduct and character that will fit us for it."[33]

We have to rise above the mind-body complex. Then only we shall be able to handle our tensions and lead a balanced life.

V

Gandhi and Environment

The concepts of environmental conservation, sustainability and survival, which the modern ecologists are embarking upon, are inherent in the ideology of Mahatma Gandhi. He was by far more ahead of his time than all modern environmentalists. In as early as 1927, he had warned the word that the large scale industrialism would create problems of the type we are confronting today. He said: "The world influenced by the western culture was going in the wrong direction and like the proverbial moth would burn itself eventually in the flame around which it was dancing carelessly." He saw the doom of India and the entire world on the development path it was going on. He was not against industrialization but against industrialism and the dehumanized machine culture. He emphasized small-scale enterprises for "production by the masses and not mass production by any individual or group of company." The latter would mean prosperity for a few and poverty for the rest and that is what has exactly happened in India and other developing countries. Small-scale enterprises are also free from any developmental conflicts between management and labour. They are less energy-intensive and therefore less polluting.

His concept of nonviolence not only meant absence of injury to the living world but also to the nature and its non-living entities such as air, water and soil. The ecological movement of the world today is essentially to preserve the nature from the onslaught of industrialization. But it will be meaningless unless it is simultaneously directed against the piling up of deadly weapons. Potential threat to environment and ecology is due to enormous arms development.

Nature is becoming victim of human greed. Indiscriminate misuse of natural resources in the name of economic development disregarding the ecological implications has landed mankind in the present impasse. Gandhi had said: "The earth provides enough to satisfy every man's need but not every man's greed". He was of the view that as long as greed prevailed and the fruits of economic development were not shared equitably among the masses, poverty and hunger would exist. He also felt that till the evils of hunger, malnutrition and exploitation of the poor continued in many parts of the world, there could be no economic stability in the human society., The present ecological crisis demands a different worldview, i.e. giving up the present life-style and reduction in consumerism. This will directly support Gandhian ideology of living and high thinking.

Affluence as a goal of development was not in Gandhi's mind. He believed that the type of development that has been achieved in the west was the result of a systematic colonization and exploitation of both man and nature.

Man must realize that he does not own nature, he is only one of its many offsprings. Nature is not due to man; man is due to nature. Man, supposedly the wisest animal on earth, should play the role of trustee of the enormous natural wealth and live in harmony with nature rather than conquer it.

There has to be paradigm shift from economic development to human development. Environmental crisis is due to adoption of western model of development. Gandhi's path of development, ecological protest movements, environmental laws and education and change in the mental attitude of exploitation are needed to protect the environment. If human beings do not like the direction in which the world is heading, they should critically examine their individual and collective behaviour and government policies and programmes to determine if they should be changed so that they continue to march towards a more "desired future".[34]

The main arguments of both the environmentalists and the establishment lobbies revolve around economic issues. The dispute essentially centres on the accuracy of cost and benefit measurements. Nobody questions the basic man-nature relationship and the right of man to exploit the nature which is taken for granted. This is because both the planners and the environmentalists have the same mind set which views man as a consumer and nature as a commodity. This mind is not only, commercial, but also ruthlessly cruel and ultimately harms the whole mankind. If the environmentalists wish to make any significant progress in conservation, they must fight on ethical and spiritual and not on economic grounds. Exploiting nature ruthlessly amounts to genocide and hence is a crime. Every living component of nature has right to dignified existence. Man, being the most evolved, should be the custodian and protector of the dignity of all.[35]

VI

Science, Technology and Globalization

We are privileged to live through one of the greatest scientific and technological revolutions in human history. We are also saddled with the ominous responsibility of warding off the disastrous consequences of the new forces, which this revolution has unleashed. Socially undermined and process-oriented, the impact of forces cutting across the entire realm of human activity and relationship is making the world in many unforeseen ways when even experts cannot comprehend, let alone the common man.[36]

The basic tenet of the scientific method enunciated by Francis Bacon in the early seventeenth century focused on carrying out experiments that would unravel linkages between the phenomenon to arrive at general laws of nature in order to control it and endow new powers to humankind. This approach led to the belief that matter is the sole ultimate reality and life is purely a chance occurrence caused by fortuitous combination of atoms. The scientific method and the materialistic philosophy of life, when adopted by social scientists like Locke, Smith and Bentham, generated the belief that the sole purpose of life is to maximize material pleasure and human welfare that can be ensured through a limitless pursuit of material prosperity, aided by the creation of more and more sophisticated artifacts. This technology, the progeny of science, came to be hailed as the great benefactor which would liberate humankind from poverty, destitution and exploitation and usher in an era of peace and abundance in society.

What, however, has become evident over the decades is that although modern technology has contributed to increased productivity, lower costs, and much else, it has simultaneously brought humankind to the brink of disaster through environmental pollution, resource depletion, and nuclear, biological and chemical weapon systems accompanied by more effective delivery systems, manipulation of genetic codes, and the rest. Having got us in a fix, technology has no control over the weapons dumps and agents, not even on ballistic rocketry, which are now within the reach of petty and power-hungry politicians, mindless terrorists, fanatics and even mad adventurers. There is no technology which can protect us from the mass destruction that ever a careless slip or an error of judgement can cause. A case like Bhopal tragedy, limited but unprecedented, thus becomes a forerunner of the ultimate disaster and sinks into the collective consciousness of the helpless citizen of the world.

A technological culture does not limit itself to the use of the machine. It generates any number of standardized means to achieve predetermined ends.

Technological advancement is often used to disempower and subjugate people, often in very covert ways. The control over technologies is an increasingly important way to control information, employment and decision-making within societies. Pilger points out to the merging of the era of 'new democracy' in the world which enables free flow of capital and provides a free environment for multinationals to set up investments. He provides examples of the major agencies of the world's financial and economic sectors such as the International Monetary Fund (IMF), World Bank etc. which collaborate with the institutions of certain nations such as Organization for Economic Cooperation and Development (OECD) and the World Trade Organization (WTO). He further points that free trade takes place not only between nations but between the 180 multinational companies. Governments legitimize the condition of free trade either through economic coercion or through co-option.[37]

These multinationals are totalitarian by nature and are labelled by Pilger as "private tyrannies". They flood the markets and control economic policies of other countries. For example, the surpluses of American agricultural products in the form of exports to poor countries can destroy the agricultural base of those countries as in the case of Korea and can cause malnutrition and starvation in many African countries. The impact on countries are further heightened by various structural adjustment programmes imposed by IMF and other such global financial bodies.[38]

The drive is for consumerism and people gain significance in relation to their purchasing power. The movement of finance is closely linked with the movement of people and the role of media in promotion of consumption through advertising.

The difficulties for many nations is the acceptance of economic rationalist arguments where surplus budgets are strived for at the expense of the 'underclass' of people who need government subsidies and welfare expenditure.

The over-reaching effect of finance-escapes in a world characterized by:

* Competition and emphasis on free markets
* Individualism
* Minimal government intervention, privatisation of public sector
* "Trickle down" approach to welfare
* Emphasis on outputs, through inputs and quantity as out-course
* Growth of supernational organisation
* Managerialism

The Multilateral Agreement on Investment (MAI) is the latest attempt to gain unlimited freedom by the institutions within the finance-escapes. Once signed, these agreements will remove the restrictions on the movement of free capital anywhere in the world. The MAI, according to Pilger, represent the most important 'imperial' advance over half a century. The effect of MAI is to transfer policy making responsibilities away from national governments to multinationals. However, under the conditions of the MAI, corporations will be able to challenge local or national laws in international tribunals but no individual or government will have the right to take action against offending corporations. This gives licence to corporations to abrogate their responsibilities in a range of areas, including citizen's rights, environmental protection or loss of employment. Also, under MAI agreements, signatory countries cannot protect their local industries, which will lead to immense job losses.[39]

From the above discussion a natural corollary follows as to why would governments sign MAI agreements under such conditions? The World Development Movement (1994) argues that in 1995 more than 80 per cent of investment ended up in twelve countries. The forty-eight least developed countries received only 0.5 per cent. The poorer countries are being faced with increased pressure to sign up or face the prospect of non-investment. This will further perpetuate the imbalance in global distribution of wealth and resources.[40]

The economic crisis which the world faces today poses important responsibilities, accountability and transparency. The market processes render both governments and multinationals unaccountable.

Impact on Human Rights

Soli J. Sorabjee writes that the impact of globalization on Human Rights was animatedly debated at the Sub-Commission on Human Rights in Geneva.[41]

Thanks to the information technology revolution and communication, transmission of ideas and their globalization has led to an explosion, promoting the right to free expression and access to information. Technological advancement in medical research, space exploration and biotechnological innovations are also of immense significance.

The crucial questions are: Who has benefited from the processes of globalization? To what extent has globalization aided peasants, disadvantaged sections, women and ordinary working people? Has it decreased disparities in wealth and income? How has globalization improved the capacities of states, particularly those with low levels of human development and lacking in economic resources to meet the basic human rights obligations to their citizens?

According to one view, while a small section of humanity is basking in the glow of globalization, the larger segment wallows in increasing despondency and despair, a phenomenon described as "the concurrence of globalization and marginalization". The anti-globalization demonstrations in cities across the world should not be dismissed as extravagant protests of misguided persons. They 'symbolise the voice of millions who lose out in the trading game'. The urgent need is to ensure that the processes of globalization are sensitive to the goals of sustainable human development, of which the promotion and protection of human rights is paramount.

Transnational corporations (TNCs) play an important role in globalizing world economy. Their activities have an impact on different rights, for example, community rights, such as clean environment, as well as individual rights, like education, health and employment. The need to subject TNCs to the discipline of fundamental rights is plain. But there are problems. What is the definition of transnational corporations? Why should other business enterprises be left out? Discriminatory practices and sexual harassment also prevail there. Is the size of the business enterprises a key element? Thus the grand debate continues.

Gandhi's views of a peaceful world is a world of small, self-reliant communities tied together in "oceanic circles" of equitable interaction with plenty of space for unlimited personal growth and interpersonal competence, in harmony with nature. Such a world has no room for central world authority. It does not need "balance of power" but an alternative defensive defence. It does not need an arms race or alliance but civil defence, not deterrence but disarmament. To facilitate this process, Gandhi advocated strengthening of non-national-state movements, forces, and institutions as countervailing and pressurizing forces and powers.

Science is supremely important so far as the question of our understanding of the world is concerned. So is technology in terms of its potential to contribute to human happiness and prosperity.

Gandhi's theory of "oceanic circle" provides a systematic way to initiate globalization from below. In this structure, composed of innumerable villages, there will be ever widening, never ascending circles. Life will not be a pyramid with the apex sustained by the bottom. But it will be an "oceanic circle" whose centre will be the individual always ready to perish for the circle of villages, 'till at last the whole becomes one life composed of individuals, never aggressive in their arrogance but ever humble, sharing the majesty of the oceanic circle of which they are integral units. Therefore the outermost circumference will not wield power to crush the inner circle but give strength to all within and derive its own from the centre.[42]

Globalization from below is to establish a clear global agenda with global structures but with initiatives of ordinary people. This requires an analysis of local and national contexts in the light of global issues and the ability to transcend the assumption of national community work practice and policy. It is crucial to make the connections across countries of the nature and cause of social problem or issues, which seem only pertinent to localized situations. It also involves the need to promote an international consciousness, which can lead to international forms of organization and community work practice on the Gandhian lines.[43]

VII

Communism, Socialism and Gandhism

Gandhi had said in *Young India* on 15th November, 1928: "Bolshevik regime in its present form cannot last for long, for it is my firm conviction that nothing enduring can be built on violence (This has been proved as the Soviet Union of Russia has collapsed). But communism means a classless society—an ideal that is worth striving for. Only I part company with it when force is called to aid for achieving it. We are all born equal, but we have all these centuries resisting the will of God. The idea of inequality of high and low, is an evil, but I do not believe in eradicating evil from the human breast at the point of the bayonet. The human breast does not end itself to that means. . . . If communism came without any violence, it would be welcome. For then no property would be held by any body except on behalf of the people, for the people. A millionaire may have his millions but he will hold them for the people. The state could take charge of them, whenever they would need them for the common cause."[44]

"To socialists and communists they can do nothing to bring about economic equality today. They will just carry on propaganda in its favour and to that end they believe in generating and accentuating hatred. They say when they get control over the State they will enforce equality. Under my (Gandhi) plan, the State will be there to carry out the will of the people, not to dictate them or force them to do its will. I shall bring about economic equality through nonviolence, by converting the people to my point of view by harnessing the forces of love against hatred. I will not wait till I have converted the whole society to my view but will straightaway make a beginning with myself. It goes without saying that I cannot hope to bring about economic equality of my conception, if I am the owner of fifty cars or even ten *bighas* of land. For that I have to reduce myself to the level of the poorest of the poor. That is what I have been trying to do for the last fifty years or more and so I claim to be a foremost communist."[45]

"We must have the ability and courage to subsist on what our soil can give us rather than depend on foreign charity. Otherwise we shall not deserve to exist as an independent country. The same applies to foreign ideologies. I would accept them only to the extent that I can assimilate them and adapt them to the Indian scene. But I must refuse to go under them."[46]

"So far as I am aware, in socialism all the members of society are equal—none low, none high. . . . Looking at society or the world, there is nothing but duality or plurality. Unity is conspicuous by its absence. Socialism begins with the first convert. If there is one such, you can add zeroes, to the one and the first zero will count for ten and every addition will count for ten times the previous number. If, however, the beginner is zero, in other words, no one makes the beginning, multiplicity of zeroes will able to produce zero value. Time and paper occupied in writing zeroes will be so much waste."

"Socialism is as pure as crystal. It, therefore, requires crystal-like means to achieve it. Impure means result in a impure end. Therefore, truthful, nonviolent and pure-hearted socialists will be able to establish a socialistic society in India and the world. To my knowledge there is no country in the world, which is purely socialist, without the means described above."[47]

Gandhi's socialism was a moral socialism based on his doctrine of nonviolence and truth.

VIII

Evaluation of Gandhi

Sharp said: "Today, Gandhi and his ideas rarely receive attention. Many who know the name dismiss him as a strange religious 'saint' of some kind, or a prudish ascetic because of his views on sex and pleasures. Others often condescendingly view him as someone who was once important but who is no longer relevant. Many of the people born in the West since 1940 or so have little idea who Gandhi was."[48]

Kumar is of the opinion that in India, much for what Gandhi stood for died with him. Indeed, there must have been tremendous relief among his camp followers, and his fellow workers. For having brought them to this point, many of them could think in terms of reaping the dividends of his sufferings and sacrifices. This old man most obligingly left them free to dip their hands in the holy waters of material gains. A thousand and one things, which he held dear were thrown overboard with scant respect. To compensate this lip service paid to him, the name of Gandhi is uttered loudly but the ideals for which he stood for, have been ignored. If Gandhi were to come back, it is a good sign, but he will swallow us all along with our arm chairs. He wanted this country to be a model nation and what we find today is no better, if not worse than the others. Justly, he might say, "celebrate nothing and let me live in peace". Gandhi had been treated by his own people irrelevantly.[49]

Thomas Weber says that the book and articles about Gandhi are now far too many to count. These can be divided into two categories. First opinion is that either Gandhi's legacy is a destructive one, holding back development in the country, his successors being eccentric or dangerous fools. Second is that the only hope for the country is to adhere closely to Gandhian principles, and the Mahatma's followers are depicted as saint. For example, in his book *Gandhi Today; A Report on Mahatma Gandhi's Successors,* Shepard asks the question about the Gandhian tradition in India, whether it has died away, and what has become of the constructive workers that Gandhi sent to the villages. He concludes that with the passing away of Vinoba Bhave and Jayaprakash Narayan, "it is unlikely that the Sarvodaya Movement will again be a major force on a national level". The book is an extremely positive account of the work and life of some of the leading stars, whose efforts constitute "the main strength of the Sarvodaya movements". But even these luminaries are fast disappearing and anyway Gandhism should not be dependent on a collection of stars. Only in passing does Shepard concede that while the movement as a whole has declined, it can still provide guidance for the new generation of leaders who "willingly look back to Gandhi for inspiration."[50]

Ved Mehta and V.S. Naipaul proclaimed that Gandhi is dead but the body is putrefied. However, Mehta and Naipaul got it wrong. The old guard Gandhians have their faults, faults the author delights in pointing out that like the rest of us they are human. Gandhism is not a reactionary force holding back development in the country, but a sign post of hope for the planet. Some like, Mark Shepard, go further and say that it is Gandhian and Gandhism that are still needed in a country where "neither capitalism nor centralized socialism has worked." Shepard notes that there is a growing interest in looking back to the Mahatma and a greater willingness among many to take the type of action which brings change. Those old Gandhians "who have upheld the traditions" could step back from their positions of hegemony and assist the young by "providing guidance and models for the inexperienced activists." [51] After all, the future of Gandhism is in their hands. Long live Gandhi.[52]

Gandhi is more relevant today than ever before. We have to choose between "Atom" and "*Ahimsa*", "nonviolence" and "nonexistence", and between "*sarvodaya*" and "*sarvanasha*" (total annihilation). There is a growing awareness all over the world that Gandhi's work, teachings and thoughts have greater relevance. This is what Dr. Nelson Mandela, former President of South Africa, said: "Gandhi holds the key to human progress". Further, "The Twenty-first century belongs to Gandhi". Ironically, there are more research foundations, groups and centres devoted to the study and examination of Gandhian thought in other countries than in India.

Julius Nyerere, former President of Tanzania said: "Gandhi was a rare person".[53] He was one of those human beings whom God sends in a millennium to remind us of the meaning of life and the dignity and responsibility of being human. His uniqueness lies in his life and in the means he advocated and adopted as matters of principle. They make the message of his life not one just for India, but one, which is relevant to human being everywhere. His message was in his uncompromising rejection of violence as a way of righting wrongs.

Daisaku Ikeda, founder President of Soka Gakkai International, Tokyo, Japan said: "What best to be emulated from Gandhi is that a good end can only be achieved through equally good means."[54] "I want to cross the ocean. I can do so only by means of a vessel. If I were to use a cart for that purpose, both the cart and I would soon find the bottom." Elsewhere Gandhi wrote: "Your belief that there is no connection between the means and the end is a great mistake." And, "your reasoning is the same as saying that we can get a rose through planting obnoxious seed."

Dr. Federico Mayor, while inaugurating the exhibition on the occasion of Gandhi's 125th birth anniversary celebrations in Paris (France), pointed out that if humanity has to survive it has to take Mahatma Gandhi seriously.

A.T. Ariyaratne, the Founder President of the Sarvodaya Shramadan Movement in Sri Lanka, said the earth-ship is in serious danger. Gandhiji showed a way to seal the hole and save the ship. We in *Sarvodaya* are applying his prescription with modification to suit the changing climate.

Dr. Martin Luther King, Jr declared: "The choice today is no longer between violence and nonviolence. It is either nonviolence or non-existence."

When Gandhi was assassinated on 30 January, 1948, Einstein along with several other world leaders felt it a personal tragedy. On 11 February, 1948, Einstein issued the following statement for the memorial service held in Washington: "Everyone concerned with better future for mankind will be deeply moved by the tragic death of Gandhi. He died a victim of his own principle, the principle of nonviolence. He died because in a time of disorder and general unrest in his country, he refused any personal armed protection. It was his unshakable belief that the use of force is an evil itself, to be shunned by those who strive for absolute justice."[55]

With this faith in his heart and mind, he devoted his whole life for the upliftment of humanity and led a great nation (India) to its liberation. He demonstrated that the allegiance of man can be won, not merely by winning the game of political fraud and trickery, but through the living example of morally exalted way of life.

The veneration in which Gandhi has been held throughout the world rests on the recognition that in our age of moral decay, he was the only statesman who represented that higher conception of human relations in the political sphere to which we must aspire with all our power. We must learn the difficult lesson that the future of mankind will be safe when our actions, in world affairs as in all other matters, are based on justice and law rather than the threat of naked power as has been true so far.

This particular statement as well as the views of other eminent world leaders substantially echo the words of Dr. Arnold Toynbee (A world reputed historian) that a chapter which had a western beginning will have to have an Indian (Gandhian) ending if it is not to end in the self-destruction of the human race. At this supremely dangerous moment in human history, the only way of salvation for mankind is the Indian way—Emperor Ashoka's and Mahatma Gandhi's principle of nonviolence and Sri Ramakrishna's testimony of the harmony of religions. Here we have an attitude and spirit that can make it possible for human race to grow together into a single family and, in the Atomic age, this is the only alternative to destroying ourselves.

IX

Eternal and Universal Future of Gandhism

In conclusion, we can sum up the future of Gandhism as eternal and universal. Its cardinal principles of Truth and Nonviolence are as important and significant as sun to our life. Gandhism exhorts us not only to believe in purity of means but to practice them to achieve our ends and goals. Gandhi said that man can find God in the service of humanity.

In Gandhi's view, cult of violence has to be rejected at all costs and at all places. He taught us that our aim should be to develop harmonious relationships between different communities, castes, religions and other groups and to replace hatred with love and affection.

The world today has not become a better place to live in despite spectacular' achievements in science and technology. The development processes adopted by us have alienated man from man. The time has come now for serious thinking on the issues facing the world. Gandhi's decision on "*Dandi March*" (Salt *Satyagraha*) was a message so simple that it reached everyone. Through the March Gandhi tried to provide means for the lowliest to undertake the change of self and take part in the change of society. In his scheme, the people were at the centre. He kept his policies and programmes to secure full support and participation of the people and to develop capacities in them to work as members of a one world community. The people felt that he was talking to them directly rather than through impersonal means of communication. He emphasized self-discipline, truth, *satyagraha* and nonviolence as some of the methods to achieve the societal goal. He said: "I am endeavouring to see God through service to humanity."

In fact, the basic principle of Gandhism in working with people is to lead them from conflicts of interests to community of interests. The goal of Gandhism is to bring about a community of interests by holding it up as the common good, by making *Sarvodaya* the motivating factor for individual action. It is a process of right discernment of the context for the sake of right action, which would help to take it from conflict to harmony without sacrificing any value.

Mahatma Gandhi won commitment from his followers. He knew the pulse of the people and the skill to get them involved. He had a keen understanding of people and their motivation, emotion, pain, trust and loyalty to deal with them.

Gandhi maintained that human need should rise above and transcend animal nature so that man could be creative and cease to be merely a creature. He had a holistic approach to life. His development philosophy revolved around man, his society and environment (nature) and their respective and simultaneous development. He believed that instead of man exploiting the society and both exploiting nature, there was a symbiotic way of life in which they were in harmony with each other. In his frame of reference for development, man is the centre of attention. The objective is the moral and spiritual development of man. His ethnics in relation to material things and property consisted in his concept of Trusteeship. Man is not a Trustee of his faculties and attainments but everything he comes by, and trusteeship consists not only in using powers and property but in using them selflessly and for the well being of others.

Gandhism is the only way to eradicate poverty, bring prosperity, and prepare people to live in harmony and peace in the world. Gandhism will remain alive so long as the Sun does not disappear from the cosmos.

Modern science and technology has produced neighbourhood, but not brotherhood and sisterhood. Distance has decreased but people have become more distant. As one leader of the world had said: "I sought my soul, I could not see. I sought my God, my God eluded me. I sought my brother or sister, I found all the three." In the contemporary world, there is reverse correlation between human relationship and the advancement in science and technology. The superiority of the materialistic approach does not help in fostering positive human relationship. Power and competition once combined in the lives of people, become potent source of destructiveness and violence. Contrary to power, "love" provides people with a profound relationship with each other. This relationship cannot be accomplished by harnessing sophisticated arms and technical force, but through man himself, working with the other man. The lesson which we can draw from Gandhism is that his ideas, methods, techniques and strategies should not remain only skin deep but should penetratc into the soul of each of us.

REFERENCES

1. Swami Vivekananda, "On Future (Sacred Space)", *The Times of India*, June 4, 2001, New Delhi, p. 10.
2. Taba Homayun, "Beyond Materialism: A Spiritual Longing", *The Times of India*, June 4, 2001, New Delhi, p. 10.
3. *Ibid.*
4. Swami Chaitanya Keerti, "Learn to Live Life Like a Lotus", *The Hindustan Times*, June 4, 2001, New Delhi, p. 2.
5. Khan Maulana Wahiduddin, "Prophet Muhammad's Vision of Peace", *The Times of India*, June 4, 2001, New Delhi, p. 10.
6. Sharma, S.K., "Betrayal of Mahatma Gandhi", *Gandhi Marg*, Journal of the Gandhi Peace Foundation, 102, September 1987, pp. 330-31.
7. Hans Gerth and C. Wright Mills, ed., *From Max Waber: Essays in Sociology*, Oxford University Press, 1946, New York, p. 295.
8. Quoted in David Beethan, *Max Weber and the Theory of Modern Politics*, Polity Press, 1985, London, pp. 230-31.
9. Punit, A.R., "Gandhi—A Study in Charismatic Leadership", *Gandhi Marg*, Vol. II, No. 7, October 1980, pp. 374-84, pp. 374-75.
10. *Ibid.*, p. 375.
11. Choudhri Kunal Roy, "Gandhi and the Paroxysm of Charisma", *Gandhi Marg*, Vol. XX, No. 4, January-March, 1999, pp. 469-78.
12. Talcolt Parsons, *Sociological Theory and Modern Society*, Free Press, New York, 1967, pp. 49-50.

13. Arthur H. Schlesinger Jr., *The Politics of Hope*, Eyre and Spottiswoode, London, 1964, pp. 49-50.
14. Lucien Pye, *et al.*, "Comparative Politics of Non-Western Countries", *American Political Science Review*, Vol. 49, No. 4, 1955, p. 1025.
15. Choudhari, Kunal Roy, "Gandhi and the Paroxysm of Charisma", *Gandhi Marg*, Vol. XX, No. 4, January-March, 1999, p. 476.
16. *Collected Works of Mahatma Gandhi* (CWMG), Vol. 25, p. 117.
17. *Ibid.*, Vol. 333, p. 167.
18. *Ibid.*, Vol. 34, p. 364.
19. For details about mesmerists and mesmerist movement, see Robert Darton, *Mesmerism and the End of Enlightenment in France*, Cambridge, Mass: Harvard University Press, 1968.
20. Choudhari, Kunal Roy, "Gandhi and the Paroxysm of Charisma", *Gandhi Marg*, Vol. XX, No. 4, January-March, 1999, p. 477.
21. Swami Ranganathananda, "Gandhi and the Future of Humanity", in *Gandhi and Future of Humanity*, ed. by Ramjee Singh, Gandhian Institute of Studies, Varanasi, 1997, pp. 1-5.
22. *Ibid.*
23. *Ibid.*
24. *Ibid.*
25. *Ibid.*
26. Krishnamurty, J., "Don't be a Slave of Your Profession", *The Hindustan Times*, June 6, 2001, p. 2.
27. *Ibid.*
28. Gangrade, K.D., "Gandhian Perspectives on Education", in *Gandhi and the Changing Facets of India*, eds., Gangrade, K.D. and Radhakrishnan, N., Gandhi Smriti and Darshan Samiti, New Delhi, 1998, pp. 119-46, 128.
29. Mehta, Usha, "Gandhi's Purifying Influence", *Gandhian Prasang*, Vol. III, No. 2, January 30, 2001, pp. 86-91.
30. Gandhi, M.K., in "Development of Body, Mind and Spirit", *Navajivan Education Supplement*, 28 February, 1926 (CWMG, Vol. 30, pp. 58-59). See also "Intellectual Development", *Harijan*, 8 May 1937 (CWMG, Vol. 65, pp. 73-75). Both these articles have been reproduced in *Gandhi on Education* by National Council for Teacher's Education, New Delhi, 1998, pp. 12-14 and pp. 88-91.
31. Mehta, Usha, "Gandhi's Purifying Influence", *Gandhi Prasang*, Vol. III, No. 2, January 30, 2001, pp. 90-91.
32. *Ibid.*
33. Bimal Prasad, *Gandhi, Nehru and JP—Studies in Leadership*, Chanakya Publications, Delhi, 1985, p. 14.
34. Gangrade, K.D., *Environmental Crisis: A Challenge to Modern Civilisation for Secularization of Environmental Stewardship*, Rawat Publications, Jaipur and New Delhi, 1998, pp. 51-61, pp. 86-95, specially p. 14.

35. Mishra, P.N. and Pandit Shailendra, "Environment Concern: The Missed Issue", *Gandhi Marg*, Vol. XVII, No. 2, January-March, 1995, pp. 487-90.
36. Bhan Susheela, "Science, Technology and Peace", *Gandhi Marg*, Vol. XVIII, No. 1, April-June 1996, pp. 44-53.
37. Pilger, J., *Hiden Agenda*, Vintage, London, cited by Hurriyet Babacan and Narayan Gopal Krishnan, in their article, "Community Work Partnership in a Global Context", *Community Development Journal—An International Forum*, Vol. XXXVI, No. 1, January 2001, Oxford University Press, Oxford, U.K., pp. 3-17.
38. Babacon Hurriyet and Gopalkrishnan Narayan, "Community Work Partnership in a Global Context", *Community Development Journal*, Vol. XXXVI, No. 1, January 2001, Oxford University Press, Oxford, U.K., pp. 6-17.
39. *Ibid.*
40. *Ibid.*
41. Sorabjee Soli, "Globalisation", Sunday, *Times of India*, New Delhi, August 19, 2001, p. 12.
42. Gandhi, M.K., *India of My Dreams*, compiled by R.K. Prabhu, Navajivan Publishing House, Ahmedabad, Seventh Reprint, 1999, p. 100.
43. Babacon Hurriyet and Gopalkrishnan Narayan, "Community Work Partnership in a Global Context", *Community Development Journal*, Vol. XXXVI, No. 1, January 2001, p. 15.
44. Gandhi, M.K., *Harijan*, 12-3-1937, see also Reference No. 41, p. 27.
45. Gandhi, M.K., *Harijan*, 31-3-46.
46. Gandhi, M.K., *Harijan*, 6-10-46.
47. Gandhi, M.K., *Harijan*, 13-7-47.
48. Sharp Gene, *Gandhi as a Political Strategist*, Gandhi Media Centre, New Delhi, 1999, p. XVIII.
49. Kumar, Ajit, "Good Bye Mr. Gandhi", *Gandhi Marg*, Vol. XX, No. 3, October-December, 2000, pp. 356-58.
50. Weber Thomas, "Gandhi is Dead, Long Live Gandhi: The Post Gandhi, Gandhian Movement in India", *Gandhi Marg*, Vol. XVIII, No. 2, July-September, 1996, pp. 160-92. Also see Mark Shepard, *Gandhi Today: A Report on Mahatma Gandhi's Successors* (Arcata, Calif: Simple Production, 1987), p. 9.
51. Mark Shepard, *Since Gandhi: India's Sarvodaya Movement* (Weare, New Hameshie: Green Leaf Book, 1984), p. 38.
52. Weber Thomas, "Gandhi is Dead, Long Live Gandhi", *Gandhi Marg*, Vol. XVIII, No. 2, July-September, 1996, p. 190.
53. Nyerere, Julius K., "Gandhi Spells Nonviolence—Total Uncompromising Nonviolence", *Gandhi in the Global Village*, (eds.) Radhakrishnan, N. and Vasudevan, N., Gandhi Media Centre, New Delhi and Centre for Global Nonviolence, Hawaii, 1998, pp. 1-2.

54. Ikeda Daisaku, *Gandhi in the Twenty-First Century—Towards a Lasting Swaraj*, p. 12, see reference No. 52 (for details about the book).
55. Otto Nathan and Heinz Norden (ed.), *Einstein on Peace*, New York, Schocken Books, 1968, pp. 467-68.

APPENDICES

APPENDIX I

GANDHI: YEARS OF EXPERIMENTS

1869 : **Oct. 2:** Born at Porbandar, Kathiawad, India. Son of Karamchand and Putlibai Gandhi.

1883 : Married Kasturba.

1887 : Passed Matriculation.

1888 : Sailed from Bombay for England to study law.

1891 : **Summer:** Returned to India after being called to the Bar, began to practice law in Bombay and Rajkot.

1893 : **April:** Sailed for South Africa to become lawyer for an Indian firm found himself subjected to colour discrimination.

1894 : Drafted first petition sent by the Indians to the South Africa Legislature; **May:** Organised the Natal Indian Congress.

1899 : Organised Indian Ambulance Crops for British in Boer War.

1901 : Embarked with family for India, promising to return to South Africa whenever needed.

1902 : Travelled extensively in India, attended Indian National Congress meeting in Calcutta and opened law office in Bombay.

1903 : Returned to South Africa at the request of the Indian Community: Established the weekly journal "*Indian Opinion*".

1904 : Organised Phoenix Farm near Durban; wrote the book "Guide to Health".

1906 : **Sept.:** First '*Satyagraha*' campaign against proposed Asiatic ordinance against Indian immigrants in Transvaal.

1907 : **June:** Organised '*Satyagraha*' against compulsory registration of Asiatics (The Black Act).

1908 : **Jan.:** Stood trial for instigating '*Satyagraha*' and was sentenced to two months imprisonment in Johannesburg jail (his first imprisonment); Summoned to consult General Smuts at Pretoria; Compromise reaches; released from jail; **Feb.:** Attacked and wounded by Indian extremist for settlement with Smuts; **Aug.:** After Smuts broke agreement, second '*Satyagraha*' campaign began with bonfire of registration certificates; **Oct.:** Sentenced to two months rigorous imprisonment.

1909 : **Jan.:** Prepared for final phase of struggle; **Feb.:** Sentenced to three months imprisonment in Volksrut and Pretoria jail; **June:** sailed for England to present Indian's case; **Oct.:** Wrote to Tolstoy regarding passive resistance; Wrote "Hind Swaraj".

1910 : **May:** Established Tolstoy Farm near Johannesburg.

1912 : Gave up European dress and milk.

1913 : **Sept.:** Helped campaign against nullification of marriages not performed according to Christian rites. Third '*Satyagraha*' campaign led 2,000 Indian miners from Newcastel across Transvaal border; **Nov.:** Arrested for third time in four days; **Dec.:** Released unconditionally in expectation of a compromise.

1914 : **Jan.:** Suspended Satyagraha following agreement with Smuts; 14 days penitential fast for moral lapses of inmates of the farm; **July:** Returned to India, leaving South Africa for ever.

1915 : **May:** Established *Satyagraha* Ashram near Ahmedabad.

1917 : Moved Ashram to new site on Sabarmati River; led successfully '*Satyagraha*' campaign for rights of peasants on indigo plantations in Champaran (Bihar); Defied order to leave area in April, was arrested at Motihari and tried, but case was withdrawn.

1918 : **Feb.:** Led strike of mill workers at Ahmedabad; mill owners agreed to arbitration after his three-day fast (his first fast in India). **March:** led '*Satyagraha*' for peasants in Kheda. **April:** Organised nationwide *hartal*—suspension of activity for a day against the Rowlatt Bill: Fasted at Sabarmati for three days in penitence for violence and suspended *satyagraha* campaign which he called a 'Himalayan miscalculation because people were not disciplined enough; Became Editor of English weekly "*Young India*" and Gujarati weekly "*Navjivan*"; Presided over All India Khilafat Conference at Delhi.

1920 : **April:** Elected President of All India Home Rule League. Successfully urged resolution for a '*Satyagraha*' campaign of non-cooperation. **Aug.:** Surrendered his war medals.

1921 : Resolved to wear only loin cloth to propagate home spurn cotton and to signify his identification with the people. Mass civil disobedience thousands went to jail, Gandhi invested with sole executive authority on behalf of Indian Congress.

1922 : Suspended mass disobedience because of violence at Chauri Chaura and undertook five-day fast of penance at Bardoli: Arrested at Sabarmati on charges of sedition for articles in *Young India*, pleaded guilty in famous statement at the 'great trial' in Ahmedabad before judge Broomfield sentenced to six years imprisonment in Yervada jail,

1929 : Arrested for burning foreign cloth in Calcutta and fined one rupee.

1929 : **Dec.:** Congress session at Lahore voted for complete independence and a boycott of the legislature, January 26 proposed as National Independence Day: Third All-India '*Satyagraha*' campaign.

1930 : **March 12:** Set out from Sabarmati with 79 volunteers on historic Salt March 200 miles to sea at Dandi, **April 6:** Broke salt law by picking up a handful of salt at seashore. Arrested by armed police men at Karadi and imprisoned in Yervada jail without trial. One hundred thousand persons arrested.

1931 : **Jan.:** Released unconditionally with 30 other Congress leaders, **March:** Gandhi-Irwin (Viceroy) pact signed which ended civil disobedience, **Aug.:** Sailed from Bombay for Round Table Conference in London, **Dec.:** Returned to India: Authorised by Congress to renew '*Satyagraha*' campaign (fourth nationwide effort).

1932 : **Jan.:** Arrested in Bombay with Sardar Patel and detained without trial at Yervada prison. **Sept. 20:** Began fast unto death while in prison in protest of British action giving separate electorates to untouchables. **Sept. 26:** Concluded 'fast' in the presence of Rabindranath Tagore after the British accepted 'Poona Pact'.

1933 : Began weekly publication of '*Harijan*' in place of '*Young India*'; **July:** Disbanded Sabarmati Ashram which then became the centre for removal of untouchability.

1934 : **Summer:** Three separate attempts made on his life. **Oct.:** Launched All-India Village Industries Association.

1936 : Settled down at Sevagram (Wardha); gave trial to his ideas about education.

1939 : Fast unto death at Rajkot and ended it on Viceroy's intervention.

1940 : **Oct.:** Launched limited individual civil disobedience campaign against Britain's refusal to allow Indians to express their opinions regarding World War II; 23,000 persons imprisoned within a year.

1942 : **March:** Met Sir Stafford Cripps in New Delhi but called his proposals postdated cheque; these were ultimately rejected by Congress; **Aug.:** Congress passed Quit India resolution. The final nationwide '*Satyagraha*' campaign with Gandhi the leader.

1942 : **Aug. 9:** Arrested with other Congress leaders and Kasturba and imprisoned in Aga Khan Palace, near Pune; revolts in many parts of the country; **Aug. 15:** Mahadeo Desai died in detention.

1943 : **Feb.:** Began 21-day fast at Aga Khan Palace to end deadlock between Viceroy and Indian leaders.

1944 : **Feb. 22:** Kasturba died in detention at Aga Khan Palace at the age of 74; **May 6:** After decline in health, was released unconditionally from detention (this was his last imprisonment; he had spent 2,338 days in jail during his lifetime); **Sept.:** Important talks with Jinnah of Muslim League in Bombay on Hindu-Muslim unity.

1946 : **Nov.:** Began four-month tour of 49 villages in East Bengal to quell provisional government.

1947 : **March:** Toured Bihar to lessen Hindu-Muslim tension, Began conference decision to accept division of country into India and Pakistan; **Aug. 15:** Fasted and prayed to combat riots in Calcutta as India was partitioned and granted Independence; **Sept.:** Visited Delhi and other neighbouring areas to stop rioting and visited camps of refugees.

1948 : **Jan. 13:** Fasted for five days in Delhi for communal unity. **Jan. 20:** Bomb exploded in midst of his prayer meeting at Birla House, Delhi. **Jan. 30:** Assassinated at Birla House by Nathuram Vinayak Godse, a fanatic in protest of Gandhi's advocation of Hindu Muslim Unity.

Arrests and Imprisonments of Mahatma Gandhi

South Africa

10 Jan. 1908 : Arrested for failing to register or to leave Transvaal and was sentenced to two months simple imprisonment. On 30 January following a compromise, released.

7 Oct. 1908 : While returning from Natal as he was unable to show his registration which he had burnt, imprisonment with hard labour.

25 Feb. 1909 : Arrested, sentenced for 3 months imprisonment at Transvaal for not producing registration certificate.

6 Nov. 1913 : After the 'Great March' he was arrested at

Plam Ford, released on 7 on bail furnished by Kallenbach.

8 Nov. 1913 : Again arrested and released on bail.

9 Nov. 1913 : Arrested and sentenced to nine months imprisonment. At Volksrust sentenced for further three months. But unexpectedly released on 18 December, 1913.

India

16 Apr. 1917 : While touring Champaran served with a notice to leave the district but was not arrested.

10 Apr. 1919 : Arrested at Palwal on his way to Amritsar and was taken back to Bombay where he was released on 11 April.

10 Mar. 1922 : Arrested near Sabarmati Ashram for writing three articles in *Young India*.
Sentenced to six years imprisonment. Released from Yervada prison on 5 February, 1924 unconditionally after an operation on 12 January, 1924.

5 May 1930 : At 12.45 a.m. arrested at Karadi near Dandi for violating Salt Law, without trial was imprisoned and released on 26 January, 1931 unconditionally.

4 Jan. 1932 : Arrested in Bombay at 3 a.m. and taken to Yeravada jail. On 8 May, 1933 as he started fast was released at 6 p.m.

1 Aug. 1933 : Arrested early morning at Bombay on his March towards Rass and released on 4 August at 9 a.m. and was asked to leave Yervada limits by 9.30 a.m. Did not comply, so arrested on 4 August at 9.50 a.m. and sentenced to one-year imprisonment. Started fast on 16 August and was released unconditionally on 23 August due to serious health condition.

9 Aug. 1942 : Arrested under Defence of India Rules in the early hours of the morning following 'Quit

India' resolution and was lodged in Aga Khan Palace jail. Released unconditionally at 8 a.m. on 6 May, 1944.

[Courtesy from the Gandhi Diary 2003, Published by Gandhi Book Centre Bombay Sarvodya Mandal, Mumbai.]

APPENDIX II

MAHATMA GANDHI

Mohan Das Karamchand Gandhi was born at Porbandar in Gujarat on 2nd October, 1869. Gandhi was in school from 1881 to 1887. After spending nine months in a college, he left for England in September 1888 to study Law. He returned home in 1891 and set himself up as a lawyer. In April, 1893 Gandhi was called to Natal in the Service of a merchant named Seth Abdulla. Soon after arrival, he experienced in person the harsh treatment meted out to coloured people by the whites. Gandhi decided to return home in April, 1894. But news appeared about a proposed legislation against Asian immigrants when he promptly decided to stay on and defend his people, the struggle in South Africa lasted from 1894 to 1914.

He finally sailed for India on 19th December, 1914 and reached Bombay on 9th January, 1915. Gandhi established the Satyagraha Ashram in Ahmedabad city on 25th May, 1915. Between 1917 and 1918 Gandhi participated in two peasant movements in Champaran (Bihar) and Kaira (Gujarat) and in he labour dispute in Ahmedabad itself. Gandhi protested against the Rowlatt Bills and founded the Satyagraha Sabha (28 February, 1919) whose members undertook a peaceful breach of the law of sedition in April, 1919.

In a meeting of the All India Khilafat Conference on 24th November, 1919 he proposed that India should respond by nonviolence, and non-cooperation. The Non-Cooperation Movement was consequently initiated in 1920. At the Amritsar Session, Gandhi had opposed those who wanted to reject the Montagu-Chelmsford Reforms and had offered to co-operate with the Government. After Nagpur session he emerged as the undisputed leader of the Congress and Indian nationalism and he retained that unique position till his death. When there was a serious outbreak of mob violence in Chauri Chaura in Uttar Pradesh, in which Congress and Khilafat volunteers were involved.

Congress was prevailed upon by him to suspend the movement for the time being.

Gandhi was arrested and sent to jail for six years on 10th March, 1922. From 1924 to 1929, Gandhi devoted himself largely to the constructive programme, several local *satyagraha* movements were also undertaken during this period. His famous Dandi March, 1930 started a country-vide movement to violate the Salt Law. Gandhi was arrested on 4th May, 1930. Gandhi was chosen as the sole representative of the Congress to the Second Round Table Conference in London which opened in September, 1931. On May 8, 1933, he announced a fast for 21 days for the Harijan cause and he was promptly released by the Government. When the war broke out and India was dragged into it without her consent, Gandhi felt it necessary to protest. It would be better for India to "Do or Die" as he realised than for her to succumb to passivity and moral degradation. The Working Committee and the AICC adopted the famous "Quit India" resolution, demanding immediate independence and British withdrawal from India. Immediately after, all the Congress leaders were clapped into prison (9th August, 1942). There Gandhi lost his life-long companion Kasturba. His release came in 1944.

Till his death in 1948 he was the acknowledged leader of the Congress and of Indian nationalism. On 30th January, 1948 he was assassinated by a Hindu fanatic while he was on his way to his prayer meeting in the city of Delhi. He has been regarded, both as a saint as well as a political visionary deeply committed to peace, nonviolence and total human development. His vision has shaped the political thinking and the development strategies of all the countries of the world.

[*Homage to Heroes Everyday* compiled by Minu Ray, Vice President, All India Centre for Urban and Rural Development, New Delhi, 1977, pp. 10-11.]

APPENDIX III

KASTURBA GANDHI

Kasturba was born at Porbandar in 1869. She was the wife of Mahatma Gandhi and was also his steadfast companion in all his experiments in India and in South Africa. A delicated, small but elegant lady, she was simple, straightforward and methodical. Her public life began after she joined her husband in South Africa in 1897. From 1904 to 1914, she was the soul of the Phoenix Settlement and became Kasturba 'mother' to the inmates, a role she continued at Kochnab, Sabarmati, and Sevagram Ashrams in India. She led the women's *satyagraha* in the final fight in South Africa. She was imprisoned and came out of jail in an emaciated condition. In 1918, she took an active part in the Kaira *Satyagraha* or 'No Tax Campaign' and taught the village women the art of nonviolent resistance. Later during India's nonviolent fight for freedom, she took up the leadership of the movement whenever Gandhi was arrested; she plunged into the struggle, addressed meetings, collected funds and kept up the morale of the people. She presided over the backward Rani Paraj community's second conference, which resulted in their giving up drinking and taking of spinning and Khadi. In 1939, she participated in the Rajkot *Satyagraha* for political reforms and was kept in detention at Tramba. In 1942, Gandhi was arrested early in the morning of August 9 at Birla House, Bombay. Kasturba decided to address the meeting which Gandhiji was to have addressed that after noon. She was arrested as *she* was proceeding to the meeting and taken to Arthur Road Prison at Bombay, from where after two days she was taken to the Aga Khan Palace detention camp at Pune to join her husband. In February 1943, Gandhi went on a 21-day fast and Kasturba looked after him day and night. She took only one meal a day of fruit and milk. She had done the same during all his previous fasts. She suffered from chronic Bronchitis, with heart failure, and a terminal Pneumonia carried her away. She attended prayers morning and evening till the end. She gave up all food except '*Ganga jal*' (Ganga water) on the last day. She wanted to hear nothing but '*Ram Nam*'. She died on 23rd February, 1944 on Maha Shivratri Day as the sun went down, with her head on her husband's lap.

INDEX